# The Monster of Perugia

## The Framing of Amanda Knox

Mark C. Waterbury, Ph.D.

## Dedication

This book is dedicated to "each unharmful, gentle soul, misplaced inside a jail."

# CONTENTS

# Preface

When I first learned about the tragedy in Perugia, I had no connection with the victim, the suspects, their families, or friends. I have never received any form of compensation, reimbursement, or offers for same, for my work on this case. My work has been independent, and the opinions expressed here are entirely my own. I have never knowingly misrepresented any facts associated with the case.

My connection to the case arose, in part, as a result of two happenstances. I happened to live near Seattle, and I happened to be a scientist/engineer with experience at reviewing a variety of forensic technologies.

Although I began with no preconceived opinion about guilt or innocence, from the early accounts of this case the involvement of Amanda Knox in such a horrific crime seemed unlikely. There is a useful, general guideline in science that extraordinary claims require extraordinary proof. It was clear that the claims about Amanda emanating from Perugia were extraordinary; that she had left her home in Seattle, gone bad in a matter of weeks, and committed a rape/murder as part of a satanic sex conspiracy. When I heard the news reports in which the prosecutor claimed these things, my impression was not, "Gosh, that's awful," it was more like, "Give me a break."

While looks can be deceiving, Amanda neither looked, nor acted the part. She had no history of violence. Over time, we learned that her entire legal history comprised accepting a noise ticket for a college going away party that got too loud. Amanda's life before the murder was exemplary. Her life after the murder, and after her subsequent arrest, has followed a similar pattern. She is deeply loved by her family and friends, as can be witnessed by their continual support. Amanda's life counts, even in the coldest calculation of guilt or innocence, because it speaks to fundamental questions of character, and of plausibility.

After studying this case in considerable detail over a period of years, I have yet to find a single, solitary shred of plausible evidence against either Amanda or Raffaele. The innocence of Amanda Knox and Raffaele Sollecito in the murder of Meredith

Kercher is not merely a matter of their guilt not being proven beyond a reasonable doubt. The degree of proof from the defense has far exceeded that standard. Amanda and Raffaele have long since proven their innocence to virtually all objective and informed observers.

Unfortunately, something is rotten in Perugia.

The thing that is rotten in Perugia has wrongfully convicted Amanda and Raffaele of murder. Whoever or whatever it is, it has inflicted a terrible toll on them, their families, and their loved ones.

A terrible, wrongful, and conspicuous toll has also been inflicted upon justice itself. What does it do to respect for laws when innocent people, good people, have their lives publicly torn asunder by a justice system that is anything but just? What does it mean for our lives and our freedoms when we see that innocent lives can be seized upon and ruined in full view of the world, with its consent, tacit blessing, and even enjoyment, as long as the ruination is performed by duly constituted authorities?

All of this leads me to move on from most questions about the murder itself, because I believe they have been largely resolved. What remains there, is for the appeals court to correct the errors made in the court of first instance.

The focal point of this book is on the framing of Amanda and Raffaele. The case for Amanda and Raffaele's innocence will be made only in passing. For those who desire a detailed refutation of the evidence-free and continually changing claims that were made by the prosecution, there are numerous resources in the bibliography.

My goal is to tell the truth about what has happened in Perugia as accurately, and as clearly as I can tell it. It is my hope that telling that truth will help to educate and motivate people to support the release of Amanda and Raffaele from a prison where they do not belong, and to advocate for investigation of what has taken place, and reforms to correct these abuses.

## Acknowledgements

The support, encouragement, and tolerance of my wife, Maureen has been particularly invaluable. Many people have contributed in many ways to developing the ideas, the information, and in the preparation of this book. I would especially like to thank, in alphabetical order by first name, Andrew Lowery, Anna Gilmour, Bruce Fisher, Candace Dempsey, Prof. Chris Halkides, Douglas Preston, Doug Longhini, Frank Sfarzo, Heather Coy, Jason Lezneck, Jim Lovering, Joseph Bishop, Dr. Kathy Fosnaugh, Krista Errickson, Lisa Rieger, Michael Becker, Mike Heavey, Paul Ciolino, Sarah Snyder, Ray Turner, Steve Moore, and Thomas Wright. This list is far from complete, my apologies and thanks also to those I have overlooked.

# PART I – 21<sup>ST</sup> CENTURY FAIRY TALES

# One - A 21st Century Fairy Tale

## Fairy tales can come true. It can happen to you.

Amanda Knox left her home in Seattle for one year of study in Perugia, Italy in the fall of 2007. Three months later Meredith Kercher, one of her roommates, was brutally murdered in the cottage they shared with several others. Amanda and her boyfriend, Raffaele Sollecito, were arrested just three days later and convicted of the murder two years after that. Unless her sentence is reduced or overturned on appeal, Amanda will not return home until the year 2033. She will be 46 years old and will have spent the prime of her life in Italian prisons.

Amanda Knox is innocent.

So is Raffaele. He too, will spend much of his life in prison for a crime he clearly did not commit. These two bright, kind, caring young people have been demonized in the press and wrongfully convicted of murder despite evidence that not only doesn't prove them guilty beyond a reasonable doubt, but that overwhelmingly exonerates them.

Why?

It has been attributed to a clash of cultures between the life-loving Seattle girl and straight-laced Perugians. It has been ascribed to people who made a bad initial call under pressure, and then sought to save face, "bad face" in the Italian expression, by refusing to change their minds when the evidence, the lack of motive, lack of prior violence, and simple, common, sense showed that they were wrong. It has been attributed to Amanda turning cartwheels, and to her not retaining a lawyer soon enough. It has been blamed on everything she said, did, didn't say, and didn't do. And it has been attributed to a grandstanding prosecutor whom many believe to be mentally unbalanced.

While all of these explanations may be factors, none of them fully fit the evidence. None of them provide a clear, complete, *satisfying* explanation, in the sense that the truth is satisfying. *The Monster of Perugia* will seek clues to such an explanation as it examines what went so terribly wrong and led to the wrongful prosecution and convictions of Amanda Knox and Raffaele Sollecito. It will examine how the tainted forensic investigations and prosecution occurred, and why Amanda and Raffaele fell victim to what investigator Paul Ciolino called the "railroad job from hell."

Meredith Kercher's murder was tragic, horrific, and senseless, but in and of itself, it was anything but exceptional. It was the kind of crime that unfortunately happens every day, a crime of opportunity, a disturbed young man assaulting and murdering a young woman. The real questions lie in what happened that led up to the murder, and why the investigation was so completely and *obviously*, twisted to achieve the desired result. That is where I believe the real mysteries lie.

The tragedy that befell Meredith must not be understated. Her life, which showed great promise, was taken from her in a heinous and cowardly act. But it does not bring justice to Meredith to punish the innocent, and it does not bring justice to Meredith to treat her actual murderer with lenience that will enable him to kill again.

### Perugian Fairy Tale

Amanda Knox and Meredith Kercher went abroad to study in a beautiful place – a small Italian city with ancient streets, picturesque vistas, and crystal skies. Perugia was a beautiful place to live, to study, and to grow. It was a land right out of a fairy tale.

Fairy tales are made of fantastical elements and a far-fetched sequence of events, and are peopled by mythical creatures like witches, trolls, and monsters. They happened, not here and now, but once upon a time, far, far away. But this is a fairy tale of the 21$^{st}$ century, and it is happening even as I write, a mere jet flight away. And although one speaks of a "fairy tale ending" not all fairy tales end happily ever after. The end of this particular tale remains very much in doubt, but it has already been a tragedy for three young people, their families, and their friends.

Bad things happen in fairy tales.

**Meredith Kercher** was born in London, England and attended the University of Leeds with a degree in European Studies. She traveled to Perugia to continue her studies as an Erasmus exchange scholar. Her father, John Kercher, was a freelance writer for British tabloid newspapers. Her mother, Arline Kercher is a housewife who was born in India.

**Amanda Knox** was born in Seattle, Washington, U.S.A. and attended Seattle Preparatory High School and The University of Washington, seeking a degree in languages. She arrived in Perugia in September of 2007. She had worked two jobs in Seattle to raise some of the money for her studies, and was eager to dive into the experience of a lifetime. She chose to study at the Stranieri, the University for Foreigners, rather than at the American run Umbra Institute, where most American students went. She found an apartment in an Italian neighborhood with mostly Italian roommates, rather than stay in student housing where most of the American students lived. She immersed herself as completely in the Italian language, culture, and life as she could.

**Raffaele Sollecito** came from the city of Giovinazzo in Puglia, the "heel" in the South of Italy. A computer science major and the son of a doctor, he was one week from completing his degree at the time of the murder. Raffaele and Amanda met at a classical music concert one week before the murder. During that time they were almost inseparable, spending every night together.

Meredith, Amanda, and Raffaele came to Perugia with their lives before them. They were working hard on their studies while enjoying the bounties of their young lives. The path for Rudy Guede was different.

**Rudy Guede** was born in the Cote d'Ivoire (Ivory Coast), an impoverished nation in western Africa. He moved to Italy when he was two years old, his father working as a laborer. Rudy was 16 when his father left Italy, abandoning him. Paolo Caporali, a wealthy businessman, informally adopted Rudy. Caporali brought him into his home and gave him a job.

Two months before the murder Paolo threw Rudy out of his home and fired him because he only rarely showed up for work. Paolo called him "a terrible liar." At the time, Rudy lived in an apartment he had rented near the cottage where the murder took place. His landlord had recently asked him for proof of employment – proof he did not possess.

In the month before the murder of Meredith Kercher, Rudy was caught or observed breaking into several places in Perugia and nearby Milan, including a residence, a lawyer's office, and a school. Incredibly, each time that he got caught he was quickly released rather than being kept in custody.

**Public Minister Giuliano Mignini** The prosecutor of Amanda Knox is a powerful and popular figure in Perugia. He is known for a shrewd and sensationalistic approach to trials – an approach that plays well in his drama-loving environment. Before this trial Mignini was most famous for his investigation and prosecutions of 20 people who he claimed were involved in a satanic ritual murder plot called the Narducci case, an offshoot of the Monster of Florence case. Mignini was charged with prosecutorial misconduct for his role in that investigation and prosecution just before this murder, and was tried and convicted during the course of his prosecution of this case. As of this writing, his 16-month sentence is under appeal.

### Introduction to a Murder

This is intended as a brief account of how the murder of Meredith Kercher occurred, based on the best information available. It is not a complete description. The goal is to provide an orientation to the case and an introduction to the people who played major roles. This will necessarily involve stating matters in brief, without simultaneously providing support. Ample supporting information is provided in later chapters and in the references in the bibliography. Many details are omitted to keep this overview short and to the point.

The evidence itself is clear and simple. Doubts about the case do not stem from that evidence, but from the smokescreen of distortions and lies broadcast by the prosecution, elements of the press, and nameless Internet trolls. The real, outstanding questions are not about the details of the murder, but about the aftermath – the framing of Amanda and Raffaele.

## Just Another Burglary

Rudy Guede murdered Meredith Kercher in Perugia, Italy in the cottage at Via dela Pergola on the night of November 1, 2007. The evidence of Rudy's guilt is clear, complete, and overwhelming. He left substantial amounts of his DNA in, on, and around Meredith's body. He left his feces in the toilet. He left his handprints, shoe prints, and footprints in her blood. He fled to Germany two days later. In contrast, no evidence, DNA or otherwise, of the presence of either Amanda or Raffaele was found in the murder room, a small space in which a violent, bloody murder occurred. That simple fact is virtual proof of their innocence.

Meredith shared the upstairs apartment with three other women; Amanda Knox and two Italian women in their late twenties, Filomena Romanelli, and Laura Mezetti, who were both interning at a law firm in Perugia. Four young Italian men lived downstairs.

Rudy Guede was acquainted with the men and occasionally played basketball with them in the plaza near the apartment. Guede was unemployed, broke, facing eviction, and had committed several break-ins in Perugia and nearby Milan in just the previous month before the murder.

On November 1, 2007, the night after Halloween, all but one of the residents of the cottage on Via dela Pergola were away at various places for the holiday, All Saints Day. Rudy may have been aware of this since he knew the young men downstairs and could know of their plans. That night of the month was also when rent payments were gathered together, usually in cash. It was a common night for break-ins.

At about 9:00 P.M. Rudy threw a rock through a window of the upstairs apartment to enable entry, a break-in method that he had used before. After waiting a while to see if anyone noticed, he used some combination (there are multiple possibilities) of a planter near the window and a security grating over a lower window to climb up, remove some remaining shards of glass from the casement, open the inner blinds, and enter the apartment.

The window was just over 10 feet above the ground, less than that to the planter. The climb was not difficult for Guede, an athletic basketball player, and a burglar as well. He entered Filomena's room and began to ransack it, probably looking for the rent money. He interrupted his search before finding the money and went to use the bathroom shared by Filomena and Laura.

Shortly thereafter, Meredith Kercher returned home unexpectedly and Rudy surprised her. In some way that may never be known, he confronted Meredith, known to be a fighter who stood up for her self, and matters escalated from a break-in to a murder and sexual assault. During the murder, Rudy clasped his hands over her face hard enough to leave bruises and stabbed her with a small knife on both sides of her neck.

Rudy washed some of the blood off himself and his shoes in the bathroom shared by Amanda and Meredith, leaving behind footprints. He removed a quilt from Meredith's bed and tossed it over his victim in a gesture of sorts, one that is not uncommon for new murderers. He laid the bloody knife down, leaving an imprint of it marked by her blood, and rifled through her purse, leaving his prints on it. He took her rent money and cell phones and left the cottage, leaving a fading trail of bloody shoe prints.

Later that same night Rudy cleaned up, a little, and went out dancing at the Domus, a local discotheque. People not only saw him dancing, but recalled that he had a very strong body odor. He went dancing again the following evening, attracting attention during a moment of silence that was held for Meredith. During the moment, Rudy, and Rudy alone, did not pause, but continued to dance. He fled to Germany the following day.

In spite of what tabloid writers and people pushing sensationalistic book and news coverage say, there is no great mystery as to who committed this murder. Tragic as it was, in and of itself the murder was not even unusual. As is almost always the case, the murder of Meredith Kercher was committed by a disturbed, young, male acting alone.

## The Calm Before the Storm

Amanda was at Raffaele's apartment nearby the evening and night of the murder. A friend of Raffaele, Jana Popovich, had asked him to take her to a train station that evening. She stopped by twice that evening, seeing both of them at his apartment the first time, and speaking with Amanda the second when she told them she did not need a ride after all.

Amanda had been scheduled to work at le Chic, a bar where she worked part time, but she received a text message from Patrick Lumumba, the owner, telling her it was also not necessary. She replied to him by text, saying, in Italian, "Okay, see you later. Good night." They then switched their cell phones off so they could be together and not be disturbed, and so that she would not be called in to work should circumstances change.

Italian investigators later interpreted the words "See you later" to mean that Amanda and Patrick had an appointment to commit murder later that night. This tortured interpretation of an ordinary expression was in spite of the fact that "See you later" has the same connotation in Italy that it has in the United States: It means, *Goodbye*.

It would not be the last time that mundane words, deeds, facial expressions, and facts would be forcibly twisted to interpret them as incriminating evidence against Amanda and Raffaele. In fact, this kind of distortion would set the pattern of the entire investigation and prosecution and play a central role in the framing of Amanda Knox.

Raffaele and Amanda watched the romantic comedy movie, *Amelie*, on Raff's computer that evening. IMDB.com describes *Amelie* as follows. "Amelie, an innocent and naive girl in Paris with her own sense of justice, decides to help those around her and along the way, discovers love." Later, the couple made dinner, had a minor plumbing leak from the kitchen sink, smoked a joint, had sex, and went to sleep. It was a restful evening, the last for a very long time.

## Compatibility Test

Italian investigators and courts often use the phrase, "it is compatible with." This means something like, *you can't prove it isn't, it might be,* or even, *it isn't impossible.* Saying that the evidence *is compatible with* some theory is a very low hurdle to clear. It is a kind of job insurance, a way of going along without putting yourself on the line. *It is compatible with* comes in particularly handy when you begin an investigation with a theory, and then try to force fit the evidence around that theory. If you actually study the evidence before you choose your suspects, not so much.

I like the phrase. It is a fudge factor for the forensically challenged that may be useful. In keeping with another phrase, *what is sauce for the goose is sauce for the gander* I will use it whenever the evidence developed in this book is *compatible with* the theory at hand.

## Two – The Crucible of Perugia

In medieval times in Europe, roughly one hundred thousand people were tried for witchcraft, three quarters of them women. With charges often based on gossip, hysteria, and accusations from other desperate victims, most were convicted and were burned, hung, or strangled. Thankfully, that dark era is past and such groundless, perverse, inhuman prosecutions no longer take place - for the most part.

A conspicuous exception has transpired in Perugia, Italy, in the trial of Amanda and Raffaele. From the prosecutor's bizarre charges of satanic sex rituals to the Italian nation's fixation on Amanda's every quirk, there has been no more egregious a witch trial in the 21$^{st}$ century. To understand this trial, then, let's begin by taking a look at the crucible of witch-hunt justice.

Medieval witch-hunts didn't just happen – they were fed by an atmosphere of superstition and fear and promoted by those who benefited from them. After getting off to a slow start, they soared after the publication of an instruction manual, *The Hammer of Witches,* one of the first printed books. "All wickedness," *Hammer* informs us, "is but little to the wickedness of a woman.... Women are by nature instruments of Satan."

Among other things, witches were believed to have powers to control and coerce men. To face such powerful and sinister adversaries, witch hunters armed themselves with far reaching powers. Wikipedia calls witch trials "a vivid cautionary tale about the dangers of religious extremism, false accusations, lapses in due process, and governmental intrusion on individual liberties.... Evidence that would be excluded from modern courtrooms – hearsay, gossip, stories, unsupported assertions, surmises – was also generally admitted." All of these violations of the normal rules of courts and justice were allowed since, when your adversary is possessed of supernatural powers, what sense does it make to play fair?

*Hammer* conferred a mantle of authority that carried great weight in the small towns and backwaters where the most ardent witch-hunts occurred – backwaters not unlike Perugia, Italy. A minor crossroads for the drug trade, the Albanian mob, and college kids, who make up one quarter of the population of 160,000, Perugia is a small, conservative city compared to cosmopolitan Rome or Florence.

## More Weight

Giles Corey was a prosperous farmer and church member in the small, conservative town of Salem, Massachusetts in the late 1600s. In an atmosphere of suspicion, a woman accused Giles of asking her to write in the devil's book. This same woman also claimed to have been told by a ghost that Giles was the ghost's murderer. He was therefore arrested along with three women. One of these, terrified and desperate to gain favor with the prosecutor, declared that Giles was a warlock, a male witch.

Turning the accused against each other was a standard operating procedure in witch-hunts. It's surprising what you can get people to confess to, and what accusations they may make when you tell them they'll be burned at the stake. Many witches opted for a quick confession and execution, rather than a prolonged process to achieve the same outcome. Spouses testified against their husbands or wives, children accused their parents, and neighbors vied to be the first to turn on each other.

Giles Corey, however, was made of sterner stuff than this. He refused to even enter a plea. He knew that if he pleaded he would be tried and would certainly be convicted. He would then be executed – his assets seized – and his family would lose everything.

To the Salem authorities, Giles' refusal to cooperate implied a lack of respect that could not be endured. Therefore, to press its point and demonstrate its power the court had him crushed under ever-greater piles of rocks. He was asked three more times, if he was ready to plea. Each time he famously replied, "More weight." It took two days for the pressure to kill him, and justice was served.

As in this case, little importance was attached to actual guilt or innocence during witch trials. After all, not one single person out of the tens of thousands who were burned, hung, or otherwise tortured to death were actually guilty of consorting with the devil. *It wasn't real.* The entire phenomenon was a figment of the imagination.

Sometimes though, the need for a witch-hunt was created by a crisis that was all too real, such as a drought or epidemic. Frightened, perhaps starving, citizens demanded action from the authorities. The leaders could lose power if they failed to respond decisively. They couldn't be hamstrung by their inability to respond to the crisis.

They needed scapegoats, and what better scapegoats could be found than witches causing mischief by casting evil spells? The community gained a distraction from their troubles, at the least, and everyone gained the entertainment of witnessing the downfall of someone even less fortunate than their selves.

To ease the path to that downfall, those selected for hunting as witches were usually "different" people who stood out from their community for some reason. They were often elderly women who had to rely on charity, and so had become a drain on resources, or midwives who might have influence outside of the mainstream. But often too, they were young and impetuous, pretty and free.

In some places, in some cases, not much has changed.

## The Perugian Witch-hunt Begins

Perugia has plenty of minor, drug-related crime, theft, and burglaries, but murders are not common. When news of a murder spread, some of the visiting college kids began to pack their bags, setting off an alarm among the townspeople. It was a crime that needed solving as rapidly as possible. If it was not, the impact on the universities – the local bread and butter – could be substantial. Mayor Renato Rocchi and Chief of Police Arturo De Felice stepped up to the challenge and announced *in advance* that the crime would be solved quickly. Like town leaders of old when faced with a crop failure, the Perugian witch hunters needed guilty people, and they needed them fast.

Giuliano Mignini was chosen to lead the prosecution. He has claimed that he was simply in the rotation – randomly selected.

Like many other aspects of the trial, that chance event was very convenient. Under Italian law, the choice placed him in charge of both the prosecution and the police investigation itself.

Mignini arrived at the cottage less than an hour after the first polizia officers. In less than three days, he would determine that Amanda, like others he had investigated before, had committed the murder as part of her involvement in satanic sex rituals.

There was no evidence of Satanism. There was no evidence Amanda had anything to do with the murder, but that was no reason not to whip up a good yarn. Mignini fed fanciful stories of a satanic sex rite gone wrong to the media, and the media devoured them. Soon the Perugian community and the world knew all about "Foxy Knoxy" Amanda's childhood nickname, somehow turned sinister, and her circle of Satanists. This wasn't the first time that Mignini's career enjoyed a boost from his skilled performance transforming a mundane investigation into a satanic conspiracy, as will be shown in the Chapter Three.

Edgardo Giobbi, head of Rome's Special Services Organization, was brought in to help with the investigation, and help he did. In a remarkable interview, Giobbi boasted about deciding that Amanda Knox was guilty – before the evidence had even been gathered.

His determination of guilt began while taking Amanda through the cottage on November 3, one day after the murder was discovered, while she tried to help with the investigation. She was asked to put on a pair of shoe covers before entering. Struggling with them for a moment before finally slipping them on, she was reported to have said, "voila," and – even more damning – to have, in Giobbi's view, *twisted her hips* a bit. For a trained investigator like Giobbi, this was enough. "My suspicions were raised," he said.

Giobbi's opinion was cemented when Amanda ate pizza with Raffaele a couple days after the murder. She had been dragged in for questioning for many, many hours during this period, and was hungry. They were in Italy. Who, in Italy, who but a guilty person would think to eat pizza when they were hungry?

"We were able to determine guilt, psychologically, without the need for analyzing evidence," Giobbi explained in an amazing television interview. The coroner's report had not yet been filed.

The DNA tests had not been analyzed. The knife wounds had not been measured. Rudy Guede was not yet apprehended or even under investigation. But Detective Edgardo Giobbi had already determined that Amanda Knox was guilty – *psychologically.*

He had found the witches' mark. Amanda was pretty, free, and *different.* She twisted her hips, he thought. She cried, but not when he thought she should. She had blue eyes: a shocking feature in dark-eyed Italy. "I've seen eyes like those in a war zone," one journalist later said. Exhaustion might have had something to do with that.

## The Interrogation of Amanda Knox

With Amanda's guilt decided in advance, it only remained to come up with a confession, some evidence to support it, and to put on a trial. Time was short. Edda Mellas, Amanda's mother, was about to arrive from the United States. If Amanda got away from Italy with her, extradition would be very difficult in the absence of evidence. Crushing her beneath rocks was out of the question, but there are subtler means to arrive at the same result.

In an all night interrogation conducted November 5th 2007 by a dozen police detectives operating in non-stop tag-team fashion, Amanda gave a confused, conflicting, and generally bewildered account of "what might have happened" as requested by the interrogators. This has come to be called her "confession," but not once did Amanda ever say or imply that she was involved in the murder.

What Amanda said was that she imagined herself covering her ears to avoid hearing screams while Patrick committed the crime in the next room. Patrick, it turned out, had an unassailable alibi, as was quickly proven. What Amanda said was all wrong, and showed no indication that she had any special knowledge of what happened. But the prosecution and the press have relentlessly pointed to the tortured statement that she made during that interrogation, and her note the morning after trying to clarify it, as proof of her involvement and of her dishonesty.

In an influential series of articles about the case, former FBI agent Steve Moore explained a simple, fundamental fact of interrogations that he learned from observing some foreign antiterrorism efforts. If you want to obtain information from a witness, you want them to be rested, awake, and clear. If you want them to say whatever you want, you want them to be exhausted, overwhelmed, and afraid. To learn something from a witness, that witness ought to be wide-awake. To coerce a witness, you push them to their limit - and beyond.

To begin to understand the interrogation of Amanda Knox, we will find it instructive to follow along with her from the time that she discovered something was wrong at the cottage, about 10:30 AM on November 2, till her interrogation ended in her arrest at 5:30 AM, on November 6. What we are looking for is the sheer summation of sleep deprivation and stress leading up to her statement. As you wonder what condition she would be in, honestly ask yourself what state *you* would be in under the same circumstances.

## To Sleep, Perchance to Dream

First, let's remind ourselves of the situation. The stress on Amanda was tremendous. Her roommate and friend had been violently murdered, and it could easily have been her. She was without legal counsel. In fact, she was actively prevented from meeting with a lawyer until it was decided that she would be held *for a year* before charges were brought. She was in a foreign country where she only barely spoke the language, and was without any local support from friends or family, aside from Raffaele, whom she had just met. It was a time when, unknown to her, every move she made – every smile, every tear, every look – was observed, analyzed, and dissected by investigators, the media, and ultimately by the world at large. It was life under a microscope: a microscope with a palpable and malevolent bias.

*Friday, November 2, 2007 (the morning after the murder)*
From 10:30 in the morning, when Amanda discovered that something was wrong at the cottage, till 5:30 that afternoon when she was taken to the questura, the polizia headquarters, Amanda was under constant pressure. She showed symptoms of being in shock: complaining of extreme cold and behaving nearly hysterically. She was questioned by the polizia until 5:30 in the

morning while having minimal food. That works out to almost nineteen hours of questioning and constant exposure to the polizia. At the end of the day she returned to Raffaele's place, ate, and finally fell asleep, at around 7:00 AM. She was asked to return to the questura for further questioning at 11:00 AM. If she got up as late as possible, at about 10:00 AM, that gave her three hours of fitful sleep the first night after the murder.

*Saturday, November 3, 2007*
Amanda reported to the questura, as requested, at 11:00 AM. The polizia drove her to the cottage where the murder took place. There, she was toured around both floors and asked questions. A famous photo was taken of her surrounded by polizia officers. Since she was not allowed to return to her apartment to retrieve any of her clothes, Amanda and Raffaele later shopped for underwear at around 7:00 PM. It was ordinary underwear from an ordinary store. There was a lingerie store next door, but they didn't choose that. Later they had pizza. These two trivial events were converted by the news media into shopping for "sexy lingerie" and eating pizza – *pizza*– after her roommate had been murdered.

Amanda's desire to wear clean underwear was turned into evidence against her. Her desire to eat when she was hungry was one of the three incidents cited by Detective Giobbi as vital clues to her guilt.

Amanda complained at this time about exhaustion and the relentless, repetitive, belligerent, and suggestive questioning of the polizia. They had fixated on a tube of Vaseline lip balm found among Meredith's belongings, believing it to be intended for use as a sexual lubricant. This was a sign of good police work to come. What else could lip balm be used for?

Amanda complained about not having had a break. Despite her exhaustion, she could not sleep because of stress. She wrote an email and sent it to her entire address book at 3:30 AM. She had approximately 3 hours of sleep in 44 hours.

That night Sophie Purton, a friend of Meredith's, told the polizia that Meredith had told her that Amanda brought men back to the house. She added that some of these were probably just friends. To Giuliano Mignini, however, bringing a man back home could only mean that she was bringing them back to have sex.

They therefore summoned Amanda for further questioning the following morning.

*Sunday, November 4, 2007*

We don't know exactly how much Amanda slept Saturday night, but we know she was up until at least 3:30 AM writing her e-mail. Then it was off to the questura the following morning. She sent a text message to Spyros, a Greek friend, at 6:19 PM on the 4th saying that she was "With the police in my house. I am very tired." Soon after, she told the woman the polizia brought in as an interpreter that she was "Not well. I can't eat. I can't sleep. And my period just started."

She spent most of Sunday at the questura, making yet another trip to the cottage where she was questioned about the kitchen knives for *some inexplicable reason*. At one point, she collapsed and began to sob. At another point, she struggled to breathe. A polizia detective, Monica Napoleoni, even asked the coroner to determine whether she required medicine.

She returned to the questura at about 7 P.M. where she and Raffaele were placed in another bugged room. She spoke with her second cousin in Germany on a phone that was tapped. It was one of a half dozen calls, every one of which was recorded. Hours passed, so Amanda was there until late that night. She wrote another e-mail to a friend, again complaining of exhaustion.

*Monday, November 5, 2007*

It would be a long day. It would be an even longer incarceration.

In an attempt to regain some sense of normalcy, and perhaps out of dogged determination to continue her life, Amanda attended her scheduled Italian class on Monday at about 9 A.M. There she wrote a letter in Italian for an assignment. Amanda avoided discussing any aspect of the case under instructions from the polizia not to. Her instructor read her letter aloud to the class and then turned it over to the polizia. It quickly found its way to the tabloids, which twisted and distorted it to sell papers.

She spoke on the phone with Patrick Lumumba early that afternoon, while she was with the polizia again. She told him that she had "spent a long, long, long, time with the police. It is very difficult, exhausting." She resigned her job at Patrick's club, explaining that she was afraid to go anywhere at night after the murder.

A candlelight procession of mourners marched that evening for Meredith. Neither Amanda nor any of the other flat mates attended, hoping to avoid the news cameras.

At 10 P.M. on Monday night, November 5, both Amanda and Raffaele were summoned to the questura, according to Inspector Giobbi, who stated with "mathematical certainty" that he had summoned them both. This contradicts statements by members of the "Flying Squad" polizia organization that performed the interrogation. They claimed that only Raffaele had been summoned, and Amanda had tagged along, perhaps in an effort to make Amanda's appearance seem a happenstance. The final interrogation of Amanda Knox *began* after 10 o'clock that night. After 4 days of questioning and three nearly sleepless nights, Amanda was utterly exhausted and would be questioned once more in a non-stop session lasting until 5:30 A.M. the following morning.

### Kind Treatment and Tea

No less than 12 detectives performed the final interrogation of Amanda Knox in a relentless barrage – almost all of it in Italian. Amanda, who barely spoke Italian at that point, had her responses recorded by an interpreter who worked for the polizia. This interpreter put distorted versions of her words into a kind of Italian police dialect. Amanda did not have a lawyer present even though she was clearly a suspect and had requested one. "It will only go worse for you," she was told when she requested legal representation.

And in a stunning and frankly unbelievable discrepancy from all the previous conversations, phone calls, and discussions – every one of which that could be secretly recorded, was secretly recorded – the prosecution claims that her final interrogation was *not recorded in any way*. This is a violation of Italian law, which requires that interrogations of suspects be recorded. It is also a violation of common sense that someone would hit the *off* switch at that critical time.

Without fear of contradiction from evidence that they claim does not exist, the unanimous and identical memories of the 12 officers that interrogated Amanda were that they respectfully bestowed kind treatment, biscuits, and tea. Does an all night interrogation by 12 officers operating in rotating shifts in a foreign language sound like "kind treatment" to you?

The only other recording was Amanda's memory, which she has recounted in consistent detail. She told of abusive behavior, threats, relentless pressure, her head being cuffed, them calling her "stupid." Edgardo Giobbi has said that he could hear her screams from the office he was in that night. But simply for testifying about being cuffed, she has been charged with defamation, a criminal offense in Italy. Many press accounts of this say that she claims to have been "beaten," a sensationalistic and inaccurate paraphrasing of her actual statements that she was "cuffed at the back of the head." It is also far less believable than what Amanda actually said.

Amanda could not maintain the resolve of Giles Corey when her inquisitors pressed her to imagine what might have happened, when they insisted repeatedly that she knew all about it and was lying, when they told her they had solid evidence that she was there. Amanda had been questioned for more than 50 hours over a four day, three-night period, finally lasting into the middle of the night, in a language she barely knew, and without an attorney. Experienced investigators have said that under those circumstances you can get pretty much anyone to say to pretty much anything.

Amanda took the bait and, as was suggested to her, she imagined the owner of the bar where she worked, Patrick Lumumba, committing the crime while she covered her ears in the next room to avoid hearing the screams. Why did they suggest Patrick to her? The evening of the murder she had sent him a text message saying, "See you later. Good night." To the Italian investigators, "See you later" meant that they had an appointment for later that night. But there may have been another reason. Patrick was black. There are a number of reasons to think that the polizia may have been looking for a black man.

As soon as possible Amanda made a written statement saying that it all seemed like a dream – that she was unsure what was real and what was imagined. Nevertheless, the witch hunters touted this as an accusation – one witch of another – and raced off to capture Patrick while ignoring the total lack of evidence against him.

Three successive nights with very little sleep combined with four long days of extreme stress is enough to leave virtually anyone in a confused, nearly delirious state. In the final interrogation, she was summoned to appear after 10:00 at night for a relentless, all night, high intensity session that would end with her breakdown at 5:30 AM. Would you call Amanda "clear, lucid, and awake?"

## Rules of Witch Trial Evidence

Coerced confessions and accusations played a vital role in witch trials, but finding evidence to support those confessions wasn't left to chance. While there might be signs of a secret ceremony, a pentagram, or a suspicious circle of ashes, sometimes these couldn't be found. Most "witches" weren't really witches, after all. They were simply people. No pentagrams left behind.

Fortunately, this problem was long ago resolved in an ingenious manner, and the lack of actual evidence no longer blocked the wheels of justice. The solution was the invention of a "witches' mark." These marks could be almost any mark on a witches' body: a mole, scar, or blemish. Its existence was proof that the bearer was a witch, making it a powerful tool in the witch hunter's armament.

To locate the witches' mark, the accused were publicly stripped, shaved to reveal anything hidden, and inspected from head to toe. Any suitable blemish could be dramatically revealed to the watching mob, hungry for revenge on the chosen victim. Occasionally there was a complete absence of any visible marks, but this was suspicious in its self and gave rise to the realization that the devil's mark could be invisible.

The blemish-free accused, were therefore further explored by piercing them with pins, searching for a spot that didn't hurt, its having been made insensitive by the devil himself. These were not slender, modern pins, you understand, but pins from the middle ages. Think about it. It is a good bet that many spots hurt like hell when probed this way before locating the devil's mark that did not. One wonders about the patience of the accused during this investigation.

If you have a mark, you are a witch. If you don't have a mark, it is because it is invisible or you have concealed it. You are a witch with an invisible mark and the Devil is on your side. Lack of evidence against you is no defense. It only indicates that you have concealed that evidence. Amanda and Raffaele thought that innocence would protect them, but in a witch trial, innocence is neither a defense, nor much of an obstacle to conviction.

## The Crucible of Perugia

Arthur Miller's play, *The Crucible*, used the example of the infamous Salem witch trials of 1692 to mount a powerful critique to the excesses of the McCarthy era in the United States in the 1950s. During that dark period, Senator Joseph McCarthy used reckless accusations, unfair interrogations, unsubstantiated evidence, and character assassination to attack his political enemies and advance his own prestige. His hunts for imaginary communists finally came to an end when McCarthy was asked during a nationally televised hearing, "Have you no sense of decency sir?" For this – he had no answer.

Wikipedia describes the McCarthy witch-hunts this way:

"Suspicions were often given credence despite inconclusive or questionable evidence, and the level of threat posed by a person's real or supposed leftist associations or beliefs was often greatly exaggerated. Many people suffered loss of employment, destruction of their careers, and even imprisonment. Most of these punishments came about through trial verdicts later overturned, laws that would be declared unconstitutional, dismissals for reasons later declared illegal or actionable, or extra-legal procedures that would come into general disrepute.

McCarthy was not only allowed to purvey paranoia and prejudice for his own personal aggrandizement, he was aided and abetted in that effort by much of the United State's government – by business leaders, show business personalities, and everyday people. Contemptible as his methods and actions were, he did not act alone, but drew about himself a whirlwind of mass hysteria, a delusion of communist threat on a grand and entirely fanciful scale.

Most of the laws he pushed through were eventually declared unconstitutional, verdicts were overturned, and some lost jobs were restored. To this day, the name, "McCarthy" is associated with extremism and injustice. And yet, lives were ruined, and tragedies occurred that can never be undone.

Like the McCarthy era trials, there was even a silver lining to the black cloud of the Salem witch trials. News of what took place in Salem spread throughout America and Europe. The result was widespread and deep, and can be summarized in one word: revulsion. No one was ever convicted of witchcraft in America again, and Europe also abandoned the practice. After centuries of such trials, they were finally brought to a halt by the clearly appalling nature of that event. People listened, learned, thought about it, and said, in a sense, "Never again."

The eyes of the world have been similarly drawn by what has taken place in Perugia, Italy. As the truth about this witch trial of the 21st century spreads, one wonders about the reactions to such a conspicuously practiced injustice by a modern European nation. What will be the outcome of the crucible of Perugia?

**The Selection is Made**

There is a famous photo of Amanda surrounded by polizia that Detective Edgardo Giobbi had posted in the hall near his office. It appears on the cover of this book. The photo was posted beside those of mafia dons before she was charged with a crime. A portrait of a twenty-year old girl with no prior crimes was framed and mounted as a trophy, surrounded by pictures of some of the most violent and dangerous criminals in the world.

Before the real questioning even began, before the evidence was collected, before the evidence was analyzed, Giobbi and Mignini made up their minds. There was never a true, neutral investigation to identify the guilty party. It was, instead, a selection process. They selected someone to be prosecuted, just as the witch hunters of long ago selected witches to be tried. Once Amanda was chosen, the process of investigating her, prosecuting her, and convicting her could not be stopped. The conviction was pre-ordained and could not be prevented regardless of the lack of evidence, regardless of the lack of motive, regardless of common sense.

The railroading and the conviction have happened, they cannot be undone. Amanda and Raffaele have now spent years in prison, and that cannot be undone. But why did it happen? Witch hunters didn't set out on witch-hunts out of the goodness of their hearts. They hunted witches because they had reasons to hunt witches.

Certainly there were people that deeply believed in their pursuit of witches, but while some witch-hunters likely believed their own lies, by happy coincidence they often benefited from the hunt. There were even professional witch-hunters who made careers by going from town to town conducting witch trials. It makes one wonder what kind of person pursues such an unusual career. What kind of person would destroy the lives of innocent people to advance their own interests?

## Three – Dr. Strangelove and

## The Madness of PM Mignini

This exercise is an effort to learn something about the psychology of the person who, far more than any other, has driven this investigation and prosecution. His actions have been at the fulcrum, the pivot point, for every aspect of this case. To understand the wrongful convictions of Amanda Knox and Raffaele Sollecito, one ultimately needs to understand some things about Public Minister Giuliano Mignini.

But first, some movie history.

In *Dr. Strangelove,* Stanley Kubrick's classic film, General Jack D. Ripper was given a little too much authority. A special protocol had been created to avoid a situation where the destruction of the United States' political structure by a surprise nuclear attack might render us unable to kill enough commies in revenge. It was called "Wing Attack Plan R." Under the terms of this protocol, carefully selected generals were empowered to launch a nuclear strike under their own authority. They were further empowered to prevent their self-launched attack from being stopped by anyone without the proper recall code.

To ensure that they are insulated from potential threats or intimidation from the mafia and other criminals, prosecutors in Italy have been given wide discretionary latitude, great presumptive responsibility, and are largely shielded from removal or sanction. This system has had some success. The mafia doesn't dominate Italy as completely as it did in the past. Italy has been dominated by the government and media empire of Prime Minister Silvio Berlusconni instead.

Even the best-laid plans can have unintended consequences.

The generals entrusted with the authority to initiate Wing Attack Plan R were carefully vetted for stability and sanity. When General Ripper launched an unprovoked surprise attack on the Soviet Union, he explained his actions as follows, requesting backup from the rest of the Strategic Air Command (SAC):

> "Yes gentlemen, they are on their way in, and no one can bring them back. For the sake of our country, and our way of life, I suggest you get the rest of SAC in after them. Otherwise, we will be totally destroyed by Red retaliation. My boys will give you the best kind of start, 1400 megatons worth, and you sure as hell won't stop them now. So let's get going – there's no other choice. God willing, we will prevail, in peace and freedom from fear, and in true health, through the purity and essence of our natural fluids. God bless you all."

Well said, but this comment not only caused the President to doubt Ripper's sanity, but to go so far as to question the program that had put him in a position to rain devastation on the world.

> President Muffley: "General Turgidson! When you instituted the human reliability tests, you assured me there was no possibility of such a thing ever occurring!"
>
> General Turgidson: "Well, I, uh, don't think it's quite fair to condemn a whole program because of a single slip-up, sir."

## The Monster of Florence

If such a human reliability test program had been in place in Italy, it is possible that some flags would have gone up when Giuliano Mignini applied for a job. In his tenure as a Public Minister, the rough equivalent of a District Attorney in the United States, Mignini has compiled a record of bizarre prosecutions, some of which are described in *The Monster of Florence* by Douglas Preston with Mario Spezi. Their book recounts a series of horrific murders of young lovers in the vicinity of Florence – seventy miles up the road from Perugia – over a period from about 1961 to 1985. The murders were never solved, at least in part because of the incompetent and bizarre nature of the investigations. For the full story, consult that excellent book. These materials are mostly drawn from that account.

Mignini's behavior in that case provides vital background information that *informs* the current matter. Here, then is a brief summary of something called the Narducci prosecutions – improbable offshoots of the Florence murders, offshoots that were only recently resolved.

At the end of the Monster of Florence slayings in 1985, a doctor named Francesco Narducci drowned in Lake Trasemino near Perugia. Rumors circulated that Narducci had been murdered because he was somehow connected to the Florence killings, but were soon dismissed for lack of plausible connections and evidence. Narducci was apparently a simple suicide or drug overdose victim. Nevertheless, seventeen years later, in 2002, Gabriella Carlizzi, an Italian blogger whose writings channeled a dead person – contacted Mignini with a revelation.

Carlizzi told Mignini that Narducci had been murdered by a satanic cult because he knew too much about the Monster of Florence murders. She further claimed that his group, which she called the *Order of the Red Rose,* was affiliated with the Masons and was responsible for the terrorist attacks of 9/11 as well as many other ritual murders throughout Europe.

Having an agile mind of his own, Mignini quickly linked Carlizzi's satanic cult with a group of loan sharks he was investigating at the time. Not much sexy or juicy in a loan shark investigation. What better way to spice it up than to tie it to one of the most infamous series of murders in Italian history, one that was committed by a satanic sex cult? A series of creative news leaks ensued that revealed cleverly revised polizia recordings from the loan sharks. The revisions changed the recorded conversations from generalized threats to specific references to Narducci and the Florentine murders. In this investigatory effort, Mignini worked with Chief Inspector Michele Giuttari, who had been placed in charge of the *Monster* investigation in 1995.

Carlizzi further told Mignini that Narducci's body had been swapped out for another one so that the autopsy would not reveal evidence of his murder. What was her basis for this claim? Spiritual insight. Mignini seized upon this baseless claim and found what he felt was support for it in the pseudoscientific analyses of a single photograph of the corpse taken on a dock in

Lake Trasemino. In that photo, Narducci's body appeared to be 4 inches too short, based on comparisons with the dimensions of planks in the dock in the same photo. This comparison was made despite the fact that no measurements of the planks shown in the photo were available because the dock had been replaced.

Acting under Mignini's orders, the polizia exhumed the body, convinced by Mignini that it was not Narducci's. They subjected it to DNA testing, revealing – to the amazement of all – that it was in fact *Narducci's body*! Conspiracy! The only possible explanation was that the evildoers must have *learned of the exhumation in advance* and swapped out the body *again*. This was the only explanation, that is, that allowed for an "out" for Mignini and Giuttari.

Rather than abandoning a theory that was preposterous in the first place, and directly and overwhelmingly refuted by the evidence, Mignini and Giutarri doubled down on their bets and *broadened* their net of prosecutions. To swap out Narducci's corpse *twice* and to learn of his exhumation in advance required a vast and incredibly improbable conspiracy of high-ranking, Satan-worshipping participants. No problem. Mignini thereupon launched a series of investigations and prosecutions that would eventually lead to the indictments and actual trials of 21 people.

After eight years of investigation and prosecution, all 21 defendants in the Narducci case were acquitted of all charges. The judges in Florence found that not only were the defendants innocent, there simply was never any crime in the first place: The bodies were never swapped. But the targets of Mignini's charges were investigated and prosecuted over a period of eight years. Imagine the emotional drain, the uncertainty, the impact on your life and livelihood, and the legal bills.

Two other defendants in a related prosecution were, however, convicted. The two? PM Giuliano Mignini and Chief Inspector Giutarri were convicted of misconduct in their investigation. Mignini was convicted of prosecutorial misconduct including illegal wiretapping and other unlawful means of investigation.

What was taken from the Narducci defendants can never be restored. Eight years of living under the threat of imprisonment. Eight years of persecution on the basis of ludicrous charges. Yet, even now, it isn't over for them. Mignini is not only appealing his own conviction, he is appealing the acquittals of the defendants he charged. That's right, the prosecution can appeal acquittals. There is no such thing as a bar against double jeopardy in Italy. If at first you don't convict, try – try – again.

## Prosecutorial Rampage

This entire debacle, this *prosecutorial rampage,* was set in motion in the mind of Mignini by a clue from a spirit channeler. Who would believe – and stake his career on that belief – that an ordinary drug overdose was actually perpetrated by a vast network of Satan-worshiping conspirators? What kind of mind latches onto such a slender thread and follows it down such a tortuous path? And even more disturbing than that is the way Mignini chose to follow that tortuous path.

An article in Panorama dated 2/11/2010 described a series of files that investigators found in Mignini's personal computer:

"From December 2005 to May 2006 a file was created and added to entitled "Attacks to Remember," in which there is another file: "Orgy of Attacks Following the Arrest of Spezi; an index of newspapers: Libero, Il Giornale, Oggi." Following that is a long list of people "To Remember" that consisted of the names of some of the most prominent judges involved in the case of the Monster of Florence, a long list of politicians, among which could be found the ex-mayor of Florence, Leonardo Domenici, the deputy mayor Michele Venturo and the Minister of the Environment Altero Matteoli, all of whom signed a petition of solidarity protesting Spezi's incarceration."

Mignini is not a man who forgives and forgets. He is a man who identifies and pursues enemies – real or imagined – with a vengeance that could be called obsession. And he is a man who has, more than once, discerned satanic sex conspiracies behind mundane crimes.

Panorama 2/11/2010

"Spezi's arrest unleashed scathing criticism by some journalists. Giuttari and Mignini responded with a series of "assessments" (later judged illegal by the tribunale) authorized under the signature of

Judge Marina De Robertis, who used a legal procedure meant only to be employed in an emergency; but these emergency authorizations were never retroactively justified as required by law."

In other words, Mignini pushed through extraordinary surveillance orders under the excuse of some pressing emergency, then didn't quite get around to explaining what the emergency was. These contingencies were the sort of thing meant to deal with mafia activities, not criticisms from journalists. It was a fundamental abuse of the power he was entrusted with.

"One of the cases involved the wiretapping of a cellular telephone owned by the daily newspaper, La Stampa, in use by the reporter Vincenzo Tessandori, who was moreover illegally investigated beyond normal judicial procedures, but who had written several articles critical of the investigation. The same illegal harassment was directed at other newspaper reporters such as Gennaro De Stefano (who has since died) and Roberto Fiasconaro."

Giuttari and Mignini ordered the wiretapping and shadowing of two police officials from the press office of the Polizia in Rome, who had earlier asked Giuttari to limit his television appearances. Giuttari, it seems, was writing a book about the Monster of Florence murders, and was beginning his media career. In his imagination, at least, Giuttari seems to run into many widespread murder conspiracies.

"But Ferrara quickly realizes that the truth is darker than that: he believes that the girl was murdered. And when he delves deeper, there are many aspects to the case that convince Ferrara that the girl's death is part of a sinister conspiracy–a conspiracy that has its roots in the very foundations of Tuscan society..." Description of *A Death in Tuscany*, Michelle Giuttari

Mignini placed wiretaps on the police officials who asked for the TV appearance cut backs. He tapped the cell phones of reporters who criticized him and his investigation. He pursued many of those who disagreed with his prosecutions and had the courage to oppose him. The criticism from journalists he called "an orgy of attacks." Well-stated criticisms were "attacks to remember," and those who opposed him were persons "to remember." Remember these reminders; you will need them to complete the final section of this chapter.

Mignini claimed to be taken by surprise by his own conviction for misconduct in 2009.

"I did not expect this inability to understand...this constant acrimonious vilification," the prosecutor complained.

"I am shocked," Mignini said in an interview with seattlepi.com after the hearing, held in an ancient, baroque Florentine courtroom with oak paneling and antique leather chairs. "It was totally unexpected."

Of course, this wasn't the first time that a person given great authority has taken even more of the same.

From Dr. Strangelove:

President Muffley: "General Turgidson, I find this very difficult to understand. I was under the impression that I was the only one with the authority to order the use of nuclear weapons."

General Turgidson: "That's right sir. You are the only person authorized to do so. And although I hate to judge, before all the facts are in, it is beginning to look like, uh, General Ripper has exceeded his authority."

Did Mignini learn his lesson after all of this? Apparently not. The blogger Carlizzi wrote a post just four days after Meredith's murder claiming that it was part of the same series of murders as the Monster of Florence case. Mignini, once again picking up Carlizzi's insight, declared in early hearings that Meredith's murder was part of a sexual, sacrificial rite associated with Halloween.

The framing of Amanda Knox follows in a direct progression from Mignini's prosecutorial misconduct in the Monster of Florence case. The framing may even have been driven by needs arising from that case.

**Closing Arguments**

To see the mind of Mignini fully unleashed, his spectacular and unbelievable closing arguments in this case cannot be matched. It was a performance of operatic dimensions, full of sex and violence and entirely a figment of his imagination.

> "There could have been an argument between Meredith and Amanda that then degenerated because of the rental money that had disappeared or maybe Meredith was annoyed by the mere presence of Rudy," Mignini's closing arguments

Notice that Mignini said, "There could have been an argument." Not that there was any evidence of one, but, you never know... and that seems to have been enough for the Court in Perugia, as will be shown in Chapter Eleven.

> "After a heated discussion, the three, under the influence of the drugs, and probably alcohol as well, decide to put into action the project they had of involving an extreme sex game."

> "Amanda has the occasion to get back at that overly serious and moralizing English girl who she felt was too tied to the closed group of her English friends, and who accused her not too subtly of not being orderly or clean, and who criticized her for being too easy with boys."

> "Amanda nurtured her hate for Meredith, but that night that hate could explode. For Amanda the moment had come to take revenge on that prissy girl. That is what she must have thought. And in a crescendo of threats and increasing violence, Meredith's ordeal begins." - Mignini's closing arguments

There is no evidence, and there was no testimony, that Amanda harbored a "hatred" of Meredith. It is pure fiction. They went to parties together, got along well, and had never been seen having a single conflict. Indeed, no evidence to support any of these closing conjectures was ever presented in court. There didn't seem to be any need to do so. The jurors were captivated and appalled, following along almost as if they were moviegoers, suspending disbelief to enjoy a film.

Mignini even played a realistic, computer-generated animation depicting Amanda, Raffaele, and Rudy murdering Meredith. It was a totally fictitious rendering of events that are completely unsupported by the evidence. The movie was interspersed with photos of the final, bloody crime scene. It has since disappeared, and has never been seen again by outside eyes. Efforts by the defense to obtain the animation to show its extremely prejudicial nature have been refused. Yet, the court allowed it to be presented in the trial.

The "extreme sex game," motive that Mignini had first proposed for the murder, which appeared to have been abandoned during the trial, was reincarnated for use during closing arguments in which the defense was not allowed to object and not allowed to cross-examine. During his closing Mignini was also allowed to claim to the jury, unchallenged, that Amanda was deeply mentally disturbed.

What kind of mind dreams up such malice-filled fiction, such lurid, fantastical tales to put two innocent people in prison for the rest of their lives? What sort of mind projects unmitigated evil into the hearts of innocents?

## Motivation

It wouldn't be right to judge Mignini's actions without considering the possible motives behind them. Indeed, Mignini appears to be motivated by no less than a desire to save the world from evil. He describes this quest in a document he wrote entitled *The Gospel and the Strength*.

In *Gospel*, he refers to the "...the task of establishing and maintaining the Kingdom of God in the world...." No small task, that. Accomplishing his goal will require power: "...achieving that end can not disregard the use of force to overcome the obstacles, internal and external, who are opposed." Opposition to Mignini's establishment of the Kingdom of God on Earth will be overcome by force. Simple enough.

I bring this motivation up lest we rush to judgment and assume that PM Mignini may have acted out of personal interest, or something less than the very highest of ideals. We should remind ourselves that General Jack D. Ripper only acted when a line in the sand was crossed:

> From Dr. Strangelove: "I can no longer sit back and allow Communist infiltration, Communist indoctrination, Communist subversion and the international Communist conspiracy to sap and impurify all of our precious bodily fluids."

## Psychiatric Help – 5 Cents

With the Narducci prosecutions in mind, and after a taste of Mignini's closing arguments in this case – which began with shrill complaints about attacks from afar before moving on to a fantastical version of events – an unpleasant question has to be raised. Is Giuliano Mignini, like the fictional General Ripper, mentally ill?

To make such a diagnosis requires expertise. For example, to analyze Amanda's psychological makeup for his closing arguments, Mignini relied on an unnamed psychiatrist who was apparently retained by the actual murderer, Rudy Guede. This psychiatrist provided insights into what he claimed was the terrible dark side of her personality, even though he had never actually spoken with her.

Following Mignini's example, and in keeping with his profound grasp of fair play, we are eminently qualified to diagnose *him*, in turn. I took a couple of courses in psychology, and I am sure there are similarly qualified armchair psychiatrists among my readers.

No one is suggesting that Mignini is a full-blown paranoid schizophrenic. That would be obvious. This is an inquiry into whether he may suffer from a more subtle condition. We read, for example, in answers.com (which, I presume, has got all the answers) that "Individuals with delusional disorder may seem offbeat or quirky rather than mentally ill, and, as such, may never seek treatment." We make this inquiry not only that we might put a stop to the obvious wrongs that are now being perpetrated by him, but also, in the event of a positive finding, to encourage him to seek aid and support.

## A Very Good Place to Start

All of which brings us to something called Paranoid Personality Disorder, or PPD. There are plenty of personality disorders to choose from, but this one seems to me to be a very good place to start. The diagnostic criteria for PPD are spelled out in the *Diagnostic and Statistical Manual of Mental Disorders (fourth edition) (DSM-IV)*.

This manual is produced and updated by the American Psychiatric Association, but it comes in handy around the world. It provides a standard language for discussing mental disorders and defines specific criteria for diagnosing them. Of course, these matters are not without controversy, and are strongly influenced by opinions and interpretations.

With this in mind, my intention is that the reader consider Mignini's words and actions, some of which were reviewed above, and compare them with these diagnostic criteria. Readers can then make up their own minds as to whether they feel there may be some correspondence.

Remember that this is not an all-or-nothing matter. Sometimes these things are a matter of degree, with individuals landing somewhere along a spectrum of disorder. Identifying four or more out of the following seven criteria is enough for a diagnosis of PPD. What if the number is only three?

Paranoid Personality Disorder (PPD) is defined in DSM-IV as:

A pervasive distrust and suspicion of others such that their motives are interpreted as malevolent, beginning by early adulthood and present in a variety of contexts, as indicated by four (or more) of the following:

1) Suspects, without sufficient basis, that others are exploiting, harming, or deceiving him or her.

2) Is preoccupied with unjustified doubts about the loyalty or trustworthiness of friends or associates.

3) Is reluctant to confide in others because of unwarranted fear that the information will be used maliciously against him or her.

4) Reads benign remarks or events as threatening or demeaning.

5) Persistently bears grudges, i.e., is unforgiving of insults, injuries, or slights.

6) Perceives attacks on his or her character or reputation that are not apparent to others and is quick to react angrily or to counterattack.

7) Has recurrent suspicions, without justification, regarding fidelity of spouse or sexual partner.

I make no judgment on this issue, but from what I can discern from afar, the behavioral traits of Giuliano Mignini are *compatible with* paranoid personality disorder.

## Four – Nineteen Eighty-Four – Perugia Style

In George Orwell's classic novel, *Nineteen Eighty-Four*, everyone was monitored, everything observed, every word recorded. Human rights were trampled under an iron boot. The government was always right, especially when it was wrong. Finding a place to speak, or even to think privately, was futile.

"The telescreen received and transmitted simultaneously. Any sound that Winston made, above the level of a very low whisper, would be picked up by it; moreover, so long as he remained within the field of vision which the metal plaque commanded, he could be seen as well as heard." - 1984

The monitoring in *1984* was ubiquitous. Everyone assumed they were watched at all times. They factored that observation into their lives, and were fearful in every move they made.

"You had to live–did live, from habit that became instinct–in the assumption that every sound you made was overheard, and, except in darkness, every movement scrutinized." -1984

According to the Italian Ministry of Justice, 112,000 phones in Italy were monitored in 2009 and 13,000 locations were eavesdropped on, likely the highest incidence of wiretapping in Europe. This is the number of publicly acknowledged wiretaps and doesn't include unpublished activity.

It is widely understood that the e-mail and telephone conversations of journalists, friends, family members, and anyone else in Perugia associated with this trial were monitored. It is certainly known that every phone conversation of the initial suspects and of anyone else close to the scene of the crime was monitored in the days immediately after the murder. Conversations that took place in rooms at the questura in those days were recorded. Skype phone calls and emails were intercepted.

This near blanket eavesdropping was an accomplishment, but progress has also been made in the *selectivity* of what was monitored. In *1984, Perugia Style*, only the right things are recorded: only those conversations that support the prosecution's case, only those camera views that support Mignini's theories. At least, that is what we have been told by the prosecution. This selectivity has been brought to our attention, in part, because of the conspicuously unbelievable assertion that the final interrogations of both Amanda and Raffaele were not recorded, as previously discussed. There are many other examples.

Controlling information by destroying it or controlling how it is recorded and presented is a page torn by the Perugian authorities directly from *1984*. It is control of the past by controlling the present. When it just happens that the only written record remaining of Amanda Knox's interrogation was the translation created, recorded, and thereby controlled by the polizia interpreter, it is not surprising. When it just happens that no recording of the interrogation exists, so we are left, only with the record they want us to have, it is nothing new. These tactics are closely in line with what Orwell anticipated and decried many years before.

**The Memory Hole**

In *1984,* Winston worked at the Ministry of Truth, which was, of course, in charge of lies. Throughout the Ministry, there were small portals, pneumatically linked to a vast furnace somewhere beneath the building. These portals were called "memory holes" because whatever passed into them was forever destroyed.

> "When one knew that any document was due for destruction, or even when one saw a scrap of waste paper lying about, it was an automatic action to lift the flap of the nearest memory hole and drop it in, whereupon it would be whirled away on a current of warm air to the enormous furnaces which were hidden somewhere in the recesses of the building."

By continually destroying all records that did not agree with the current party line, the party maintained control of the truth.

"And if all others accepted the lie which the Party imposed – if all records told the same tale – then the lie passed into history and became truth. 'Who controls the past' ran the Party slogan, 'controls the future: who controls the present controls the past.'" - *1984*

## Format C:

Back in the day, "Format C:" was the death command for hard disks in MS-DOS computers. You'd tell an annoying computer novice asking too many questions to type that into the command line. They'd never ask for help again. The command erased all information from the main operating drive of the computer. I know people who accidentally did it (I did *not* suggest it).

Some of the most important evidence in this case was recorded in the computers of the victim and the accused. What was their personal relationship like? Did they get along? Did they hang out? Were there pictures that showed Amanda and Meredith together? Did Amanda have dark musings about savage attacks, or ruminations on how pretty the cottage was and how nice her roommates were? Could there be emails that described terrible conflicts and building tension – conflicts that the prosecution claims, but for which no shred of evidence was ever found? The computer memories were vital evidence in establishing this information, critical to the defense, and perhaps to the prosecution as well.

Unfortunately, the computer forensic experts of the polizia completely destroyed three out of the 4 computer hard disk drives that they examined in their investigation. They destroyed Amanda's, Meredith's, and one of Raffaele's two computers. It took Italian experts, whose skills have been lauded in recent testimony, to achieve this remarkable 75% rate of total failure. Perhaps it would have been good for them to glance at the Wikipedia article on the subject before they began. It follows.

"Only use tools and methods that have been tested and evaluated to validate their accuracy and reliability."

"Special care must be taken when handling computer evidence: most digital information is easily changed..." Wikipedia, Computer forensics

Creating an exact copy of a computer drive is called imaging. This process duplicates all data on the drive – it doesn't just make copies of the current files. In this way, data from files that previously existed but have been "deleted" are available for analysis. Every little buffer, cookie, and backup are available for analysis. Imagine the polizia computer expert hard at work making these precise duplicate copies of the data on these critically important pieces of information. As an expert, he must be aware of the requirement to "only use tools and methods that have been tested..." He is therefore using the utmost caution, using only tested techniques.

He somehow manages to fry all the vital data on the first disk drive. Oops. That critical disk swirls down the memory hole. He then proceeds to the second drive. And fries it as well. Hmmm. Something is not going right here. Yet, another drive went down the memory hole. What does he do? Does he ask for help? Does he reconsider his methods? Of course he doesn't. Practice makes perfect. He examines yet another disk drive, using the same tools and techniques, and sends it down the memory hole as well. Apparently, this was all in a day's work for these computer experts. During the appeals, the prosecution has claimed that their services are clamored for.

Urban legend has it that Einstein defined insanity as doing the same thing over and over and expecting different results. That is doubtful, but it is fairly certain that no Einstein worked for this computer forensics team. All of this is amazing, unbelievable... how could someone be so foolish, so incompetent – unless, of course, the erasures weren't accidental at all.

The defense has stated that Amanda's computer contained pictures of her happily socializing with Meredith, directly contradicting the prosecution's claim that they were at odds. Meredith's computer would likely have stored similar pictures, and perhaps emails and comments that she made about Amanda. The prosecution has controlled the past by erasing it.

They have since fought a defense motion to have the drives shipped to the manufacturer to see if they can restore the data. Was this a coincidence between the incompetence of the investigators and the convenience of the prosecution (which ran the investigation, remember)? Or was it a deliberate case of tampering with the evidence?

The same experts that destroyed this evidence then testified that Raffaele's remaining computer did not show signs of use during the period that he said he used it on the night of the crime. How much credibility should this testimony be afforded?

> From 1984: "The past, he reflected, had not merely been altered, it had been actually destroyed. For how could you establish even the most obvious fact when there existed no record outside your own memory?"

To interpret this mishandling of the evidence, one must consider the implausibility of a computer expert making such a fundamental, egregious error three times in a row alongside the probability that those drives contained information that would have aided the defense. These facts are compatible with the deliberate destruction of evidence favorable to the defense by the polizia and prosecution.

## Thoughtcrime Leads to Facecrime

> "It was terribly dangerous to let your thoughts wander when you were in any public place or within range of a telescreen. The smallest thing could give you away. A nervous tic, an unconscious look of anxiety, a habit of muttering to yourself – anything that carried with it the suggestion of abnormality, of having something to hide. In any case, to wear an improper expression on your face...; was itself a punishable offense. There was even a word for it in Newspeak: facecrime..." - 1984

Every expression on Amanda's face has been analyzed *ad nauseam* by the media and even by the court throughout this case. Her smiles have made headlines worldwide. Her outfits, hair length, tears or lack of tears, the quality and character of her Italian language skills, everything has been picked through. When she greeted her family at the start of each day's court proceedings, the photographers were there to capture every smile at her family and friends, amplifying them to portray her as glib, uncaring, and insensitive. The mere fact that her eyes are blue was enough to fuel speculation.

Amanda is clearly guilty of committing facecrime. She even wore an "All you need is love" shirt to court one day. In *1984*'s Newspeak, I guess this might be called "shirtcrime." It was as if she didn't want to be utterly consumed by the court. She tried to assert her own individual, loving self rather than to knuckle under and be consumed by the ordeal she was immersed in. For this she was pilloried, yet again, in the press and in Perugian public opinion, perhaps even contributing to her conviction. Her wearing that shirt, though, clearly was an effort to assert her individuality, and in *1984,* individuality was a crime.

## A Little Sorcery

Amanda stated in her interrogation that she and Raffaele had been reading a Harry Potter book in German at Raffaele's place the night of the murder. This was contradicted by leaks from the polizia of photos showing a Potter book at *her* apartment. This apparent contradiction was pounced upon and repeated – proof that Amanda had lied about her activities. The polizia photos of Raffaele's place, however, clearly showed that a German language Harry Potter book was at Raffaele's place, exactly as Amanda said.

In fact, there were two HP books in German, one at each apartment. Try to find that fact in a news article. It is easy to find news articles that cite the Harry Potter book as evidence that Amanda lied about her whereabouts the night of the murder. See, for instance, The Times of London article entitled "Harry Potter clue revealed in Meredith Kercher murder":

"A Harry Potter book which Amanda Knox, the American student suspected of involvement in the murder of Meredith Kercher, claimed to have read at her boyfriend's flat on the evening of the murder has been found – not at the flat but at the cottage where the British student was killed."

If you try to find articles explaining that there was no discrepancy, that the Potter book was right where they said it was, it will be a much longer search.

"But you could prove nothing. There was never any evidence."
"I tell you Winston, that reality is not external. Reality exists in the human mind, and nowhere else.... Whatever the party holds to be truth, is truth." *1984*

With the media's cooperation, the Ministry of Truth had done its job.

## Alone With Her Thoughts

At the end of *1984,* Winston's rebellion against authority is discovered and he is arrested. He serves time in the Ministry of Love, which was entrusted with the task of torturing enemies of the state.

> From 1984: "Never again will you be capable of ordinary human feeling. Everything will be dead inside you. Never again will you be capable of love, or friendship, or joy of living, or laughter, or curiosity, or courage, or integrity. You will be hollow."

PM Giuliano Mignini demanded that not only should Amanda receive a sentence of life in prison, but that it begin with nine months of complete isolation during daylight hours; solitary confinement. Nine months without contact with people, while looking forward to spending the rest of her life in prison. Amanda had already been confined for 23 hours a day before even being charged, and she was not allowed to speak with the other prisoners during the one hour she was not confined.

What was the goal of this demand? Was it to cut her off entirely from the outside world, so that she could no longer proclaim her innocence? Was it so she would be forgotten? Or was it to crush her spirit by destroying all hope?

Stuart Grassian, M.D., a board certified psychiatrist who has extensively studied solitary confined prisoners in a number of prisons, made the following observations about this practice.

> "...confinement of a prisoner alone in a cell for all or nearly all of the day, with minimal environmental stimulation and minimal opportunity for social interaction – can cause severe psychiatric harm."
>
> "...many – including some who did not become overtly psychiatrically ill during their confinement in solitary – will likely suffer permanent harm as a result of such confinement."

*Severe psychiatric harm... permanent harm.* Remember that Mignini's request for solitary confinement wasn't in response to violent, uncontrollable behavior in prison (which Amanda has never exhibited), but was requested at the *beginning of her sentence,* before the appeals process had even begun. This, in spite of the fact that under Italian law defendants are not even considered to be convicted until their appeals have been exhausted.

The *Sourcebook on Solitary Confinement* by Sharon Shalev states:

> "The potentially damaging effects of solitary confinement are also recognized by national and international instruments and by monitoring bodies, which view it as an extreme prison practice which should only be used as a last resort and then only for short periods of time."

And yet, Mignini wanted this crushing, extreme punishment used upfront, before it could be stopped. It was not only a rush to judgment, it was a rush to inflict harm as quickly as possible before the appeals had any chance to overturn the verdict.

Giuliano Mignini sought to inflict punishment that might have caused permanent psychological damage to Amanda Knox, and he sought to do so as soon as possible. Why?

Fortunately, the court rejected solitary confinement, along with a life term, and gave her a sentence that Mignini called "lenient" – 26 years in prison. Mignini appealed this sentence, again demanding life in prison, and used his appeal as part of an excuse (along with alleged complexity) to remain involved in the prosecution, an involvement that would normally be a violation of Italian law. Of course, Italy has something on the order of 200,000 laws, which they appear to use selectively.

> Prisoners in solitary "begin to lose the ability to initiate behavior of any kind–to organize their own lives around activity and purpose," he writes. "Chronic apathy, lethargy, depression, and despair often result. . . . In extreme cases, prisoners may literally stop behaving, becoming essentially catatonic."

Tens of thousands of prisoners are currently in solitary confinement worldwide, many of them in the United States.

"So I wait. The waiting is pain because it is waiting without life, as life passes me by, but I'm waiting still, because it is all I can do. I think about my freedom and it is what I do to keep going, because I know I will be free. I will be with my family and my friends and I will be able to live the life I've always seen myself living: traveling, marrying, having children, writing, speaking, helping, dancing, free, loving." Amanda's Prison Diary

# Part II – BLEEDING EDGE FORENSICS

# Five – Sherlock Holmes and the Adventure

# of Forensic Science

(Author's Note) In writing this chapter, I faced a dilemma. If the material were presented in detail, many readers would lose track of the narrative of the book. On the other hand, if the material were stripped down to the essentials, useful content would be lost. To resolve this, I have written short and long versions of the same material. A brief, essential précis follows, while a more complete version appears as the forensic science appendix. The same split has been used for the same reason in Chapter Seven - *DNA – A Simple Twist of Fate*, a brief version is included in the main narrative, and a more complete version appears in the appendices.

Sherlock Holmes, the world's first investigative detective, could discern your occupation from the way you wore your hat. Sir Arthur Conan Doyle's famous character could sniff at your tobacco and determine that you had fallen on hard times, or glance at your shoes and know which borough of London you resided in. His skills and insights were nothing less than remarkable. Of course, they were also pure fiction.

> "Pipes are occasionally of extraordinary interest," said he. "Nothing has more individuality, save perhaps watches and bootlaces. The indications here, however, are neither very marked nor very important. The owner is obviously a muscular man, left-handed, with an excellent set of teeth, careless in his habits, and with no need to practice economy." *Sherlock Holmes*

Some of today's forensic scientists say they have similar skills. They claim they can tell how many people were involved in an attack from the number of wounds, can deduce a day's activities from a few cell phone calls, and improve the fundamental performance of analytical equipment with the twist of a knob. Unfortunately, this is also pure fiction. On a worldwide basis, the quality and reliability of forensic evidence has all too frequently been distorted, blown out of proportion, and not properly vetted by scientific methods.

In fact, the entire field of forensic science is currently under review – some even say it is under attack. This review isn't just led by defense attorneys, but by governments, scientists, and others who believe that the proper role of forensic science is to assist in identifying and convicting the guilty– that they might be stopped– and freeing the innocent. Not the other way around.

That is placing it in stark, simple terms of course, but forensic science has been at the heart of a fundamental and ongoing failure of the criminal justice systems of even the world's most advanced nations. For those nations that are on the borderline, the situation is far worse. Far from the public's common CSI show-inspired misconception that the field comprises brilliant and attractive forensic scientists operating state-of-the-art equipment to solve intractable cases by the end of the hour, the reality is a hodgepodge, patchwork quilt of over-worked investigators with wildly varying capabilities, training, and facilities.

In the wake of discoveries of wrongful convictions that were at least partly caused by mistaken forensic science work, the U.S. Congress requested a review of the field by the National Academy of Sciences. That report concluded that there are serious and fundamental issues that require reform, and made recommendations. Even within the United States, forensic science facilities vary enormously in their capabilities and staffing, ranging from sophisticated purpose-built laboratories to the back room at the county courthouse. Expand the view to an international perspective and the variation is even wider. The result is a far-too-common failure to identify and convict the guilty and to free the innocent.

I do not mean to criticize the great majority of the world's forensics experts, who try their best to honestly do their jobs. They need help, and often, they are not receiving it. Many of the most critical problems in this field could be addressed with adequate funding and proper support.

But there are also problems that result from shortcomings in the techniques of forensic science, and from a failure to separate the responsibility for performing forensic science investigations from the responsibility for convicting criminals. This results in a fundamental and systemic conflict of interest between the funding and career prospects of forensic researchers and the judgment calls they must make.

Before we explore these issues, a basic question: What is "forensic science"? What does that term really mean and how does it differ from "regular" science? In general, forensic science is defined as a set of scientific, or *scholarly,* methods used to investigate matters of interest to a court. The word "scholarly" is of interest here, because that means learned, but it does not necessarily mean scientific, and there can be a world of difference. More specifically, forensic science is a set of different investigative disciplines such as fingerprint analysis, ballistics, bite mark analysis, and DNA profiling.

The ultimate objective of forensic science is to apply the powerful techniques of modern science in the service of justice. To better understand forensic science let's take a fairly large step back for a brief review of science itself. I do this because it appears to me that there isn't a lot of understanding of the relationship between science and forensic science, and because that lack of understanding seems to be common among the Polizia Scientifica. So let's go back to school for a bit and talk about *science.*

**The Scientific Method**

Scientific research is performed by a fairly well defined set of methods that have been developed mostly over the last century. As part of that method, theories and experimental techniques are subjected to a rigorous process of peer review in which other researchers ask probing and difficult questions about the work. Peer review takes place both by presenting the experiments and explanations in a public forum before other investigators with credentials in the field, and by publication in the peer-reviewed technical literature.

If an experiment produces results that are interesting enough to pursue, other researchers will reproduce it in an independent facility to validate, refute, or refine the research and its conclusions. This comprises the vital step of determining reproducibility. If an experiment cannot be reproduced, it cannot be said to be valid, it is irreproducible. The famous *Journal of Irreproducible Results*, a satirical science magazine, is full of outrageous experiments that could never be reproduced (nor would anyone want to). The JIR recently held a contest for funniest graph, for instance. The winner: *All Theories Proven With one Graph*. It's a very impressive graph.

People perform science. As a result, it is blessed and burdened, as is any other human endeavor, by our strengths and weaknesses. But the design of the scientific method is intended to achieve a real understanding of existence that is independent of the researcher. The method was conceived to harness human insights and abilities while transcending human foibles and failings.

Real science benefits from exposure, criticism, and review. The light of day is welcomed, demanded, it is a fundamental part of the process. Pseudoscience hides its dirty work in the shadows while putting on a pretentious show. It is like a magic act in which your attention is directed toward the beautiful woman, while the magician pulls the sleight of hand behind his back. A pseudoscientist wants you to look at the fancy machine, the impressive graph, while somewhere out of view the books are being cooked and the results compromised.

## Guilds and Craftsmen

The power of scientific methods to unlock information cannot be disputed. Unfortunately, not all of the techniques that comprise forensic science were developed that way. In fact, some of those techniques are skills that were accumulated over time in a manner more closely resembling a medieval craft than a science.

When people confuse the abilities of full tilt scientific research with a technique cooked up by some guy that took a correspondence school course, you have a problem. When someone makes up a brand new test method that hasn't been subjected to *any review whatever*, let alone fully vetted by a peer review process, and then pretends that it is "scientific," you have the potential for grossly misleading judges and jurors, leading to terrible miscarriages of justice.

## They Blinded Me With Science

From the adventures of Sherlock Holmes at the turn of the last century to the popular and numerous crime scene investigation series *CSI* many of the common conceptions of detective work in general and forensic science in particular have been shaped by fictional accounts rather than the far-more-mundane reality. Real investigators are human beings; they are not all brilliant analysts with superhuman insight. Real "forensic scientists" often aren't even scientists at all, but "practitioners" who may have little or even no formal scientific education.

This isn't too important for the plot of a TV adventure. The crime will be solved before the final station break no matter what. But if you happen to be a suspect in a murder case, or if a loved one was the victim of a crime, the gulf between the reality and fiction of forensic science takes on critical importance. It is important because the actual abilities of forensic science to lay bare mysteries and solve crimes simply do not begin to approach either the expectations of non-technical persons or the claims of some forensic scientists. It is also important because the final determination of innocence or guilt is made by some of the same lay persons who are fundamentally ill informed on the matter: the jurors.

This misinformation is a double-edged sword. It can cut the prosecution, or it can damn the defense. Having seen neat, clear, convincing scientific evidence on CSI type shows, many jurors now expect a scientist to walk into the courtroom and present rock solid DNA evidence. They expect a beautiful full color chart or a computer animation that tells who did what and how and that points a virtual arrow of guilt at the defendant. There is even a name for the phenomenon: the "CSI effect." This helps the defense, because real world evidence is rarely so cut and dried, nor so impressively presented.

On the other hand, jurors can also regard forensic practitioners with unwarranted reverence, accepting their word as the word of "science" rather than seeing it as what it sometimes is, an opinion voiced by someone who is in league with the prosecutor, and whose livelihood depends on coming up with material to support the claims of that prosecutor. Such a practitioner may be anything but objective – anything but fair. This conflict of interest has led to calls for the separation of forensic laboratories from police, prosecutors, and other parts of the criminal justice system. The NAS report, in particular, has urged for such separation.

## The Advent of DNA Profiling

In the 1980s, a technique called *DNA profiling* was developed. For the first time, it provided a genuinely scientifically developed technique to *individualize* evidence from a crime scene. Individualizing evidence means that it was possible to specifically connect physical evidence from a crime scene with a particular individual as the source of that material. That's different from methods that merely suggest a class of people, such as a male in his thirties or a left-handed suspect. When biological traces are left behind that are clearly associated with a crime, DNA profiling could often label a specific person as the source of that material.

This new ability brought with it an unintended benefit. Not only could this technique give powerful evidence to aid current investigations, it could be used to reanalyze evidence from crimes that had been committed years – even decades – before.

This was a great boon to prosecutors, who could look at cold cases from the past and finally bring criminals to justice, but it had yet another consequence. The new technique of DNA profiling was also applied to cases in which people loudly proclaimed their innocence. Many of these people had been convicted, at least partly, on the basis of forensic science techniques. Yet, when DNA profiling was used to review the evidence, hundreds of convicted people in the United States alone *were proven to be innocent*. The stunning implication was that the results from these other forensic techniques were wrong. Moreover, while those hundreds of overturned convictions were important, they were just the visible tip of the iceberg. Many times that number of false convictions must exist, but simply weren't amenable to review by DNA profile techniques.

*Innocence Projects*, which were organized in many cities, performed much of this work. Defense lawyers who had run up against dead ends teamed up with the new DNA forensics experts and tested the biological evidence left behind in many of these serious crimes. In hundreds of cases, the DNA proved them right. And they were set free.

All of this raised a fundamental question. If the results from some of these other forensic science techniques implied that innocent persons were guilty, what did that say about those techniques? It said that they did not work as advertised. Their reliability was called into question by the unequivocal discovery that in many cases their application led to the wrongful convictions of innocent people. Which makes one wonder; where did these forensic science techniques come from? Why were they applied for decades when they didn't really work?

Although forensic practitioners frequently use the term "science," it is sometimes a bit of an exaggeration. In fact, there are wide discrepancies between the various forensic science disciplines as to how carefully they were developed in the first place, and how well they have been reviewed, tested, and analyzed over the years. The result is that a few of them are quite sound, such as the analysis of fingerprints, but several others are on far shakier ground. Yet, they are routinely applied in cases that affect people's lives and freedom.

When techniques are applied even though they are not really understood, their results, interpretation, and evidentiary value are simply not reliable. When verdicts are rendered on the basis of these unreliable results, innocent people go to jail, and guilty, dangerous people are free to commit further crimes. The loss to society is tremendous. The loss to victims, past and future, and to the wrongfully convicted, may devastate their lives.

## The Drive for Reform

As a result of this discovery of flaws at the heart of forensic science, the United States Congress requested a review of the field from the National Academy of Sciences, one of the most prestigious scientific bodies in the world. The NAS performed that study and released *Strengthening Forensic Science in the United States: A Path Forward.* For more on that important report including a link where you can read the original document, see the forensic science Appendix.

In the United States, the court ruling that determines the admissibility of forensic evidence is called the *Daubert Test,* it was established in 1993. It reads as follows:

> (1) whether the theory or technique can be and has been tested, (2) whether the theory or technique has been subjected to peer review and publication, (3) the known or potential rate of error, (4) the existence and maintenance of standards controlling the technique's operation, and (5) whether the theory or technique enjoys general acceptance within a relevant scientific community.

These are standards and ideas that apply to U.S. law, not to Italian courts, but the common sense, logic, and scientific validity has application anywhere. Science and logic sometimes cross borders with ease. Other times, not so much.

**Inculpation and Exculpation**

Exculpation is the process of ruling a suspect out by suggesting or proving their innocence. Evidence is said to be *exculpatory* if it suggests or proves innocence. Inculpation is the inverse, implying that a suspect may be guilty of the alleged crime. Inculpatory evidence suggests guilt, but it does not prove it. For more on these important concepts, again, see the appendix and bibliography.

**Probative Value**

*Probative value* is an important aspect of evidence because information doesn't help a bit in an investigation unless it has that. Although this may seem obvious, I believe that failure to understand it lies at the heart of some of the most important misunderstandings in this case.

Consider two fingerprints left at two different crime scenes. The first print – call it "Print A," was found at an apartment where a murder occurred and is an exact match to someone from a community 50 miles away. That person had no business ever being in that apartment. He had no relationship with the apartment: he wasn't the landlord or a former tenant. There is no innocent explanation for his print being there. This fingerprint is clearly inculpatory. It suggests that he may have been present at the crime, and therefore involved in it.

Now consider a second fingerprint, "Print B," found on a random item at an apartment that was shared by several people and where a crime was committed. It is found to be a match for one of the roommates at the apartment. So what? It probably doesn't mean anything relevant to the case. The roommate lived there, and there is nothing surprising that he left traces of his presence at the scene. The evidence matches, but it is not inculpatory because it doesn't really provide any information that he was involved in the crime. There is, in other words, a perfectly innocent explanation for the fingerprint to be present at the place where the suspect lived. Your fingerprints are present at your home, for example, and yet you probably haven't committed any heinous crimes lately.

The difference between these two fingerprints is captured by the idea of whether the evidence is *probative*, whether it tends to prove a *relevant* point. Print A appears to have been left behind by someone who had no legitimate business being in a place that was a crime scene. That discovery has significant value in determining guilt or innocence. Print B was left by someone on a mundane object at his own home, where he had every right to be. It provides no information that is relevant to the case. The probative value of evidence is whether it is useful to prove, or contribute to proving, something important in a trial.

## A Man's Gotta Know His Limitations

Sherlock Holmes may not have needed Dirty Harry's edict, "A man's gotta know his limitations," but mortal forensic scientists might benefit by keeping the Clint Eastwood character's insight in mind. Crime scenes almost invariably bear evidence of what took place during the crime. One of the fundamental ideas of crime scene investigations, and one that has proven extremely useful, is that it is nearly impossible to be involved in a violent act without

65

leaving some kinds of traces behind. They might be fingerprints, or DNA traces, footprints, tire marks. If they look carefully, investigators can find clues as to what happened and who was there when it did. But that record is imperfect. It does not provide some kind of video recording of what took place.

In a crime scene the pattern of blood, glass, footprints, etc. might have resulted from any of a number of possible events. You can't figure out exactly which one happened no matter how long you look at the evidence. You can get the general picture, but if you know your limitations like Harry, you recognize that a general idea of what happened is the best you can do. This fundamental limitation appears to be sometimes lost on some forensic scientists, who must work on the edge of this information boundary and are often pressed to give answers that they just don't have. Failure to resist such pressures has led many forensics experts to give testimony that exaggerated the certainty, or sensitivity of lab results, often leading to wrongful convictions.

## Control Experiments

Scientists are serious control freaks, when it comes to experiments anyway. Without proper controls, you have no idea what you are measuring. Control tests are such a fundamental matter that they are almost lost in the grass, yet an experiment without a control is like an old style thermometer without a scale. You see the mercury inside, but you have nothing to compare it with. There are two choices at this point. You can understand that the mercury level is meaningless, because there is nothing to compare it with, or you can point at it and make up any temperature you want.

Positive and negative control tests are vital checks that help to ensure that a test is testing what you think it is testing. If you include the factor that you are testing for, you had better get a positive test result. This is a *positive control test*. If you don't include that factor, you had better not get a positive result. This is a *negative control test*. If can't get the results you expect when you are controlling what goes into the test, how could you expect to know what the results mean when you have an unknown variable?

"Scientific controls are a vital part of the scientific method, since they can eliminate or minimize unintended influences such as researcher bias." Wikipedia

## Blind Experiments – The Blind Leading the Blind

Careful scientists also take steps to keep their own researcher bias from influencing results. They perform what are called blind and double blind experiments to avoid introducing experimenter bias, whether deliberate or not, into their results. In a double blind experiment, even the researcher doesn't know which specimen is which. Careful researchers do this to prevent themselves from knowing what the results "should be." That way, when they get a result, they can trust it, because they know they didn't unconsciously choose it. In any experimental situation where there is any kind interpretation or data massaging possible, it is important that the experimenter not know which results are hoped for.

## Forensics at the Crossroads

This has been a very brief primer on the state of forensic science in the early 21$^{st}$ century. It is a discipline at a crossroads. There have been great successes and important advances, but there have been terrible abuses as well. Opportunities to better exploit scientific advances to identify and convict guilty people have been missed because of inadequate funding, and inadequate attention to the needs of the field. Innocent people have spent their lives in prison because of inadequate techniques, shameful incompetence, and sometimes deliberate wrongdoing on the part of investigators. Other people have become victims when an innocent person was convicted and the guilty person went on to commit more crimes.

Consider that situation. If a guilty person is simply not yet identified and captured, at least they are on the run, fearful, and concerned about bringing attention to themselves. But when an innocent person is convicted of a crime that someone else committed, the person who is actually guilty is, in a powerful sense, liberated, nearly free from legal pursuit. The authorities are no longer after them. They have a conviction for that crime in hand, and, with limited resources will usually move on to other matters.

Freeing innocent people who have been wrongfully convicted is often seen as something in the province of liberals. But for every innocent person wrongfully serving time for a crime they did not commit, there may be a guilty person still at large: A person who is likely to commit additional crimes. For every wrongful conviction, there may be multiple future victims of crimes. It is a terrible price for those victims and a terrible price for society – not just a price for the wrongfully convicted.

Forensic science has reached the point at which the demands that are made on the discipline and the people practicing it often exceed the resources and the body of knowledge that are required to do a proper job. And we have a situation where fundamental conflicts of interest were built into the forensic science system from day one, contaminating many of the findings that can determine the safety of our citizens, and threatening the liberty of innocent suspects.

This has been a look at where things stand in forensic science on a good day, with good faith efforts being made all around. Now let's take a look at what happens under less favorable conditions. Let's take a look at forensic science, Perugia style.

## Six – Methods of the Polizia PseudoScientifica

## A Knife, a Clasp, a Glow

Procrustes was a clever mythical bandit. A son of Poseidon, god of the sea in the Greek pantheon, his name means "the stretcher." Procrustes had a decidedly uncivil way of providing hospitality. He would graciously offer guests the use of his rigid, metal bed – with just one catch. If they happened to be too short, he stretched them to fit. If they happened to be too tall, he cut their legs off. Procrustes had an idea just how tall guests ought to be and he made sure that his preconceived ideas were agreed with by the facts. To say that something is Procrustean is to say that it has been forcibly made to comply with some predetermined result.

There are as many ways of stretching things as there are "stretchers," but let's keep our eyes open for Procrustes as we look at the methods used in this case by the Italian forensic science unit, the Polizia Scientifica, which I call the "Polizia PseudoScientifica" for reasons that will be clear.

We have seen that there can be serious issues with forensic determinations even when performed in the best of situations. We have seen that, far from forensic science comprising a set of straightforward, standardized, orderly procedures that yield concrete results that can always be relied upon, they are sometimes a hodgepodge of unproven techniques and subjective interpretations performed by poorly trained investigators in ill-equipped laboratories. Even on a good day, it is a difficult business – one with people's lives hanging in an unsteady balance.

We must also keep in mind that forensic science is performed, and testified about, by people – not by impartial, implacable machines. Like Procrustes, these people often have preconceived ideas – they have their own interests, and they have bosses who may even possess a thought or two. They are part of a culture, and part of a political realm. Thinking of forensic test results as if they were produced in a manner that is somehow isolated from these realities is a fundamental mistake. This chapter is about forensic science performed in that less-than-perfect world, a world like Perugia, Italy, for example.

## Sorting Pepper from Fly Shit

But first, let me take a moment to talk about sorting pepper from fly shit. Since we're going to discuss pseudoscience, *pretend science*, I should preface this chapter with a brief explanation of my background in the area. I have a decade or so of professional experience at spotting technical exaggerations and distortions. It was acquired in the course of reviewing technologies, both real and – as it sometimes turned out – pseudoscientific, for investors, for businesses considering acquisitions, and for some of the largest companies in the world.

The technologies I reviewed (and still do) were mostly in the field of forensic identification, (anti-counterfeiting, shoplifting prevention, and identification), but the methods used for those purposes come from many technical fields – electronics, optics, physics, radiochemistry, DNA, nanotechnology, and others.

At those meetings, there would typically be one or more Ph.D.s presenting the technology they had developed over the previous several years. It was often my job to listen to what they had to say, witness the technology or device in action, and cut through the complications to understand what was really important. Did it really work as advertised? What issues were likely to crop up as it passed from the laboratory to the field? What were the real shortcomings and difficulties? As a general rule, what the technical people would tell you at these meetings was true. But sometimes, there were important things that they did *not* tell you. That was the type of distortion that I learned to look for. At the "meeting after the meeting," I would explain and evaluate what we had all heard.

One co-worker, a former military intelligence officer, called this "sorting pepper from fly shit." It was figuring out which science was real, and which was unsupported, unworkable, and occasionally downright pseudoscientific. After doing that in many such meetings, and many, many technologies reviewed, I believe I have some expertise at recognizing pseudoscience.

**Let's Pretend We're Scientists!**

I described that expertise because when one examines the methods of the Polizia Scientifica in the Knox/Sollecito investigation, they appear to have been not merely unscientific, but *pseudoscientific*. That means *pretend* science: it is not the real thing. We see this because a consistent pattern emerged. It was not a pattern of innocent mistakes made under the stress of time, although there were plenty of those. Neither was it one entirely of incompetence, although there was plenty of that as well.

The pattern in the Knox/Sollecito investigation was something like this: The Polizia Scientifica plucked an item from the field, often with much fanfare and a great show of force. They subjected it to some sort of *scientific* testing. Then they *cherry picked* the results and presented these selected results in the absence of anything to compare them with. That is, without any control experiments.

This method of operation is *compatible with* pseudoscience. It appears to be an attempt to create the appearance of scientific certainty while producing absolutely unscientific results.

> "...pseudoscience is any subject that appears superficially to be scientific, or whose proponents state that it is scientific, but which nevertheless contravenes the testability requirement..." Wikipedia

What is this "testability requirement"? It means that if you can't *test the test*, if you can't repeat an experiment to see if it happens again, and yet they claim that it is a scientific result, it isn't science. It is pseudoscience.

**The Object of the Game**

To understand forensic science in a less-than-perfect world, (and I know this may seem like a cart before the horse), let's *begin* by thinking about what might happen if an investigator's intentions were less than honorable. What might one do if the desire was to produce a particular result, rather than to objectively analyze evidence? What if the result was preordained, and it was your job as a forensic scientist to support it by drumming up some damning evidence? Assume that you accepted such a mission... regardless of whether your motives were high minded but uncritical support for higher ups in your organization, or morals be damned, let's get these guys. What would you do?

The idea here is that thinking about how an unscrupulous scientific investigator might proceed may be helpful down the road. I am not deciding in advance that such a thing has occurred, but only trying to point out suspicious activities to watch out for. If we are to spot Procrustes in action, it will be helpful to have his description, as it were. As we do so, we should take great care not to become Procrustes ourselves, forcing our own interpretations into a pre-ordained mold.

Here are some thoughts as to what the methods of such investigators might be.

1) Make it look *scientific*. You'd want to knock the socks off the judges, the jurors, and – perhaps most of all – the greater audience of people who are watching. Impressive looking outfits, charts, and equipment would be essential. Fancy shows are nice for real science too, of course, but if you're faking it, they are essential.

2) Do it in secret. You certainly wouldn't want the defense to know what you did or how you did it. If they knew the details of your experiments, they could attack them in court and show that they didn't prove what you claimed. Therefore, you wouldn't document any more than you had to, but just enough to make it look good. The rest of the process you would do behind closed doors and you would refuse to release the details. That way your work would make a big splash while leaving a small, difficult to discern footprint. Secrecy about the process is, perhaps, the clearest sign that something is amiss.

3) Milk the crime scene. Find the "proof" you need by milking the site for every useful tidbit. The crime scene is out there, and you know whom you're supposed to convict. Begin by finding the evidence that matches the suspects. There was plenty of natural background "evidence" available, since the targets either lived there (in Amanda's case) or visited (Raffaele). All that was needed was to find stuff that associated them with the crime. *In situ* evidence is the best kind.

4) If at first you don't succeed, try, try, again. If you failed to find what you needed in the first passes, you would make damned sure that you came up with the evidence the boss demanded, no matter what it took. If you couldn't trump up the evidence you found at the scene, you'd work something out.

I want to make it clear that I am not stating that the Polizia Scientifica actively participated in a deliberate, coordinated conspiracy to frame Amanda and Raffaele. After all, these sensitive polizia toss off defamation charges like a cat sheds hair. Their actions were probably more haphazard, perhaps making things up as they went along, like bumper cars bouncing off one obstacle after another. As for their motives for what they did on this case, we may never really know. This is another area for readers to arrive at their own judgments. Keep a mental scorecard for the scientific police to see if their actions align with some of the methods of pseudoscience. Also, make a little note of whether their actions happened to work in support of the framing of Amanda Knox.

## Pass the Collection Plate

The polizia collected evidence with a flare for the scientific. One can view excerpts of the videos taken at the time on youtube.com (See links in the bibliography. I've reviewed the raw footage from which these were excerpted). Looking at these videos, there appears to be an effort to impress without the substance behind it. The investigators wore Tyvek "moon suits," latex gloves, and breathing masks. But they do almost nothing to prevent cross contamination from those same outfits.

They rarely, if ever change their gloves, a standard precaution to avoid transferring contaminating material from item to item, thereby corrupting the condition of those items. In fact, there is no video evidence of any glove changing in the entire evidence collection process. Instead, they picked up item after item using the same – sometimes visibly contaminated – gloves. The head of this effort, Dr. Patrizia Stefanoni, later testified in court that she only changed her gloves after handling something that was "particularly soaked in blood." Small, or inconspicuous bloodstains and other contaminants were ignored. The gloves were used to keep their hands clean, not to prevent contamination of the evidence.

The number of investigators that was packed into the tiny cottage was amazing. At times, they could barely move without getting in one another's way. At one point investigators are seen carefully pulling material out of a wastebasket, acting with great gravity as if they are revealing material that might have bearing on the murder case of the century – only to find that the basket was full of gloves and other items discarded by a previous round of investigators. It wasn't merely contaminated evidence – it was an entire basket full of contamination. Investigators themselves had introduced almost all of the contents of the wastebasket. This isn't contamination measured in picograms or milligrams; this is contamination measured in kilograms.

Sometime shortly after the first inspection of the crime scene, the beds and other convenient surfaces in the cottage were covered with piles of clothing and other items that simply weren't there when the scene was fresh. Major rearrangements of personal items and even furniture had been done by previous droves of investigators. And yet, the massively disrupted crime scene was inspected anew as if it were still in pristine condition. Going through a disrupted scene isn't what's wrong here, sometimes that is unavoidable. What is wrong is equating the evidence so collected with the original state it was in after the crime.

The swabbing collection process for the DNA profiling tests was another area with more show than substance. In one case, an investigator meticulously swabs away at a stain, only to drop the swab directly onto the floor. Without missing a beat or apparently thinking, he picks it up off the floor and continues carefully swabbing the spot on the wall. It is as if he observes a "three second rule" for swabs. In other cases, the investigator decided that stains were associated, and so used one swab to collect them all. The so-called, "mixed blood" or "mixed DNA" spots in the bathroom Meredith and Amanda shared were collected at this time.

Let's walk through the Polizia PseudoScientifica process for three critical items, a knife, a clasp, and a glow. Two of these, the knife and the clasp, were tested with DNA profiling, which will be explained in more detail in Chapter 8. Here we are focused on things like evidence collection and interpretation. Why are these items so critical? It isn't because they provide damning evidence. They don't. It is because they are essentially the *only* physical evidence that is *claimed* against Amanda and Raffaele.

## A Knife

Perhaps the most impressive example of the Polizia Pseudoscientifica manufacturing evidence out of next to nothing was the Knife, a large, clumsy, ordinary kitchen knife that was retrieved from Raffaele's ordinary kitchen drawer where it lay among ordinary can openers, spoons, and forks. From this humble origin, it was transformed by scientific mumbo jumbo and prosecutorial incantation into "the Knife," a monument to deceptive over-simplification.

The investigator that retrieved the Knife stated that he chose it from among the other knives and implements, because it "looked especially clean." Apparently, this keen observer was accustomed to drawers full of *dirty* implements. The knife was stainless steel, which is... stainless. The protective oxide coating that makes it stainless forms very rapidly, which it would do almost immediately after cleaning. From that point, the appearance of stainless steel does not change visibly for a long, long time. There is simply no way that it could have looked "especially clean," it was apparently seized upon for other reasons.

The Knife did not match the wounds on the victim, it was simply too large to have inflicted them. The Knife did not match a knife imprint left in Meredith's blood at the scene. The Knife was at Raffaele's place, not at the murder scene. Transporting the Knife to Amanda's apartment would not have made sense. No marks or cuts were in Amanda's purse, which the court claimed at one point was the transportation enclosure. The court also stated that the crime was not premeditated, so... why would they have carried a kitchen knife to her place? It simply makes no sense. The Knife had nothing to do with the murder of Meredith Kercher.

But to the Polizia Pseudoscientifica and the prosecution, facts and common sense seem to be inconveniences. By the time they were through stretching and distorting the truth about it, the Knife had done more damage than any other piece of evidence. It was made into an avatar for the damning phrase, "Amanda's DNA on the handle, Meredith's on the blade." That phrase is as simplistic as it is meaningless but after endless repetition by the media and the prosecution, it came to sound like a death knell for Amanda's freedom.

Nancy Grace, for example, said "Amanda's DNA on the handle, Meredith's on the blade. Case closed!" in her nasal, insinuative tone. Nancy was not the first to make this claim. The capo, the head jailer, where Amanda was first imprisoned repeatedly sneered to her, "Your blood on the handle, Meredith's on the blade!" even as he made improper and unwanted sexual advances.

The Knife was retrieved from Raffaele's kitchen drawer some five days after the murder, *after* Raffaele and Amanda's arrest. It was taken to the police station where it sat on a detective's desk for a day or so, then was mailed to a laboratory in Rome in an ordinary envelope inside an ordinary box. No sealed evidence collection bag, no special handling, no precautions against contamination. Essentially no precautions against contamination were taken. The handling was completely inadequate for evidence slated for the tremendously sensitive technique of routine DNA profiling, let alone the hypersensitive and unprecedented low template profiling it was subjected to. Stefanoni's unique test method is described in detail in Chapter Eight – *Canary in the DNA Mine Shaft*.

However, after the prosecution decided that the Knife was the murder weapon – its handling escalated to a reverence normally reserved for an art masterpiece. When presented in court, long after it had been swabbed down for any DNA and long after any evidentiary value was removed, The Knife was ensconced in a special glass box. It was not to be handled by mere mortals. This public display of *sciencey* behavior, this charade of carefulness without content rings a bell. It all smacks of the first Method: Make it look *scientific*.

The Knife was swabbed for DNA testing despite the observation that the Knife was clean. Remember the rules of witch trial evidence. If you have a witches' mark you are guilty, if you don't have a witches' mark you are guilty *and* you have concealed the evidence. The fact that the random kitchen knife was clean was viewed as evidence that it must have been *specially* cleaned to remove the murder blood! Think about this for a moment. Do you have a knife in your kitchen drawer? Is it clean? If so, did you clean it to conceal evidence? The whole thought process is preposterous, and is predicated upon an assumption of guilt.

### The Curious Incident of the DNA in the Night Time

Let's return briefly to Sherlock Holmes because one of his most famous observations may be instructive to us now.

> Inspector Gregory: "Is there any point to which you would wish to draw my attention?"
> Holmes: "To the curious incident of the dog in the night-time."
> Gregory: "The dog did nothing in the night-time."
> Holmes: "That was the curious incident."
> -Sherlock Holmes - Silver Blaze

The blade of the kitchen knife was swabbed by Stefanoni and subjected to DNA profiling. The results came back negative. "Too Low" read the output from the Applied Biosystems profiler. What did the resourceful Stefanoni do? Knowing that there wasn't a single speck of evidence against Amanda, Stefanoni overrode the machine controls, blowing up the noise at the bottom of the graph until she could see a trace.

That over-amplification directly contradicts the instrument maker's specifications, which set limits on the machine sensitivity for a very good reason, *to avoid garbage results*. That was why the readout said "TOO LOW," as it had for a number of other test swabs. But this time, with her forensic back against the wall, Stefanoni ignored all the carefully established protocols, laboratory procedures, and the scientific method itself. She made up a brand new, completely untested technique, on the fly, and presented the results as evidence in a murder trial. The irreproducible results from this one-of-a-kind test would not be admissible as evidence in any court with integrity. The details of this atrocity of science will be discussed in the *Canary* chapter. The question here is; how did she get away with performing such an outlandish test?

Remember that Italy is a nation of laws – some two hundred thousand of them from which they pick and choose as desired. The Court of Assizes in Perugia found a law that allowed the results to be entered as evidence in spite of the fact that they could never be duplicated or tested in any way. They did this by noting that Stefanoni performed the test after *informing* the defense to allow them to attend. That notification, in the court's opinion, served as a substitute for reproducibility. If the defense had objections to the procedures, it was said, they should have attended the testing and made their complaints at that time.

Now what about that dog? It did nothing. It didn't bark, didn't make a fuss. That told Holmes that the dog knew the person who committed the crime. It was the *nothing* that was important, the nonevent that was critical to that case.

Now what was so special about the Knife? Nothing. It was a random, insignificant item. A kitchen implement so ordinary and insignificant that no one would give it a second thought. So – the defense didn't waste time sending anyone to Rome to observe the testing. Why would they? It had nothing to do with the crime.

But since the defense wasn't there to watch, and scream out objections, the Polizia Pseudoscientifica had free reign to do as they wished during the testing. Stefanoni blew up the signal, possibly fiddled with the peaks, including some, excluding others, *cherry picking* them, and generally adjusted the system to settings that it was simply not designed for. We don't know for sure, to this day, because the prosecution refuses to release the documentation of exactly what she did.

All of this is *compatible with* Method #2. *Do it in secret.*

This has always been one of the mysteries of this case. What was so special about a random kitchen knife that was retrieved from a place a quarter mile away from the murder scene? Why would the prosecution seize upon that knife as the murder weapon? It doesn't match the wounds. It was not at the scene. It would have been awkward for Amanda and Raffaele to carry it from Raffaele's place to the cottage, commit the "spontaneous murder" in the Court's words, and then carry it back to his place. Awkward and unnecessary, since there were plenty of knives right there handy in the Via dela Pergola cottage kitchen. Why didn't the polizia choose those? Could it be because the defense would have had observers present?

We now see that the knife may well have become the Knife precisely *because it was a random, unimportant item*, and the defense failed to show up to monitor the testing, allowing the Polizia Pseudoscientifica to work in secret and produce the results they wanted. The results that were presented fit the definition for pseudoscience perfectly. There is a claim that they are the results of scientific test methods, but they are not. They were produced with an untested, un-vetted technique that can never be reproduced. That is not a scientific technique.

There may have been another factor in the choice of this awkward kitchen knife to play the role of The Knife for the prosecution. The other reason will be discussed in Chapter Sixteen – The Inevitable Unexpected.

## Probe This

Recall now the section on probative value in the last chapter, because this is another reason that the Knife is more like a crock. Recall that the probative value of someone's fingerprint, for example, being found in a place where they have a right to be is essentially nothing. It just doesn't tend to prove anything of importance in a trial. Yet, "Amanda's DNA on the handle..." goes the often repeated refrain. Amanda's DNA was also on the handle of the can opener in the same drawer. And the spoons, forks, etc. because she had spent every night for the previous week with Raffaele and she used them for cooking at his place where they had privacy. There is nothing surprising or incriminating about her DNA being present on the handle of the can opener, nor is there anything incriminating about her DNA being on that knife handle. This evidence has no probative value. It is an ordinary object that does not relate to the crime. It should have been left in the drawer with the can opener.

## A Clasp

Forty-seven days after the murder, the prosecution faced a problem that called for thinking outside of the box, and perhaps outside of the law as well.

The only trace of Raffaele Sollecito found at Via dela Pergola during the main searches for evidence was on a cigarette butt that was in the living room, not in Meredith's room. Can't convict on a cigarette butt found where he had every right to be. No trace of Raffaele whatsoever was found in Meredith's room. No DNA, no footprints, no fingerprints, nothing. The reason is simple. He was never in Meredith's bedroom. Not during the murder. Not ever. No trace of Amanda Knox was ever found in Meredith's room either. Neither was there any trace of Meredith's blood on their shoes or clothing.

The absence of any physical evidence for the presence of Raffaele and Amanda at the crime scene is overwhelming evidence that they *simply were not there*. It is virtually impossible for someone to commit such a violent crime as a stabbing – blood everywhere – in a confined space, without leaving any trace of them selves. This is the ultimate bottom line of the case. Amanda and Raffaele could not possibly have committed the murder, because they weren't there when it happened.

This awkward fact placed the polizia and prosecution in a difficult position. They had already declared victory. They had raced Amanda and Raffaele off to prison in a parade around Perugia with their car horns blaring in triumph. They had posted Amanda's picture on a wall alongside mafia bosses (the exact date of this is unknown but it was up by mid February). It was "Mission Accomplished" Perugia style. How embarrassing then, that when they actually got around to looking for evidence against the pair, they found nothing.

True, by that time they had identified and captured the actual murderer, Rudy Guede, and had decided to keep him in custody this time rather than releasing him as they had repeatedly done before. One would think that they could substitute Rudy for Amanda and Raffaele, so to speak, and so have a murderer and avoid "bad face." Instead, for some *as yet* inexplicable reason, they swapped Rudy out for Patrick, but kept their eyes fixed on the prize, Amanda and Raffaele.

## Hail Mary Clasp

Faced with this lack of evidence, the Polizia PseudoScientifica sprang into action. Forty seven days after the murder, after teams of researchers had completely trashed the crime scene, rearranging everything, piling things onto beds, filling the wastebaskets with their discards, shoving furniture and carpets around on the floor, Patrizia Stefanoni led the team that went back in on a *hail Mary* mission. Their main assignment was to recover a single item: the clasp.

The clasp had been cut or torn off from the bra Meredith was wearing when she was murdered. It was spotted during the initial crime scene investigation, recorded on video, and specific, close up photographs were taken. So, its existence was well known by the polizia and prosecution from the first days. The only new information was that the fingerprints, footprints, DNA analyses, and other tests had all come back negative for the presence of Amanda and Raffaele in the murder room. They had "milked the scene" for evidence, as in Method #3, but they had come up empty, aside from the creative work they had done on the Knife.

At that point, if the prosecution had been honest, they would have looked at the lack of evidence, rethought their case, and admitted they had made a mistake. They would have dropped charges and Amanda and Raffaele would have been released. What they did instead was come up with the idea to go back in after that clasp. Perhaps, that one item, out of the dozens of items of evidence in the murder room, perhaps the one item they had left behind, held the key to the convictions! So, they called what might be referred to as the Hail Mary clasp play. In football, remember, you call a hail-Mary pass play when you are about to lose. You throw the long bomb to the end zone and see if your side catches it. You have nothing to lose, because you know you're about to lose anyway.

The clasp spent 47 days on the floor in Meredith's room. During that time unknown numbers of unnamed investigators passed through the room doing unknown things. Who was there doing what is unknown because the prosecution does not appear to have kept any records. So, we have no way of knowing what might have happened to any evidence left there. It shouldn't have mattered, actually, since evidence retrieved from an infamous, and long unsecured crime scene wouldn't be admissible in a normal court.

During those 47 days, as before and after photos show, the clasp moved across the room in some manner. Again, we don't know how – kicked, probably. It wound up under an old throw rug. This is evidence that would be subjected to exquisitely sensitive DNA testing. Would you trust the results?

What would happen to any random object left on the floor and kicked about for 47 days? In particular, what would happen to an object with cloth attached, which made it a virtual dust mop. It would be covered with dust, and the DNA that comes with that dust (roughly 30% of house dust is dead skin cells). Raffaele was at the apartment visiting Amanda on several occasions. The presence of his DNA there at the same contamination levels as that of two or three other people, simply means nothing.

Incredibly, in the *Motivation Report*, the document filed by the Court to justify the convictions of Amanda and Raffaele (Chapter 11 – *Through the Motivation Report*), the reasoning was that since the clasp was found under a rug, it had been *protected from contamination* by that throw rug.

We can do a test to decide for ourselves whether this line of reasoning is… reasonable. We need an object to represent the clasp. Something that will pick up any contaminants that happen to come its way so we can check to see if a rug really does protect things from contamination. I suggest a piece of chocolate. It won't be *too* sticky, just enough to help decide whether an object kicked around on the floor for 47 days and then discovered under a rug might have picked up any contamination.

Here's the plan. Take a piece of chocolate, unwrapped, perhaps a Perugina chocolate. Toss it on the floor. Leave it there for 47 days. Kick it around a bit. Toss an old throw rug on top of it to *protect it* as the court suggests – say, halfway through the 47 days (to be unbiased). When you retrieve this goodie for testing, pick it up with visibly grubby latex gloves, as the investigators did, and drop it back on the floor, as the investigators did, then pick it up again and carefully drop it into an evidence bag, going through the motions as if you were careful, as the investigators did.

Inspect the chocolate carefully. Do you own any pets? Look for their hair on the chocolate. If you do not believe that significant contamination may have occurred over the 47-day period, eat the chocolate. Remember that DNA testing is vastly more sensitive than your tongue, and will pick up traces that you cannot begin to sense. Send me an email to tell me the results of this test – taste, texture, etc. I will compile the answers and post them in my blog.

The handling of the clasp when it was retrieved from the scene can be seen in youtube.com videos. I've reviewed the originals from which these were made. The investigators, dressed in fancy white outfits, seem to play some kind of game with it. Why the outfits? They are standard garb, but they do nothing to prevent mixing contamination of material at the scene. As shown in close-up pictures, the outfits, and their gloves, quickly became contaminated from various sources at the scene.

Raffaele's DNA profile was reported to be on the bra clasp but, interestingly, it was not on the bra itself. How could his DNA turn up on the clasp, but not on the bra? This is nearly impossible to account for if it occurred as a natural consequence of the commission of a crime. Of course, it makes perfect sense if Raffaele's DNA was on the bra clasp because it was put there. That would be evidence tampering, a serious charge. But it wasn't the only outside-the-box action of the investigators during that visit. Something else was done that confirms the prosecution's commitment to convict at any cost.

**A Little More Sorcery**

While they were there, the same investigators that recovered the hail-Mary clasp took a snapshot. Then they apparently leaked it to the press, which would be in violation of Italian law. It was a picture of a Harry Potter book, in German, at Via dela Pergola. Amanda and Raffaele had stated that they had read Harry Potter, in

German, at *his* apartment on the night of the murder. It was part of their alibi story.

Voila! Their alibi was destroyed by this single news leak! This was just what the prosecution wanted in a country where the jurors are not sequestered or shielded from the news in any way. How could they have been reading this book at *his* place when, in fact, the book was at *her* place? The media loved it. It made for many lurid and lucrative headline stories. "Amanda's Alibi Demolished!"

Actually, though, there was a very simple explanation. They had two copies. Another picture of a Harry Potter book, in German, laying on a table at *Raffaele's* apartment where they said they were reading it, had long since been taken by the polizia. *They knew about it.* The book was conspicuous placed, it appeared in their videos as well. The polizia knew perfectly well that the Harry Potter book found at Raffaele's place *confirmed* Amanda and Raffaele's alibis. It didn't contradict them.

During the same visit to the crime scene that brought back the Hail Mary Clasp, the same group of investigators, led by Dr. Patrizia Stefanoni, took that picture. But perhaps someone else leaked it... maybe they weren't really responsible for the illegal lie. But if so, why did they photograph that particular object in the first place? It was a four-bedroom apartment, full of objects, but *that* team documented *that book.* The leak to the press occurred within the day. Soon after, Stefanoni's DNA testing confirmed the miracle of the hail Mary clasp by producing a DNA profile that was positively lush with contamination, and *some of it*, by incredible coincidence, was compatible with Raffaele.

The framing of Amanda Knox was back on track.

### A Glow

If you want to make something to look *sciencey*, nothing beats a good glow. If the glow lights up from blood... you have the stuff of a true crime novel. Luminol does just that. It is catalyzed by blood, and by a number of other substances called "peroxidases," to emit a glow that's closely related to the common glow sticks that light up when you snap a glass vial inside of them. Investigators spray a luminol solution on surfaces in a darkened crime scene and look for the emission of light. If any of these substances are present, the luminol glows briefly.

When the apartment at Via dela Pergola was sprayed with luminol, a random hodgepodge of a half a dozen footprints lit up in the apartment hallways. Amanda may have left some of these prints, it's hard to know for sure because they were only compared with her feet, and found to be "compatible" with them. None of the other resident's feet were compared to these footprints. Not Meredith's, Filomena's, or Laura's. Only Amanda's feet were compared, and found to be roughly the same size as the prints. They were roughly the same size as the other women's feet, too, so the prints could have been left by any of them.

But, they weren't trying to frame the other residents for murder, so they didn't bother to check them. In a sense, the other women's feet would have served as experimental controls. Had they all been compared, and, as seems likely, all found to be compatible with the prints, it would clearly show that there was no way of knowing who left them. Instead, they did something that was like finding a smudged fingerprint and simply assigning it to the defendant. Someone left a smudge! It must have been the defendant!

Amanda's DNA was found in a couple of these footprints. Did they also test a couple other spots a foot or so away from the footprints, to see if her DNA was simply all over the floor of the apartment where she lived? No. They tested the particular spots on the floor where the luminol glowed. Had they performed tests on other sites it would have provided control experiments to see if it actually meant something that her DNA was in those particular places, or if it was simply a random coincidence. Was the DNA actually associated with the footprint, or did it just happen to be there, because the resident's DNA was all over their apartment, as people's DNA usually is? We will never know. They skipped the control experiments, and presented the results without any reference points.

The "compatibility" of the prints and the DNA found, are examples of presenting results without context that might have made them meaningful, in an effort to cast a general pall of guilt that has no basis in the evidence. Something glowed! Horrors! And a finger is pointed at the defendants. One can almost see the gasps on the gullible and cooperative juror's faces. The defendant's DNA was found in two of the spots! Surely, she must have committed a murder or something for her DNA to be on the floor of the cottage where she lived! This is classic pseudoscience. It is a melodramatic, *sciencey* presentation of information that doesn't actually mean a damned thing.

## Another Bloody Lie

When luminal glows, it might, or might not, have been catalyzed by blood, so the next thing a good investigator does is collect samples and perform more specific tests with TMB (tetramethylbenzidine) or a similar test to find out which it is. That is why it was extremely puzzling when Dr. Patrizia Stefanoni testified in court that she had not tested any of the luminol glows for blood. It was even more puzzling when it discovered, months later, that she *had* performed the TMB presumptive test for blood, and every single result indicated that the luminol glow spots were not comprised of blood.

It turned out that Stefanoni didn't test for blood *type*. She had split hairs in her testimony and left everyone puzzled as to why she did not test for blood. She did, in fact perform the TMB blood test, why would she test for blood *type* when the test for blood itself had come back negative? Her testimony was apparently, deliberately deceptive. Has the court or prosecution complained? No, they are too busy charging Amanda with defamation for testifying truthfully. Patrizia Stefanoni's testimony left the impression that the luminol spots might have been left in Meredith Kercher's blood, even though she knew perfectly well that they were not.

Since the spots weren't catalyzed by blood, they had nothing to do with the case. When an item of evidence is tested with TMB and the result is negative, the standard procedure for a forensic investigator is to simply move on. Since the stain is not blood, the item is not relevant to the case. But, not to let all that effort go to waste, the *Motivation Report* (Chapter Eleven) made the astonishing assertion that they *"could"* have been blood, because, maybe, every single test came back negative, because... well... they just didn't work or something.

Maybe, just maybe, there was *just* enough blood present to trigger the luminol, but to go under the radar of the TMB. This would have to be in spite of the fact that the TMB test benefited from being swabbed up and so concentrated. Maybe this happened with every single footprint. The Court actually concluded this, and went on to assume that the footprints *were definitely* blood.

Some have called me a conspiracy theorist (see Chapter Fifteen) because I have come to believe that some of the folks in Perugia worked together on the framing of Amanda and Raffaele. Think about this particular matter. It reeks to high heaven of some form of collusion between the prosecutor, the forensic whiz, and the judge that wrote the *Motivation*. Just this one sequence of deception, probable perjury, and judicial malpractice exposes these proceedings for what they were.

## Glow Sticks

Some further details about what luminol does are in order because dubious statements have been made about supposed observer experience. One of the major sources of misleading forensic science results comes from claims to be able to tell something just on the basis of experience rather than for any documented and tested reason. While experience is a valuable thing, it can also be a catchall excuse for bias.

The statement has been made that the investigators could tell that the luminol glow was triggered by blood, because they were experienced investigators. They could tell just by looking. Let's analyze that claim in some detail, because it is typical of the claims of remarkable expertise made by the Polizia PseudoScientifica in this case.

Luminol effectively carries its own energy; it only awaits a trigger to go off. The color that it glows with is a broad band that is largely fixed by the luminol, the color of light emitted does not change significantly with different catalysts. If a large amount of blood is present, however, the blood can *absorb* a portion of the emitted light, slightly changing the apparent color. It has been claimed that the investigators could tell just by looking that these spots were blood-triggered spots, presumably this was the method they used.

But, as we have just seen, the sensitive TMB test for blood came up negative for every spot. That means, even if the evidence does miraculously thread the needle of concentration discussed previously, there certainly wasn't enough blood present in any of the spots to absorb any significant amount of emitted light. On the basis of visual evidence, an experienced observer would have seen an emission color indicating that the spots were *not* comprised of a substantial amount of blood. Yet the story went out that the spots were in blood, and that became the lodged-in-place misinformation.

Follow the circular logic generated by a whole chain of players, but culminating in the very specific, damaging, and wrong finding that the spots were in blood, and were therefore evidence against Amanda. First, the investigators could tell just by looking at the luminol glow that the spots were blood – therefore, they were blood. Next, all of the test results with TMB came back negative for blood, so – something must have come up short in the TMB tests, since the spots were blood.

Stefanoni then neglected to mention their existence while testifying. Remember what I said about spotting technical people who are not being forthcoming. What they tell you is usually *literally* true. What you have to look for is what they don't tell you. Finally, since the tests failed, the spots were blood. The pattern is very clear. As far as this court was concerned, those spots were going to be blood no matter what the evidence.

These are just three examples, there are many more. Enough to discern a clear pattern, that the forensic methods and interpretations of results in this case are *compatible with* pseudoscience.

## Seven – DNA – A Simple Twist of Fate

This chapter is a brief summary of Appendix D – DNA Profiling. The intent is to provide just a brief introduction to DNA profiling with an emphasis on aspects of that technology that are relevant to this case. For a slightly longer treatment, see that Appendix. There you will also find a bibliography of more complete resources. One more caveat, I am a materials scientist and I've developed some experimental techniques so I know a bit about scientific instrumentation. I am not a molecular biologist or forensic DNA practitioner. I consulted with a couple of those to fact check this material.

### The Secret of Life

In both plants and animals DNA and its cousin, RNA, work together with proteins and other organic molecules to create the molecules we are made from, organize them into cells, organize those cells into organisms, and reproduce the entire system. Not only are they the blueprints of life, they are the architects, the engineers, and the construction crews.

With just a few exceptions, every cell in the human body contains two copies of that person's DNA, organized into units called chromosomes. Each chromosome is a single chain of DNA and protein, coiled up and then coiled up again to wind an extremely long, incredibly slender chain into a fairly tight unit. This double coiling of DNA makes it practical to fit it into a cell and to move it around, otherwise, handling it would make handling a single strand of a spider's web seem easy. This is important in the present matter because DNA is a relatively compact, stable material that is encapsulated within a cell nucleus, and that nucleus is encapsulated into a cell. These layers provide some protection, and also make it a fairly "portable" material, it can be moved around in dust, etc.

There are 23 different chromosomes in people. Regular cells are "diploid" containing two of each for a total of 46 chromosomes. Sperm and egg cells are different, containing only one copy of each, so they are called "haploid." Aside from this difference, all somatic (body) cells in the human body contain the same kind and form of DNA. Red blood cells, a major constituent of blood, don't contain any DNA. Their job is simply carrying oxygen and carbon dioxide efficiently so don't have room for the rest of the equipment. The DNA in blood comes entirely from the white blood cells, which comprise only about 1% of the total blood.

The elegance of this system for producing and reproducing organisms is without parallel. It is, at once, perhaps the most beautiful, simple, complex, robust, sensitive, and spare system that exists.

DNA consists of extremely long chains made of four kinds of nucleic acids, called "bases." Those bases are bonded end-to-end to form long chains. They are also loosely bonded to pair with each other, following particular rules. Between the bonding and the pairing, extremely long, spiraling chain molecules are formed.

The longest grouping of human DNA, Chromosome 1, contains about 220 million of these bases, 110 million in each side of a double chain, the famous double helix. The exact nature of these nucleic acids isn't important to us. What is important is that they are shaped in such a way that adenine pairs only with thymine, and guanine pairs only with cytosine – A to T, and C to G. These combined bases are called "base pairs" because they always go together in the complete DNA molecule. The whole molecule, the entire double helix, resembles a ladder that has been twisted about its center.

Because of the selective bonding of bases, DNA has a remarkable property from which many of its other remarkable properties stem. It can make copies of itself.

When you unzip this ladder and cool it again in a "soup" of free nucleotides and a polymerase, those nucleotides add onto the open sides of the ladder, rebuilding each side of the original double helix. You now have two double helix chains where before you had one. The DNA molecule has duplicated itself. It has split into two halves, taken up separate bases from a soup, and formed two complete molecules.

This is a simple version of what happens when something called the polymerase chain reaction (PCR) takes place. This reaction is used to replicate DNA in a laboratory. PCR proceeds in a cyclic process, with each cycle doubling the DNA. Here's the thing. If you can make 1 DNA molecule into 2, you can make those 2 into 4, those 4 into 8... and after 28 cycles of this, the typical number performed in a PCR reaction for profiling, you have roughly $2^{28}$ power molecules of DNA for every single one that you started with. That's roughly 268 million copies made of every starting molecule.

To perform the PCR process, you first need extracted DNA from a forensic sample. That sample needs to be carefully collected from a certain, specified source. The association between the DNA and the source is critically important, as we will see in the next chapter. You need to know what it is that you've got a sample of.

**Short Tandem Repeats (STRs)**

The portions of DNA that are now used for identification are called "short tandem repeats" or "STRs." These are short sequences of DNA, 4 or 5 bases long, that are repeated some variable number of times in a particular location on a person's DNA. For example, in one person a sequence might be repeated 5 times, in another, it might be repeated 7 times.

Because of the different number of repeats, these STRs are of different lengths. Because they are different lengths, they can be separated by a technique called electrophoresis. By compiling a list of the different lengths of several different STRs in a DNA sample and comparing that with the lengths of the same STRs from different people, the source of the sample can be identified. In a nutshell, that is how DNA profiling works. There are some more tricks involved, but this is a simple starting point to understanding it.

By comparing a number of different STRs one can be fairly certain what DNA came from who, provided that some other things are done right. The STR locations are called "loci" in plural form or "locus" in singular. The usual number of loci to be compared is 13, depending on the "kit" used to find, amplify, and measure them.

## The Polymerase Chain Reaction (PCR)

The process of splitting the two halves of the DNA double helix apart, then adding complementary base pairs onto each, doesn't just happen on its own, it is initiated by a molecule called "DNA polymerase." When PCR is applied to PCR-STR profiling, the entire chain isn't replicated, but only those portions of interest, the STR loci that are used to distinguish one person from another. This is done by yet another clever trick that was developed by molecular biologists, the use of DNA primers, which are used to spot an exact location on a strand a hundred million bases long.

## Primer School

Primers are tools for recognizing a particular, exact point along the millions of bases that make up a DNA strand. They are about 20 base pairs long, and they will only bind to the complementary set of pairs on the strand being worked on. By making the recognition sequence long enough, the replication of the DNA can be restricted to a single point in the entire base sequence of DNA in the human genome. This is because the number of possible combinations of 4^20 base pairs equals about one billion. Only one such combination out of a billion random base pairs will fit the bill and be replicated.

Yet another trick to speed up the analysis involves deciding how far away from the STR region will be the point at which the primers will select. Once one has settled on 10, or 13, or more STR regions to use for identification, it would be nice to be able to process all of those regions simultaneously, in a single operation.

For these reasons, the primers are chosen so that the lengths of non-STR DNA on either side of the STR segment are of different lengths for each STR region. The final molecule winds up with a length that is the sum of the variable STR locus, plus the two non-STR regions on either side of it. By deliberately selecting different lengths for the adjacent regions, one can create non-overlapping DNA segment lengths that can all be measured at the same time.

One last trick before we measure the results (I know, you're tired of tricks). By using three or four different colored fluorescent markers with the different primers, you produce different length DNA fragments, tagged with different colored fluorescent markers. You now have two different ways of distinguishing things, color, and length. Point an ultraviolet light at the fluorescent markers and they light up in different colors. A detector can sense these different colors and distinguish them.

**Electrophoresis for Fun and Profit**

Once the PCR process is complete, you have hundreds of millions of fragments of DNA with different lengths, depending on the number of repeats in the original STR segments, and on the length of the side chains. Those STR lengths are characteristic of the particular person the template DNA came from. There are also four groups of different fragments, with each of those groups labeled at the end with a different color fluorescent dye that is part of the primer that began the replication of the DNA in the first place.

Four groups of different length DNA pieces, each group tagged in a certain color. Now how can you measure the lengths of all those molecules? That's where electrophoresis comes in.

In capillary electrophoresis, a very fine quartz tube, the capillary tube, is filled with conducting liquid and a small amount of the sample DNA is introduced at one end. An electric field is applied to the tube causing the negatively charged DNA fragments to move through it at different speeds, depending on how long they are. You start out with a mixture of different lengths of DNA all bunched up together at the beginning of the tube, and wind up with different lengths of chains flowing past the end of the tube at different times.

That's where you detect them. As each length of DNA fragment flows past the detector, it is exposed to a very bright ultraviolet light that excites the fluorescent dyes attached to the ends. The dye glows, and each color of glow is detected and recorded, making a little peak on a graph.

What you wind up with is a series of peaks as each group of selected, amplified DNA fragments tagged with different colored dyes flows past the detector. The height of each peak indicates how many fragments are in that group. The time that each peak passes the detector indicates how long the fragments were.

A DNA profile, then, is a series of peaks on a graph. Each peak represents a bunch of fragments of DNA that have some number of short tandem repeats in it. The position of that peak tells you how many repeats. The size, or area of the peak gives an idea of how much of that fragment was present. And the color tells you which one of the fluorescent tracers it was tagged with.

## Jigsaw Puzzle

Each person's DNA profile has either one, or two, alleles, genetic variants, at each STR locus. The mother and the father provide one allele each. If these happen to be the same, the individual has only one allele present at that STR locus and they are said to be homozygous for that site. If they are different, they are said to be heterozygous at that locus. Among a population, there are many different alleles for each locus. By producing a DNA profile for a suspect, and comparing the alleles that are present to the alleles that are present in a profile drawn from an item of evidence, it is possible to establish, or reject, a match.

To be a match, the correspondence must be perfect. Every allele in the suspect must correspond to an allele in the evidence item. This is a bit like matching pieces in a jigsaw puzzle. For a piece to be the correct, matching piece for a location, it must correspond in every, single respect. It must agree with the shapes of all the pieces around it. It must agree with the color at the edges, for all pieces around it. If it is merely close, it is not the correct piece and does not belong there. If it agrees on three sides but does not match in one, single sense on one single side, it is not the correct piece. Stuffing it into that position would leave another jigsaw puzzle piece, one that *does* belong there, with nowhere to go. Similarly, making an incorrect match of a DNA profile can put an innocent person in the position of a felon, and let the felon walk free.

Performing identifications by matching up DNA profiles is often compared to identifying people by their libraries. If a suspect has a copy of *Catcher in the Rye*, and so does a perpetrator, that's one match, but doesn't mean much in itself. If both suspect and perpetrator also have copies of *Moby Dick*, *All the President's Men*, and a dozen other books, with no differences, then you are likely to have a match. The analogy isn't perfect for a number of reasons. If ones library is very large, you are likely to have all of the above books. A more accurate analogy would have a limited number of possible books in every spot (locus) on the bookshelf, just as there are only so many different alleles at each STR locus.

**And The Point Of All This Is....**

If all this sounds a bit complicated, that's because it is. That is the point I am making. DNA profiling doesn't just happen, it is a process that has to be performed to produce a result. The process has to be performed in what amounts to a specialized wet chemistry laboratory, with laboratory apparatus, beginning with evidence collection bags (ideally, anyway), and continuing with swabs, centrifuge tubes, PCR reaction tubes, sample tubes, and electrophoresis capillaries. These vessels are stored, handled, and cleaned in the real world, not in outer space somewhere. That same laboratory, and some of that same equipment, may have processed many samples of the victim's blood. Things can, and do, go wrong in this process. The possibility of contamination of DNA samples in forensic laboratories is a fact of life that must be dealt with.

## Eight – Canary in the DNA Mine Shaft

It wasn't very long after canaries were first bred in Europe that a new use was invented for them. Someone discovered that they were sensitive to gases like carbon monoxide and methane. These gases seeped into mines and caused the deaths of many miners. From that time forward the gases caused the deaths of many canaries as well. The canaries provided a cheap, effective early warning system. If you could hear them singing, you were okay. Once they stopped, you knew it was time to get out of there fast. It worked out very well – except for the canary.

It wasn't long after DNA profiling was developed that researchers discovered that they could push the technique into entirely new realms of sensitivity, while paying – but a subtle price in the integrity of the results. Partly as a result of that push, a couple human canaries named Amanda and Raffaele have stopped singing, having been sentenced to decades in prison – at least in part because of an abuse of DNA tests.

A new technique called *Low Copy Number* DNA (LCN-DNA) profiling is fermenting in the world's forensics labs, in a drive to test tinier and tinier traces of material. That's a reasonable objective to pursue, because sometimes the amount of material left behind is extremely small. But the issues raised by testing these incredibly small samples are complex and manifold, with problems potentially stemming from any of a number of issues. The results of such tests can be completely wrong.

The potential complications from LCN-DNA profiling don't just come from the details of the test itself, the profiling, amplification, etc. There are also problems stemming from far more fundamental and less easily controlled issues, like sample acquisition, transfer of material to the scene, and contamination during handling and processing. The method is not a simple extension of the current methods. LCN work fundamentally changes the nature of the entire system, not just the lab work – but throughout the process of collection, handling, processing, and interpretation of results.

## Astronomical Odds, Brought Down to Earth

We've all heard about the remarkable discrimination abilities of DNA profiling. We have been told that the odds of a mistake being made are "billions and billions" to one in impressive Carl Saganesque terms. But this new twist on the technique radically changes those odds, and not in a good way. It can bring these astronomical odds right down to Earth.

Conventional DNA profiling is done with a microscopically small, but still significant sample of DNA, on the order of 1 nanogram (1 billionth of a gram). This quantity provides enough material to ensure that it is *physically associated* with the actual evidence at a crime scene – a smear of blood, a tuft of hair, a cigarette butt. You extract a sample from the specimen, amplify part of it, and profile a portion of that amplified material. You still have most of the original specimen, and the rest of the extracted material. You can extract a second sample, and test it again. Or pass it to the defense for their analysis. The experiment is *reproducible* because there is enough material present to perform the test more than once.

> "Interpretation of DNA profiles is assisted by the use of systems that are not too sensitive. This is important because the scientist often needs to associate the presence of a bloodstain (or other evidence) with the DNA profile itself." Peter Gill, Forensic Science Service, U.K.

This passage, written by one of the leading experts in DNA profiling, explains what may be the most critical issue with the new hypersensitive DNA profiling techniques. When an item of evidence is substantial, when you can see it, measure it, it is possible to work with it in a reliable, conventional manner. You might extract nanoscopic samples from it to perform tests, but you have a real, physical sample to point at, do repeated tests on... you have something *real* that can be worked with, validated.

Conventional DNA profiling has gone through an extensive validation process to prove that it works. Many researchers have devoted years and careers to understanding the method, how reliable it is, what exactly it does, and what it does not do. It has been subjected to a peer-reviewed, scientifically methodical development and testing process. The results obtained by the tests have been shown to be valid, reproducible, and reliable. All of that is critically important for trusting the method. You can believe the results, as long as you trust the investigators that collect and process the evidence.

The quantity of material involved in these tests is outside the range of normal human experience. Just as Carl Sagan tried to hammer home astronomical times and distances to people who will never experience a billion years or traverse the distance to the next galaxy, we need to find ways to somehow get a feel for these miniscule amounts to understand what some of these unexpected complications might be.

So let's work our way down to the realm of LCN-DNA by starting with things we know about. A small mosquito weighs about 1 milligram, or 1/1000 of a gram. It can still cause misery. A small grain of sand comes in at about one third of that, 350 nanograms, or billionths of a gram. One can see it, just, and you know it if it gets in your eye. The amount of DNA used in a conventional profiling test, the amount you want to have to make sure you've got plenty, is about 1 nanogram, so that would be 1/350 of a small grain of sand.

We enter the realm of LCN-DNA at about 1/10 of that, 100 picograms. A picogram is one *trillionth* of a gram. That would be 1/3,500 of a single grain of sand. The amount of DNA that was *claimed* by Dr. Stefanoni to have been on the Knife blade was about 1/3 of this, equivalent in weight to 1/10,000 of a single grain of sand.

## LCN, LTN, NT

The term, "LCN-DNA" has been adopted by groups that are working to establish standards for the technique that will make it acceptable as evidence. Those standards, discussed below, are an attempt to put the method on firm, scientific footing. For that reason, I will use LCN-DNA to refer specifically to tests performed according to those emerging standards. DNA testing that is performed with vanishingly small amounts of starting DNA that is *not* tested according to the LCN-DNA protocols is now termed "Low Template Number DNA" (LTN-DNA, and sometimes just LT-DNA). The templates in this term refer to the original DNA material that provided the template for all subsequent reproduction.

So, perhaps somewhat confusingly, we have LCN-DNA, which means ultra high sensitivity testing that follows the new standards, and LTN-DNA, which more or less means, any man (or woman) for their self, testing. Another way of looking at these terms is that any testing with a very small sample of DNA is low template, but only those tests that are done while following the emerging protocols deserve to be called LCN-DNA testing. Yet another term that is in use is "touch DNA" which refers to testing very small amounts of material transferred by a touch, as in fingerprints. These terminology matters are still somewhat in flux, and may change in the future, but this is the consensus as of this writing.

When enough DNA is available as the starting template, the copying process is performed on a large number of molecules right from the start. Any small variation in whether a given STR copies is washed out because there are a lot of templates available. If you miss one in one hundred, you only have a 1% error. Low copy number DNA profiling is usually performed by increasing the number of replication steps compared with conventional DNA testing, so that a very small sample is blown up to a large enough quantity for electrophoresis

If you only have a few template molecules, and any locus is missed in the first stage, that error continues to be amplified throughout the PCR process. Miss one in five, and the error for that single step jumps to 20%. Some profile peaks may be diminished, some may drop out entirely, and "stutters," false peaks, may occur when things don't work out quite right.

The statistical variation resulting from the tiny number of starting templates can be significant. In fact, LTN-DNA profiling is usually defined as either testing with a very small amount of starting material, say 100 picograms, or less, or as profiling with results that fall below the normal stochastic limits of the technique. "Stochastic" means that an element of chance is involved, so that the system contains a significant amount of random noise. As a result, repeating the same LCN-DNA tests on identical starting samples of material does not produce nearly identical profiles, unlike conventional DNA testing. Some alleles may have dropped out without a trace. Alleles that are not real may have dropped in. The STR numbers at some of the loci may be wrong, throwing a serious wrench into any comparisons.

If you divide the tiny sample into multiple samples, and replicate and profile them separately, these differences will show, and can, ideally, be accounted for. But if you test the entire sample in a single run, you have nothing to compare it with, and no way of knowing whether there is significant variation or not. This is why the LCN-DNA protocols require that a sample be split up and each portion tested independently, on different equipment.

The main objective of this chapter is to compare the testing performed by Stefanoni on the knife blade sample with these two classes of profiling to evaluate the validity of her work. The first step in that is to estimate the amount of DNA she was testing.

Although there has been debate among DNA forensics experts as to how much DNA was in the knife blade profile test, they are agreed that the amount appearing in the test result was well down into the range of LTN-DNA testing. Almost all (21 out of 29) of the profile peaks were between 20 and 50 RFUs, a level that would normally be excluded from consideration.

But that is the DNA that was in the test apparatus. It is the amount of Meredith's DNA that turned up inside an instrument that was operating in a laboratory that was effectively awash in samples of Meredith's DNA. It is critically important not to confuse the quantity of DNA in the *apparatus* with the amount that was actually present on that knife blade in the first place.

To control for this possibility, when DNA testing must be performed on very small samples it is a standard procedure to run negative control tests, blanks that have no DNA in them, to make sure that material hasn't been carried over from prior test or transferred in some other way into the test. It is not unusual for these negative controls to produce DNA profiles, even though none was added. A very low quantity of DNA showing up in a test does not necessarily mean that *any* was present in the original sample.

For these reasons, the real question, to me, isn't how much found its way into the test apparatus, but *how much DNA was actually on the blade*. Let us think about what else we know about the knife to find an answer for this.

First, we have the fact that the TMB test for blood came out negative. TMB testing is extremely sensitive. It can detect blood in dilutions as low as 1/10,000. If the knife had been used to commit the murder, the blade would have had blood on it, not some other body tissue. But we know from the TMB that there was no blood on the knife. No blood, and no other tissue, means no DNA.

We also know that the knife did not match most of the wounds on Meredith, it was simply too large to have inflicted them. The prosecution has tried to fudge over this glaring fact by suggesting that maybe there were *two* knives, an assertion for which there is no evidence. Experts in the field have said that it would be one of the first cases on record in which an assailant started a murder with one knife, and then switched to a second. It just doesn't make sense.

We know, too, that there was an imprint left at the crime scene by a knife blade, in blood. It does not come close to matching Raffaele's kitchen knife. It is also problematic that the knife was at Raffaele's place, not at the cottage. The prosecution has proposed that Amanda was carrying it around with her, in her purse, for protection. It is more than a foot long, and would be an extremely unusual choice for self-defense. There are also no cut marks of any kind in Amanda's purse, no evidence whatever to support this theory.

What this means is that there is no corroborative evidence to support the involvement of the knife. Contrast this with a different situation, in which a knife was dropped at the scene, or discovered in some other way that actually tied it to a crime. You would have good reason to believe that such a knife might have traces of the victim on it. No such reasons exist in this case.

All of this gives us a solid basis to arrive at an estimate of the amount of DNA that was present on the blade of Raffaele's kitchen knife. None. There was no DNA on that knife. The polizia could have pulled the knife out of a bath of sulfuric acid and the profile tests would have come out the same. The DNA in the profile came from Stefanoni's laboratory, or, possibly, the extremely clumsy handling and shipping, it did not originate from the knife.

All of that leads me to propose yet another classification of DNA profile test. Since there was *no* valid template DNA, this test should be classified as No Template DNA, *NT-DNA*. In keeping with the science tradition of naming experimental methods in honor of the originator, I propose that this test be called the *Stefanoni NT-DNA* test.

To further acknowledge that innovation, and to give her more than the benefit of the doubt, let's further review the *Stefanoni NT-DNA* profile test as she performed it on the knife blade sample. In the process, we can compare it with the nascent standards for its cousin, the LCN-DNA test.

## Science at the Improv

Just for fun, let's suppose that your life is on the line. You will spend most of it in prison if a mistake is made. Let's place your life on the line depending on the outcome of a brand new experimental technique that I just made up! Are you excited yet? I sure am. I get to try out my new test. Oh, BTW, I am palpably, manifestly, biased against you.

When people's lives and liberty are on the line, you hope the people on the job get it right. That is part of what is so disturbing about the technical work of Dr. Patrizia Stefanoni of the Scientifica Polizia. When Amanda and Raffaele's liberty was at stake, Stefanoni made it up as she went along. She performed science improv. Her techniques were at odds with both accepted scientific methodology and with simple common sense.

There was so little DNA present in the knife blade run that the instrument indicated no DNA until Stefanoni overrode the machine limits. This amplification increase was not achieved by the PCR technique. Once the sample has been selected, amplified, and subjected to electrophoresis, it is too late for additional amplification. The increase was performed by a far cruder method, simply by blowing up the scale until the tiny fluorescence peaks were visible.

This makes the testing performed by Dr. Stefanoni much worse than the various methods being experimented with to perform normal LCN testing. In those cases, the experimenter knows that the sample is tiny, and tenuous, so they use a higher number of PCR multiplication steps, typically 34 compared to 28, resulting in 64 times as many molecules for the electrophoresis and fluorescence observation.

But remember that the main problems with LCN are introduced during the first few cycles of replication when there are very few molecules and any difference in replication becomes a major artifact. That happened with the kitchen knife – or contaminant – DNA so all of those errors are well represented. In this case, however, not only were those artifacts introduced, but additional artifacts from the high amplification of the weak fluorescent signal also added noise to the vanishing weak signal. So, that's one shortcoming, a deficiency of the *Stefanoni NT-DNA* profile compared with LCN-DNA testing.

A deeply troubling question is raised by this mid-course change in experimental methodology. Since Stefanoni did not originally expect to perform LCN profiling, but only conventional profiling, she did not observe any of the far more stringent protocols that are observed by other laboratories performing LCN tests. These include extreme efforts to avoid contamination, provision of control tests, retention of a portion of the sample for subsequent testing, performance of the test on two samples for comparison, and clean up processing steps.

The following quote is all from the Forensic Science Service in the U.K. The FSS has just fallen victim to budget cuts in the U.K.

"The FSS LCN test requires an ultra-clean laboratory and so is more expensive and less widely offered than the standard test.... The site of this bespoke laboratory is remote from other DNA Units, operates stringent entry requirements, is fitted with positive air pressure and specialist lighting and chemical treatments to minimize DNA contamination."

Stefanoni's procedure, in sharp contrast to these requirements, was performed in an ordinary DNA analysis laboratory with other DNA testing units present. Ultra-clean laboratories, positive air pressure systems, and photo (UV light) and chemical DNA sterilization systems are essential facilities to avoid contamination of samples within an LCN-DNA laboratory. None of these facilities and procedures appears to have existed for Stefanoni's test. That makes four more deficiencies. In fact, the prosecution has refused to release the critical electronic data files from these tests. These files are essential to understanding what really happened and are being withheld. They have also refused to release information about what sample were tested on what dates and in conjunction with what other samples, critical information for determining the probability of cross contamination.

"In LCN testing, each sample is divided into three parts or aliquots, and two of these are tested. The third is retained for further testing in the event of a failure or to confirm the presence of a mixture.... Only those DNA components that are seen twice are included in any calculation, to show that the result is reproducible."

Stefanoni used 20% of the sample to test for blood using TMB, which came out negative. Whatever was on the knife, it wasn't Meredith's blood. Then she tested all of the remaining material at once, so there was no possibility of comparing two results, and nothing left for further testing. By the standards of the Forensic Science Service, Stefanoni's results would be thrown out by either of these criteria. And that makes two more deficiencies.

We're not through. Laboratories performing LCN rely heavily on what are called "negative controls." The following quotes are from The Law Society of Scotland's publication.

"In forensic science the fact to be established is that the DNA profile originated from the material recovered from a crime scene or a suspect, not the investigator, the laboratory, packaging, or analytical instruments.

A "negative control" is set up by simply processing a "blank" sample that has no DNA. All being well, this control will not show any DNA. The presence of DNA in the negative control illustrates that there has been a source of contamination in the analytical method. It does not, of itself, show where that occurred, merely that it has. The tradition over many years has been, for very sound reasons, that anything found in the "negative control" invalidates the analysis."

...even in a tightly controlled analytical procedure a significant number of supposedly negative controls give a positive result, i.e. they indicate the presence of DNA."

Stefanoni apparently did not perform any negative controls with the same system parameters as those used for the kitchen knife DNA. That's another deficiency. Or, perhaps, as happened before with the luminol spots, she performed such tests, didn't like the results, and so she will not reveal them.

And note here, the statement, "It does not, of itself, show where that (contamination) occurred, merely that it has." When Sara Gino was pressed, under cross-examination, to say where and how Stefanoni contaminated the samples, she could not give a specific answer, but only cited, "the literature." This was seen as a weak response. In fact, some observers took this as an indication that Gino was less convincing than the assured Stefanoni. But how could Gino possibly know at what point in the handling or processing, contamination by 30 picograms of material may have happened? This is something you test for the presence of, not something you can possibly see happen. Even if someone followed the sample with a microscope in real time, it would be virtually impossible to witness the inadvertent transfer of such a minute amount of material. "The literature," which lists typical sources of contamination to guard against, was the correct response.

Negative controls do not check for all sources of contamination, they only check for contamination originating in the laboratory. If the kitchen knife were contaminated before being chosen at random from Raffaele's drawer, this type of control won't catch it. If it was contaminated while being picked up, while being transported, or anywhere else along it's path, this method will not show that.

To control for that kind of contamination, you would have to perform additional negative control tests. These might have been on the spoons and spatulas in the drawer, or on other potentially deadly kitchen implements, handled in the same manner as the kitchen knife. When working with a stain on a surface, for example, these controls are called substrate tests. Either none of this was done, or, as we have learned before, it was done, but the results were kept secret. In either case, that's yet another, major deficiency.

So, we see that in roughly nine distinct ways, the *Stefanoni NT-DNA* profile technique was deficient compared with LCN-DNA profiling tests.

1. The DNA wasn't amplified with PCR enough; the very weak fluorescence was simply blown up.
2. The test site was not remote from other DNA tests to avoid contamination.
3. Specialized LCN-quality entry procedures to avoid contamination were not used.
4. A positive pressure environment was not maintained to exclude contamination.

5. Special LCN sterilization procedures to destroy errant DNA were not used.

6. The entire sample was consumed in a single test; no comparison of tests was possible.

7. No sample was retained for future reference. The test can never be reproduced.

8. No negative control tests were run to check for contamination. (Or, none were revealed)

9. No control tests to check for field contamination were performed.

The Stefanoni NT-DNA profile was performed with a unique, irreproducible, untested, un-vetted, never peer-reviewed technique that was made up, on-the-fly, by an overzealous investigator.

There could be some mistakes in this analysis. I make honest mistakes, and I admit it. It may be eight deficiencies, or an even dozen. We do not know the exact details of how samples were handled in the laboratory of Patrizia Stefanoni. In fact, when you see the clear discrepancies between what was said to have happened, and what you can see happening on the specimen collection video tapes, it appears that not even Stefanoni really knows what transpired during the collection, transportation, storage, and subsequent analysis of samples in this case.

But, perhaps most importantly, in this realm of sensitivity, in this extreme, almost ethereal realm where picograms determine everything, it is just not possible for ordinary handling measures to prevent contamination of the results. The DNA in the kitchen knife blade test is far more like to have come from contamination, than from the knife.

### Fatigue Failure

Back in graduate school one of my first research projects was a fatigue test on a superalloy material used in jet turbine engines. I had programmed an analogue computer to provide feedback that controlled the servo-hydraulic test. Unfortunately, although I correctly followed a wiring diagram, the diagram itself was wrong. Months later, millions of fatigue cycles later, many expensive specimens shattered later, we discovered the error.

We had fed back something like 1/3 of this plus 2 of that, when it should have been 2/3 of this, plus 3 of that, or some such thing. It wasn't what the fatigue testing protocols required. The results would never have been comparable to any of the other tests done in the field.

The test results would have been worthless, or worse, misleading, having been performed with a brand new, never before tested, never validated test technique. So, we threw out the results, at least a thousand hours of work and started over. It was the right thing to do. My professor didn't even blink. He shook his head a few times, as he looked at the diagram that was wrong. But he never thought twice about making the right decision.

Turbine blades fail, you see, and if they fail too soon, people die. This wasn't a special, courageous thing that professor did. It was what any researcher with integrity does.

Making up a brand new, untested experimental technique in the middle of a critical test is not good science. It is not brilliant. It is not cutting edge. It is incompetent. And when people's lives depend upon the outcome, it is just plain wrong.

"I think people are mystified by me. But it doesn't matter. After the Polizia Scientifica are finished they will be able to say the truth for me. And I will go home!" Amanda's Prison Diary

# III – TRIAL AND ERROR

# Nine – The Media Lottery

## Fifteen Minutes of Guilt

In Shirley Jackson's classic short story *The Lottery,* the residents of a small town participate in a lottery that no one seems eager to win.

"Bobby Martin had already stuffed his pockets full of stones..."

The entire town was involved, as if it were a square dance or a Halloween party but with less enthusiasm.

"The (men) stood together, away from the pile of stones in the corner, and their jokes were quiet and they smiled rather than laughed."

The lottery slips were drawn from an old black box made from shards of an even older black box.

"Mr. Summers spoke frequently to the villagers about making a new box, but no one liked to upset even as much tradition as was represented by the black box."

A brand new lottery box has finally been made, and it's a beauty. It doesn't have sides or a top, but it was surely built from shards of black boxes going back to ancient times. It is vast, and varied and even less fathomable than that ancient, black box. We'll call it the "Media Lottery."

When you won the lottery in Jackson's story, your fellow townspeople stoned you to death. When you win the Media Lottery, the outcome isn't much better.

To see how the Media Lottery works, let's play a little game. To keep it from becoming personal, we'll leave you out of it. The Media Lottery has selected a winner: Your daughter. You play Parent; they place Ace Journalists. This is the object of the game: Let's see if the Ace Journalists can write articles full of lies claiming that your daughter has a wild sex life and murderous psychological makeup faster than you can refute them.

Here are the rules. The Ace Journalists make money telling the sensationalistic lies. Magazines, newspapers, and websites make money spreading them. The more sensational the lies are, the more money they make, and the longer your daughter rots in prison for a crime she did not commit.

How do you like the game so far?

This may sound exaggerated, and I don't mean that the entire media behaves this way. After all, this *is* the media. There are dedicated journalists who have worked hard on this case to get the facts straight and to present them honestly, although most of the *real* journalists fled when the tabloid crowd descended. Who wants to file a serious story only to have it upstaged by tabloid slime? But much of the Media Lottery game has been played every bit this badly, with Amanda and Raffaele finding themselves being buried alive by a blizzard of lies. Moreover, this was done, not only by the tabloid press where it might be expected, but by much of the mainstream media as well. To show this, let's begin with an excerpt from an article in people.co.uk, dated December 6, 2009.

*"Amanda Knox: Inside the Sex Crazed World of the American Killer Student"*

Nothing sensationalistic about that. Perhaps I have overstated.

> "Evil Amanda Knox was yesterday branded a 'cold, calculating man-eater' by a teacher who was shocked at the killer's promiscuous lifestyle. Sonia Giugliarell said the sex-crazed American was bedding FIVE lovers when she was arrested for murdering fellow student Meredith Kercher, 21. Language tutor Sonia, 41, said: 'There was a demon inside her that nothing could control. Knox slept with different men to make herself feel important and powerful.'"

To create this smear, the writer has interviewed a language tutor who barely knew "evil" Amanda, and who is apparently moonlighting as a psychiatrist or a mind reader. Nice. But where did the tutor get these ideas that Amanda was "bedding" many lovers? Even nicer.

**Doctor Death Calling**

A month or so after Amanda was captured she got some bad news from the doctor. Well, not a real doctor, just someone the polizia or prosecutor sent to pretend to be a doctor. This impersonator informed Amanda that she was HIV positive – carrying the AIDS virus, essentially a slow death sentence. It was a lie: a shameful, baseless lie. These same people deny using undue pressure to coerce Amanda during her interrogation.

How did Amanda respond to this terrible lie? She did the right thing. At the request of the "doctor," she listed every sexual partner she had been with in her entire life so that they could be notified that they might have been exposed to HIV and could receive treatment to slow its advance. She also wrote about it in her prison diary in an effort to come to grips with her fears. She'd been with an average number of partners, but in much of the press her entire sexual history was collapsed into her two months in Italy, portraying her as the wanton young sexual predator that fit their story lines, if not reality.

Yet in spite of Amanda's cooperation, the polizia did not get what they apparently wanted most: she did not list Rudy Guede, the murderer of Meredith Kercher. This was because Amanda barely knew him, let alone had sexual relations with him. The HIV lie became just another cruelty inflicted on her, one more legal and ethical violation among many. But, not to let a good lie go to waste, they leaked her diary to the press, in violation of Italian law. The article above is just one example of how this leak became a slander in the press. That article came out nearly two years after the initial leak, plenty of time for the reporter to get the facts straight.

### The Book of Barbie

Some of the sharpest stones thrown in the Media Lottery of Amanda Knox have been hurled by travel and dining columnist Barbie Latza Nadeau, who writes for *The Daily Beast (TDB)*, a money losing internet tabloid edited by Tina Brown. For that reason, and because Barbie has written a book that is just as bad, let's look at several of her pieces.

Barbie has almost completely ignored the actual murderer, Rudy Guede. Not much of a story there, and certainly nothing to build her career on. The real facts of the case are fairly ordinary and far less marketable than the manufactured ones. She has only paid cursory notice to Raffaele. But Barbie seems to have a special fascination for Amanda, one source in Perugia called it "a hatred."

Here's what Barbie did with Amanda's diary entry about the HIV lie, in a Newsweek, online article dated July 14, 2008.

> "And by her own account in a prison, she details her sexual escapades with at least seven men she'd been with in her three months in Italy before her arrest. She even wrote that she might have HIV and then she uses a process of elimination to narrow down who might have given it to her."

Think about this paragraph for a moment. The contempt for the truth is breathtaking. It begins with "she details her sexual escapades," an expression designed to titillate readers. Amanda does no such thing. Her diary comprises eighty pages of clinging to hope, fighting back despair, proclaiming her innocence, believing that her innocence will ultimately prevail, and pleading "please, please, please" to regain her freedom and resume her life. It is painful and heart wrenching to read. No objective reader could go through Amanda's prison diary and describe it as "detailing sexual escapades."

Barbie moves on to say, "She even wrote that she might have HIV..." as if it were a whimsical thought, yet another indication of Amanda's wild behavior, rather than a horrific torment, a terrible fear.

How would you feel in her position? You're in jail in a foreign country for a murder you did not commit, facing likely conviction anyway, at which point you'll spend the most of your life, perhaps all of it, in prison. But you've just been told that you are HIV positive, so your life won't be that long. Good time for carefree sex talk.

Here is some of what Amanda actually wrote in her diary as she went through the agonizing process of trying to determine whether she might have contracted HIV:

> "I had a raging headache because this is by far the worst experience of my life. I'm in prison for a crime I didn't commit, & I might have HIV....

I don't want to die. I want to get married and have children. I want to create something good. I want to get old. I want my time. I want my life. Why why why? I can't believe this....

Thirdly, I don't know where I could have got HIV from...."

This is where Amanda tries to figure out how she might have been exposed.

"Oh please please let it be a mistake. Please oh please let it not be true. I don't want to die."

Judge for yourself. Look at what Amanda wrote, and compare that with how Barbie described it. Are these the words of a young woman "detailing her sexual escapades" as if it was a lark, or has Barbie Nadeau seriously misstated matters? A young woman was desperately hoping that her life wasn't about to end tragically, while Barbie hurled stones at her with a mixture of self-righteous moral indignation – and glee.

An Italian reporter interviewed Mignini about the HIV lie. Here is how he evaded the issue:

Paglieri: "And let us speak of the 'HIV.' Amanda, while in prison was told that she was HIV positive and she was asked to make a list of her former lovers to warn them of the danger. Then she discovered that it was a 'false positive' and became suspect that it was a trick."

PM Mignini: "I did not ask anything of the kind of Amanda. We always have the utmost respect for suspects. Why should I?"

Paglieri: "Why then, was the list all over the press which helped to create a negative image of the girl as an 'easy' woman?"

PM Mignini: "Nobody has created an image of Amanda as an 'easy' girl. Why would I need to?"

Mignini says, "I did not ask anything of the kind...." Who said he did? The fake doctor asked her. He further says, "Nobody has created an image of Amanda as an 'easy' girl." How can he possibly make such a statement after years of press smears on two continents? Read the media quotes in this article to decide whether anyone has created such an image.

Barbie Nadeau hasn't limited herself to distortions fed to her by the prosecution. She also makes up her own material. In *The Daily*

*Beast* on December 4, 2009, she writes about the announcement of conviction:

> "At one point the stepmother of Raffaele Sollecito, Knox's former boyfriend who was sentenced to 25 years for his part in the murder, yelled out 'F__k you!'"

No one else in the courtroom heard those words. Everyone else heard "Forte, Raffaele!" which is Italian for "Strength, Raffaele!" That makes sense; the curse doesn't. Were it not for Barbie's lack of concern for accuracy, this error could have been easily checked and corrected simply by asking other observers.

Here's an especially clever attack by Barbie in *TDB* Dec. 6, 2009.

> "When the two got into the prison van at the end of each hearing, the press had bets on whether or not they got to have sex the whole way back, or whether they just talked dirty to each other through the bars."

Imagine riding back to prison in a police van after spending the day on trial for murder. Whee. This, in Barbie's mind, is a sexy atmosphere. The passage paints yet another nasty picture of sex-crazed fiends, and does so without any evidence. She didn't actually say that the two had sex in the back of the van or talked dirty, only that "the press had bets." So, it leaves no tracks. How can it be refuted?

Well, for one thing, they didn't ride in the same van. They were transported in two separate vehicles, so the whole notion is fabricated. It states nothing factual, while slamming Amanda just the same. "The press had bets...." Which press? Can you refute this smear faster than Barbie can tell it?

As long as we are making things up, I have my own speculation about what Amanda and Raffaele would have said to each other if they actually had ridden back to prison together after each day in court. Through the bars of the police van, en route to the bars of Capanne prison. The conversation is purely hypothetical, but it would go something like this:

"I can't believe this is happening. It just goes on and on."

"Try to stay strong. Try to keep your spirits up. We'll make it through this."

"How can they believe that we did it? There's no evidence!"

"They don't. They're in it to save face. Or for the fame, money...."

"Who would do that? Who would ruin our lives – our *lives* – just to make a fast buck?"

"Barbie Nadeau."

Like I said, it's purely hypothetical.

Remember Barbie's two false options from this, each as bad or worse than the other, because this is a trick she has played before. Take a look at the title of her piece in *TDB Dec. 6, 2009.*

> The New Face of Evil
> "Is the real Amanda Knox the sex-obsessed, cold-blooded murderer that the prosecution depicted? Or worse?"

This raises a few questions. Shouldn't there be another possibility? How about... innocent? How is it possible to be "worse" than a "sex-obsessed, cold-blooded murderer"? Would you call this fair, balanced reporting? Could it be that Barbie is more excited about advancing her own prospects by sensationalizing someone else's misfortune than she is about factual reporting? Is she merely determined to make the move from travel reporting into real journalism, or is she is hurling stones at the winner of the Media Lottery with real enthusiasm?

> "Knox's infamy will only continue to grow as details from the trial make titillating headlines for the next year or longer."- Barbie

For an Ace Journalist on the case, these words are golden. Growing infamy! Titillating headlines! A year or longer! Think of all the stories, the exposure, think of fame! Of course, for an innocent young woman being stoned to death by a media mob, they are less exhilarating.

A final entry from the Book of Barbie; it highlights her taste for making it sensational at the expense of getting it right.

February 18, 2009, *TDB,* "Sex and Murder in Italy"
Barbie misquotes Amanda's diary as follows:

> "In one entry, she describes the night of the crime: 'That night I smoked a lot of marijuana and I fell asleep at my boyfriend's house. I don't remember anything. But I think it's possible that Raffaele went to Meredith's house, raped her and then killed. And when he got home, while I was sleeping, he put my fingerprints on the knife. But I don't understand why Raffaele would do that.'"

Barbie wrote this in February of 2009. She had a year to get the quote straight, but failed to do so. The quote she used is from a bad Italian-to-English translation of a bad English-to-Italian translation (I'm not making this up) of Amanda's actual diary entry. The real quote from Amanda's private diary had long been a matter of public record when Barbie wrote this piece because it was leaked to the press by the Perugian authorities. What Amanda actually wrote, taken from her diary word-for-word, meant the exact opposite of what Barbie wrote.

> "So unless Raffaele decided to get up after I fell asleep, grabbed said knife, went over to my house, used it to kill Meredith, came home, cleaned the blood off, rubbed my fingerprints all over it, put it away, then tucked himself back into bed, and then pretended really well the next couple of days, well, I just highly doubt all of that."

". . . I just highly doubt all of that." Amanda clearly explains that it doesn't make any sense that Raffaele would have done such a thing. It would be impossible, and preposterous. Barbie, along with some others, turned the quote on its head, making it sound like an accusation of Raffaele. It served her purpose, and that purpose evidently wasn't the truth.

Finally, Barbie refers to "several accounts" that Amanda gave, apparently expanding her marathon tag-team interrogation without a lawyer or translator into multiple events. But, not to sink to this same level, Barbie gives only one account. When she makes an error, even a specific, indisputable error like this one, she never seems to do anything to correct it. She has apparently never issued a retraction, correction, or clarification for a single one of her many reporting errors on this case.

Barbie has been relentless in her vision of the evil that must lie beneath. She has even spoken in an interview of the orgies and group sex she imagines are the typical entertainments of college kids nowadays.

"Those who find ugly meanings in beautiful things are corrupt without being charming." - Oscar Wilde

## A Higher Power

Having looked at some of Barbie's articles and compared them with what actually happened, there appears to be a clear and palpable bias towards guilt and sensationalism at the expense of accuracy. What is not clear is what is behind that bias. What is the motivation for demonizing an innocent young woman in article after article, helping to condemn her to an undeserved life in prison? Perhaps, in attributing her malign work to herself, I am being too hard on Barbie. After all, she's just a reporter at *The Daily Beast* (TDB), a travel writer until her recent anointment as a journalist. For all of the lurid stories she has told, Barbie Nadeau has to answer to a higher power – Tina Brown, the Editor of *The Daily Beast* and one of the most famous names in publishing.

Tina is the former editor of *Vanity Fair, The New Yorker,* and – shortly before *Beast* – *Talk* magazine. Don't remember *Talk*? It was a short-lived failure, beginning with a lavish party at the Statue of Liberty, attended by all the literary glitterati and ending in huge losses. Tina and her husband, Harry Evans, have undergone one of the most spectacular rises – and falls – in the history of publishing. Their trajectory is chronicled in *Tina and Harry Come to America: Tina Brown, Harry Evans, and the Uses of Power* by Judy Bachrach.

*Talk* never achieved critical mass, despite frantic – and some would say floundering – efforts by Tina.

"Let me put it this way: I think this is my last magazine," Tina said. "At the end of this one, I hope to have built a great asset and a great magazine, and then I will melt into the European sunset." – "Ten Years Ago, an Omen No One Saw" - NYTimes, 08/03/2009

The Daily Beast was launched in October 2008, with a party peopled by bloggers rather than international luminaries, and to the claim that advertising could wait while the reader base was built. One year later, there was a flurry of press releases and Brown interviews in which she said that they were on the brink of signing major advertisers. The interviews included acknowledgments that *Beast* was running on Barry Diller's investment and could not do so forever.

More than a year later Tina still presides over a publication that is almost completely unencumbered by revenue. It's the classic Internet business model: lose money on every unit but make it up in volume.

And volume she will have, as the Newsweek franchise, another fallen media star, has just come under the gentle hand of Tina Brown. After being purchased by the audio magnate Sydney Harman of Harman/Kardon, for the sum of one dollar (plus a few tens of millions in debts payable) Newsweek has drifted and lost money for a year or two. Now, after lengthy negotiations about editorial control and such, Tina has been named editor of the near-death former top tier magazine.

Will *Newsweek* be Tina's next, and final, failure? To what lengths will she go to turn *it* around and come out on top?

## Roman Holiday

"Roman holiday" sounds like a wonderful thing. It's the name of a charming old movie starring Audrey Hepburn, after all. But the phrase has a darker meaning. It is derived from the enjoyment of gladiatorial contests in ancient Rome in which even the winners were often hacked to pieces during the performance.

Roman Holiday:

    1. Enjoyment derived from watching others suffer.

    2. A violent public spectacle in which harm, degradation, or humiliation is inflicted on a person or group.

Trials are an ideal opportunity for the press-fed public to engage in dark entertainments of this sort. For example:

> "Murder and mystery, society, sex and suspense were combined in this case in such a manner as to intrigue and captivate the public fancy to a degree perhaps unparalleled in recent annals. Throughout the pre-

indictment investigation, the subsequent legal skirmishes and the nine-week trial, circulation-conscious editors catered to the insatiable interest of the American public in the bizarre. . . . In this atmosphere of a `Roman holiday' for the news media, Sam Sheppard stood trial for his life."

Sound familiar? The trial of Amanda Knox isn't the first time this kind of spectacle has been whipped up by a feeding frenzy of journalists aided by complicit judges, prosecutors, and police. The above quote is from the Ohio Supreme Court's ruling in the case of Dr. Sam Sheppard in 1954, a trial that formed the basis for the TV series, *The Fugitive*.

From the United States' Supreme Court ruling on the same trial:

"Much of the material printed or broadcast during the trial was never heard from the witness stand, such as the charges that Sheppard had purposely impeded the murder investigation and must be guilty since he had hired a prominent criminal lawyer; that Sheppard was a perjurer; that he had sexual relations with numerous women; that his slain wife had characterized him as a "Jekyll-Hyde"; that he was "a bare-faced liar" because of his testimony as to police treatment; and, finally, that a woman convict claimed Sheppard to be the father of her illegitimate child. As the trial progressed, the newspapers summarized and interpreted the evidence, devoting particular attention to the material that incriminated Sheppard, and often drew unwarranted inferences from testimony. At one point, a front-page picture of Mrs. Sheppard's blood-stained pillow was published after being "doctored" to show more clearly an alleged imprint of a surgical instrument."

Wanton, illicit sex, biased news coverage, doctored evidence, leaked testimony and evidence, and defendants whose lives depended on the outcome: All of the same elements were there in 1954, and all of the same lessons could have been learned. But they weren't.

From the Economist, one of the most respected news magazines in the world, June 10, 2010:

121

"Something else to which Italians are largely oblivious is the routine trampling on the rights of suspects and others caught up in investigations. Information is selectively leaked to reporters before the accused come to trial, often creating a presumption of guilt that is difficult to reverse, whether in court or in the public mind. An example is the case of Amanda Knox, an American student, and her Italian boyfriend, Raffaele Sollecito, who were convicted last year of the murder of Ms. Knox's British flatmate. Much of what was published before the pair's trial (heard by lay as well as professional judges) was irrelevant to the case. But it gave an impression of two young people lusting after extreme thrills."

George Orwell wrote in 1984 that Roman holidays would make a useful tool for controlling the masses, a pleasant diversion from a life of repression.

"Some Eurasian prisoners, guilty of war crimes, were to be hanged in the Park that evening, Winston remembered. This happened about once a month, and was a popular spectacle. Children always clamored to be taken to see it." *1984*

One wonders if the government of Silvio Berlusconni sees any advantage in the Roman holiday of Amanda Knox as a diversion from the endemic corruption and endless legal battles of the Italian political environment. After all, along with his government, he does have a media empire to nourish.

### A Free Press

These appalling distortions are sad and unfortunate, but, hey, it's the cost of doing business in a free society with a free press. Right? Perhaps, but here's the thing. The jury in this trial was not sequestered; they were free to read every piece of trash published. They had lots of time to do so, since the trial met, at most, two days a week.

The Italian press, working with an ample stream of leaked material, gave them plenty of trash to read. Here's an example from the Italian newspaper, *The Republic,* just five days after the murder.

"Amanda is a liar. For four days, she never stopped lying. And perhaps she will continue for the next few hours. At least in part. The morning the corpse of Meredith was discovered, she is 'surprised' to see neighbors and police while she's 'shocked' going back into the house to 'discover' what happened there in her absence."

All of this was stated as fact. Amanda was labeled a "liar" just five days after the murder – making "innocent until proven guilty" seem like a quaint idea. In fact, that concept is new in Italy and not widely understood as yet. Here are a couple of article titles from the Italian press in the days after the murder, to give a flavor for how the Italian Media Lottery treated Amanda Knox.

"Amanda Wanted Only Sex"
"Amanda's DNA on the Crime Knife" ("It's the weapon that killed Meredith.")

It has been claimed that the judges and jurors in this case were somehow immune to influence, untainted by the media, as if they weren't human beings and didn't really pay attention to what they read or heard. It has been said that they were "professionals" who could rule without bias. But the pattern of rulings in the first level trial has been one of consistent prejudice against Amanda and Raffaele. It is a prejudice so deep and consistent that you could cut it with a kitchen knife.

It is a fundamentally different system of "justice" – and a fundamentally unfair one – when the prosecutors, polizia, judges, jury, press, and stone-hurling townsfolk are all part of the same tightly knit, freely communicating, justice inflicting community. But lest we in America feel superior, we must remember that we had something similar for many years. We called them "lynch mobs."

**The Media Mantra of Guilt**

A "mantra" is a sound, word, or phrase that is recited to accomplish a transformation. Usually the change is of a spiritual nature, these media mantras have been recited for less lofty purposes.

Many of the public's misconceptions about this case come from reports that, while incorrect, have been repeated over and over again. These reports, like a spiritual mantra gone terribly wrong, have transformed two innocent young people into murderous demons. Take a closer look, for example, at the erroneous reports that Amanda nonchalantly took a shower in a bathroom awash in blood the morning after the murder.

It sounded terrible. Amanda blissfully showered amid a vast sea of blood, a scene right out of *The Shining*. This has been repeated in article after article. It is nonsense. It is a kind of "mashup" that combines Amanda's reflection on the tiny amount of blood that she actually saw, with a photograph of the bathroom when it was coated with a pink protein visualization tool days later. In fact, when Amanda went to use the shower she shared with Meredith, there was only a small amount of blood in the bathroom. It was almost entirely on the bathmat where Rudy left his footprints, and a small amount he left smeared on a faucet handle.

The actual scene was only mildly concerning, exactly as she described. When the Postal Police arrived on the scene the morning after the murder, they saw the same scene witnessed by Amanda, and found it so uninteresting that they refused to even break down Meredith's door to see if she had come to harm. It was left to one of the young men who lived downstairs to break down the door.

It's just one example, but this single distortion, repeated many times in many venues, was enough to convince countless people that Amanda Knox must be guilty. Yet, the truth might still have won out, and Amanda might now be free, or at least widely understood to be innocent, if that were all there was. But this was just one distortion among the many mantras of guilt recited. The media reported a "cleanup" that did not happen, performed with bleach that was never purchased. It reported that Amanda was sighted with Rudy, which never happened. It said that she engaged in lurid talk with Raffaele, somehow overheard in English by a clerk who spoke only Italian, while buying sexy lingerie. The simple fact that she needed clean underwear after being kept out of her apartment for three days was not as compelling a story.

But the most devastating distortion of all has been the endless repetition in the media of the mantra-sound bite, "Amanda's DNA on the handle and Meredith's on the blade." This phrase has about as much probative value to the case as the phrase "drill, baby, drill" has to a viable energy policy. First recited menacingly to Amanda by the "Capo" in Capanne prison (even as he repeatedly hit on her), it was adopted by mainstream reporters and Nancy Grace alike.

A sound bite treatment of a complex technical issue, the simplistic phrase takes whole paragraphs to dispute. Reporter after reporter has fallen for the temptation and hurled the stone, solemnly reciting the misleading but dramatic sound bite while ignoring the science that contradicts it.

## Pleased as Punch

In Perugia, it seems, it isn't enough to convict someone of a crime they clearly did not commit. It isn't enough to send them to prison for 26 years when the evidence is abundant that they weren't even present at the crime.

They make the claim that you are happy about it.

Walter Verini, Member of Parliament of Italy, visited Amanda's jail and spoke with her briefly after the verdict. Here is what he subsequently claimed about the conversation on The Today Show:

> "She had nothing to complain about the functioning of the legal system," he said. "She thinks her rights have been granted."

ABC news took up the same line in a piece entitled "Amanda Knox Says Her Murder Trial Was 'Correct.'"

This smug declaration of self-satisfaction by an Italian politician has been smeared all over the planet by our own media. Not the tabloids. Not the hate bloggers. *The mainstream media* repeated Verini's lie again and again. Amanda's rights were utterly savaged by people who had no qualms about destroying her life to avoid losing face. She is in prison because her rights have been violated by a deeply flawed process, and she is not pleased, no matter what some politician says.

What did Amanda really say? Here is how she described her conversation with Verini shortly after it happened.

Verini: "What are you doing?"
Amanda: "Reading."
Verini: "I am a friend of Ghirga's."
Amanda: "He has a lot of friends."
Verini: "What did you think of the trial?"
Verini: "I think my lawyers did an amazing job."
End of conversation.

She said nothing about her wrongful conviction being "correct." She said nothing about feeling that her rights had been respected. She said almost nothing at all, but even that was enough to be twisted.

You may remember how Amanda's voice broke and she fought back tears as she made her final statement to the court. You may recall how devastated she looked when the verdict was read. Did she appear to you then to be pleased as punch with her treatment at the hands of Perugian justice? Yet, a broad swath of the mainstream media ran this story without any counterpoint or fact checking whatsoever. Case closed, justice served, let's move on. Aren't we fine reporters?

Once the same wrong information has gone out through several outlets, it must be true. An effort to obtain a correction or retraction from the BBC ran into this dead end. When a clear, and significant error regarding the case was pointed out in their reporting, their reply was simply, "It has been widely reported...." They left the error.

## Fifteen Minutes of Guilt

Again and again and again, the winner of the Media Lottery has been soiled with lies, smears, and distortions that have no basis in fact. It's made for the daunting task of fighting an endless cavalcade of lurid smears with the powerful, but far less interesting weapon of the truth.

If the truth doesn't work, even for Amanda – someone with family, friends, loved ones, and total strangers all pulling for her – who can it work for? How can it work for the many other "unharmful, gentle soul, misplaced inside a jail," in Bob Dylan's words? Have we reached the point in history where truth is no longer transcendent? Have we reached the point where all that matters is a lurid story?

Amanda Knox is just one victim of the much broader phenomenon of character assassination by the Media Lottery. This wasn't a senseless crime; it was driven by the profit motive. They made millions by ravaging her reputation and life. The lies didn't just happen. They were twisted into shape from leaked information, or created from whole cloth. They were honed by experts for optimal shock and maximum sales, and smeared on the pages of both tabloid press and mainstream news by journalists, editors, and publishers. People did all of this – people who have sons and daughters of their own, people who should have known better.

Andy Warhol famously said "In the future everyone will be famous for 15 minutes." We may now be coming to an age where everyone will be guilty for 15 minutes. And they may spend the rest of their lives trying to prove their innocence.

## Ten – The Seven Deadly Sins of the Knox/Sollecito Trial

"Abandon all hope, ye who enter here" No, that's not the inscription over the courthouse doors in Perugia. It's the inscription over the gates of hell in Dante's *Divine Comedy,* widely considered to be the greatest literary achievement in the Italian language. In fact, the Italian language is based on the language Dante used in *Comedy*, an epic poem that described a guided tour through hell, purgatory, and heaven.

Along the way Dante learned about man's path to God and also about the Seven Deadly Sins, which had been handed down, revised, and improved upon for nearly a thousand years before the writing of *Comedy*, in around the year 1300. The Sins are a kind of a mother lode of vice, the source from which other sins, both venial (minor) and cardinal (big time) spring. They are the temptations that await us all, to which any man or woman may succumb.

The medieval version of hell described by Dante was organized into nine concentric circles in the order of the Seven Sins (and a couple of vices). Each circle bore sinners being punished by a particular *contrapasso*, a poetic inversion of the sins they had committed. Fortune-tellers, for example, walked about with their heads on backwards so that they could only see what lay behind them. Perhaps Carlizzi wanders there today.

Another point that may matter to some, the sinners who suffered eternally in hell were those who sought to justify their sins, never admitting to errors during their lives. In other words, they were those who sought to avoid "bad face." People who sought forgiveness during life were sent to purgatory where they got another shot at redemption.

### Let's Get Organized

The tragedies in Perugia are both the result of, and have fed into, a multitude of sins by a multitude of people. Perhaps we will find Dante's organizational scheme helpful in categorizing them.

In his tour through hell, Dante had the Roman poet, Virgil as a guide for his journey. Virgil is no longer available, so allow me to offer myself as a humble substitute.

Of course, it is not for me to judge. I don't have the power to do so. I merely nominate the following candidates for consideration for entry into various levels of the seven circles of hell. I leave it to readers to arrive at their own judgments, or to come up with their own write-ins. In most cases, I offer a brief nominating speech. In cases that need no further introduction, the name alone appears.

## The Sin of Pride: Excessive Belief in One's Own Abilities

Nominee #1 – Edgardo Giobbi determined, in his mind, the guilt of Amanda Knox and Raffaele Sollecito before he had even begun to acquire, let alone analyze any actual evidence. He boasted of the feat. "We were able to establish guilt by closely observing the suspect's psychological and behavioral reactions during the interrogations. We don't need to rely on other kinds of investigation as this method has enabled us to get to the guilty parties in a very quick time." This was achieved before he even heard of Rudy Guede. In fact, just hours after the murder, when he handed Amanda a pair of shoe covers, "As she put them on she swiveled her hips... my suspicions against her were raised."

Giobbi's keen psychological insights are especially impressive when it is considered that other Italian investigators were baffled by the meaning of Amanda's enigmatic text message to Patrick Lumumba, "See you later. Good night." They thought it meant, "Let's meet later tonight and commit murder." Giobbi soon posted Amanda's portrait in the hall outside his office, alongside the mafia dons.

Nominee #2 – Dr. Patrizia Stefanoni has taken has taken DNA profiling to an unprecedented level. In a fast moving field with many new developments, she has made more progress in less time than any actual scientist in the field. Stefanoni essentially claims to have developed a unique test of unprecedented sensitivity, and to have accomplished this feat, on the fly, in the middle of a critical test with near life and death implications for the subjects.

Nominee #3 – The Flying Squad took Amanda and Raffaele for a ride when they were first arrested. They were subjected to a public humiliation in a parade of polizia vehicles, horns blaring, as the polizia did a victory lap winding through the streets of Perugia. It happened shortly after arrest, prior to any appearance before a judge, and a full year before they were charged. For this despicable and unprofessional display, the Flying Squad of Perugia earned this nomination.

## The Sin of Lust: an Unnatural Obsession With Carnal Desire

Nominee #1 – Giuliano Mignini's theory of the crime provided a compelling story in which to wrap the guilt of Amanda and Raffaele. It revolved around a satanic sex orgy gone wrong. There was no evidence of this. No prior history, no testimony, no pentagrams. It was entirely a product of the imagination of Mignini. This was his second discovery of a satanic sex conspiracy. We've all bumped into them once in our lives, but twice – you've got to wonder where Mignini's mind is.

Nominee #2 – Barbie Nadeau has written more carnally oriented trash based on less evidence in this case than any other journalist. Her sniffing, self-righteous, moral indignation might be amusing were it not damage she has done to people's lives.

Nominee #3 – The readers of tabloid trash everywhere.

## The Sin of Wrath: Emotion of the Falsely Righteous – Vehement Denial of the Truth

Nominee #1 – The interrogation squad brought Amanda in day after day, forty some hours without a lawyer, without a decent night's sleep, without an interpreter, interrogating her in a language she barely knew. How long would you have held up? In the interrogation of Amanda Knox, the result was preordained, the wrath of her interrogators fixed on her in advance, the only question was how long would it take, how much pressure it would require, to put the words into her mouth to seal her fate. No matter how many times Amanda said she didn't know, that she had no idea who had done this thing, they told her that she did, and that she'd spend 30 years in prison if she didn't say what they wanted her to say.

Nominee #2 – Giuliano Mignini

**The Sin of Greed: Hoarding by Trickery or Manipulation of Authority**

Nominee #1 – Mignini and Commodi have withheld evidence from the defense as a powerful, ongoing tactic. You can't refute the data if you can't analyze it. You can't analyze the data if you don't have it. The prosecution was finally forced by the judges to release information they had previously withheld on July 30, 2009, more than a year and a half after it was gathered. But their hoarding continues, critical pieces of information remain under wraps.

Nominee #2 – The polizia cling to the recording of Amanda's interrogation while denying that it even exists. The polizia recorded everything. Phone calls, conversations, chats. It is not credible that Amanda's interrogation was not recorded. Yet, the recordings have been conspicuous by their absence.

Nominee #3 – Dr. Patrizia Stefanoni would not reveal such critical information as the dates that DNA profiles were performed, the data files that show what that actual, undoctored results were, the machine setting, or any of the information that would allow an unbiased review of the DNA data. How can we be certain that she is as masterful as she claims without the evidence of her work?

**The Sin of Sloth: The Avoidance of Work**

Nominee #1 – The Italian justice system is a comfortable thing. Trials in Italy take place at a notoriously leisurely pace. While Amanda and Raffaele languished in prison, their trial met, at most, once or twice a week. The summer? Take a pleasant month or two off. Pleasant, that is, unless, you are condemned to sit and wait in Capanne prison with it's 100°+ temperatures. The trial dragged on for a full year while Amanda and Raffaele could do nothing but wait. Justice delayed is justice denied.

Nominee #2 – The jurors enjoyed the prosecution's dramatic, if largely fictitious presentations during the cool mornings in court. Afternoons – well, it is often hot in Perugia in the afternoon, you see. The courtroom was no exception. That is why many, *including the jurors*, slept during the afternoon sessions. What was happening during their pleasant naps? That was when the defense was scheduled for its presentations.

Nominee #3 – Many of the tabloid journalists didn't even bother to remain at the court in the afternoons. When the tabloids descended on the trial like the monkeys in Wizard of Oz, the real journalists fled. Who wants to write a serious news article only to have it run, and lose, in competition with trash? That left a coterie of class-free columnists who waited for Mignini's sound bite-of-the-day then simply got up and left. With juicy, salacious lies presented during the prosecution's morning session, they had what they needed for their articles.

Nominee #4 – The Polizia Scientifica found changing gloves to be such a chore, they simply didn't bother. Why do it unless you've got blood dripping from a "particularly blood-soaked item," as Dr. Stefanoni testified? Their collection of evidence was sloppy, haphazard, failed to follow established protocols, and more than anything else, slothful.

**The Sin of Envy: Someone Else Has Something You Lack**

Nominee #1 – Stefanoni had neither the proper equipment nor the proper laboratory to perform low copy number DNA profiling, but she did it anyway. There are only a few such laboratories in the world, as it is a very new and as yet unproven technique. Her own lab was not even certified to perform ordinary DNA profiling at the time these tests were performed. The result was that she performed tests that did not conform to any standard, anywhere.

Nominee #2 – Barbie Latza Nadeau's evident hatred of Amanda, a younger, prettier woman, is almost palpable in her writing. Her sentiments expressed toward the young college students of Perugia, viewing them as immersed in drugs and sex, reminds one of the definition of a puritan, afraid that someone, somewhere, is having a good time. Fleeting though it may be, they have something she can never have again, their youth.

## The Sin of Gluttony: An Inordinate Desire to Consume

Nominee #1 – Giuliano Mignini had a decent career as a prosecutor, but it was not enough.

Nominee #2 – Tina Brown's role in this case has been behind the scenes, but as editor of The Daily Beast, and a hands-on editor at that, she has undoubtedly played a role in its continual campaign of smears, salacious half-truths, and outright falsehoods. Why does this justify a nomination for Glutton? Tina had one of the most successful careers in the history of journalism, with top-notch performances as editor of first rank publications like Vanity Fair and the New Yorker. But it was not enough. She failed famously to make Talk magazine a success, and then, as if falling, headlong, flaming from the publishing sky, she took up the Beast, fighting to make it a success at any cost in damage to lives and reputations.

Nominee #3 – Silvio Berlusconi, Prime Minister and moral compass of Italy, may rank as the most accomplished glutton in all of Western Europe. Berlusconi's remarkably trashy media empire, which dominates the print and broadcast media in Italy, took the lead in spreading early, and inaccurate word of Amanda's horrific sex life, poisoning public attitudes towards her while pleasing the audience desires they have helped create. One might think that Berlusconni's dominance of Italian politics for a decade would be enough for him. It is not, as the young women and girls who perform at his "bunga bunga parties" are increasingly revealing. Silvio is a tough competitor in this category.

Nominees #4...– The detectives, judges, attorneys, and the rest of the Perugian powers that be that have advanced their careers through their participation in this spectacle. There were careers to be made in such an infamous case. There are multi-million dollar lawsuits, all of which hang on a guilty verdict for Amanda and Raffaele. Rudy, you see, he has no money.

## Feast of Innocents

The world has witnessed a feast of innocents in Perugia – gorged upon by a circle of gluttons. It was a large, and festive table, with Mignini at its head. There were the civil suit attorneys, working almost feverishly as wannabe prosecutors. There were those hoping for career enhancement, and even the ordinary polizia wanted shares, received medals, filed lawsuits. Amanda has been sued by those who paraded her like a trophy kill through the streets of Perugia before taking her to prison, their car horns blaring in celebration.

The gluttons had only to commit two innocents to life in prison and they had what they desired. They have tasted fame, and they desired more. They had money, but they wanted more. They had positions of power, but one can never have enough power. Gluttons are never the ones to say, "Enough!" That word must come from higher powers. But who will finally intervene here?

Surely, the professional judges we had heard so much about, would see the charade of justice that had been presented to them by the prosecution. Surely, the court's ruling and Motivation Report would finally bring reason to bear, and put an end to these clear excesses.

## Eleven – Through the Motivation Report

The Motivation Report from the Court of Assizes in Perugia, Italy attempts to justify the wrongful convictions of Amanda Knox and Raffaele Sollecito for the murder of Meredith Kercher. It does so in spite of the lack of evidence, lack of motive, and lack of common sense. Producing such a lengthy and impressive document that justifies doing something terribly wrong is not an easy task – it requires inspiration.

After careful study, it appears to me that the court's inspiration was Lewis Carroll's *Through the Looking Glass and What Alice Found There*. In that classic work, the characters inverted reality and tortured logic with tenacity undaunted by reality. The Court of Assizes found a similar challenge before it. Without valid evidence, without anything resembling a believable motive, without any prior history of crime or violent acts whatsoever, it is unbelievable that Amanda Knox committed such a crime. So, the Court turned to pure fiction to justify its actions.

In *Through the Looking Glass*, Alice speculated about what it would be like on the other side of a mirror. To her surprise, she was able to pass through to that other side, but when she did, she found herself trapped in a world where everything was backward, where logic itself was inverted.

The *Motivation* arrived at the outlandish conclusion that a rock that was clearly thrown through a window from the outside to break into the cottage, was instead thrown from the inside of the cottage to simulate a break-in. Once that rock passed through that window backwards, logic in the Perugian court was turned into its mirror image, and outrageous conclusion after outrageous conclusion was reached. With those conclusions, Amanda Knox passed through the looking glass and was found guilty in spite of overwhelming evidence of her innocence.

Nevertheless, the *Motivation* is important evidence. Very poor evidence against Amanda and Raffaele, but very telling evidence against Giuliano Mignini and the judges that made this decision. As we analyze it, we see a pattern of contortions that go well beyond bad judgment calls or mere incompetence. Instead, we see sign after sign of willful and deliberate twisting to achieve a desired result.

The *Motivation Report* is compatible with the framing of Amanda Knox and Raffaele Sollecito.

## Meandering River

The 400+ page long *Motivation* begins by meandering about through almost random observations as if to take up space, or perhaps to lull its readers to sleep. At times, no real attempt was made to develop a coherent narrative from these observations. They are like postcards from the edge of a murder.

> "Meredith was very attached to her family and very affectionate; she had bought some presents and had a case full of chocolate she had bought in Perugia that she wanted to bring for her sister, Stephanie Arline Lara Kercher." *P-24*
>
> "She loved pizza very much and at times went dancing." *P-24*

These and similar insights must have served to guide the Court's reasoning. To avoid putting *my* readers to sleep, this chapter will walk through the perverse logic that was applied to just a few important aspects of the case. Of particular importance are the Court's findings that the break-in at the cottage was staged rather than actual, and that while Rudy seemed to break in everywhere else, he would never have done such a thing as break in there.

To make these assertions, the Court reached conclusions that fly in the face of common sense, all the while cloaking itself in a guise of reason. Tweedledee and Tweedledum, rotund twin brothers imported from a nursery rhyme to the looking glass world, were masters of this.

> "Contrariwise," continued Tweedledee, "if it was so, it might be; and if it were so, it would be; but as it isn't, it ain't. That's logic."
>
> "I was thinking," Alice said very politely, "which is the best way out of this wood: it's getting so dark. Would you tell me, please?"
>
> But the little men only looked at each other and grinned.

The *Motivation* is also called the *Massei Report* because Judge Giancarlo Massei wrote it. In it, he disagrees with the contentions of prosecutor Giuliano Mignini on many major points of evidence and witness testimony, even calling some unbelievable. These two little men disagreed on many fundamental points, except for one thing on which they agreed: guilt. There is a precedent for this.

> Tweedledum and Tweedledee
> Agreed to have a battle;
> For Tweedledum said Tweedledee
> Had spoiled his nice new rattle.

> Just then flew down a monstrous crow,
> As black as a tar-barrel;
> Which frightened both the heroes so,
> They quite forgot their quarrel.

Even though the court did not accept the prosecution's proposed motive, much of its evidence, or the scenario for how the crime occurred, these little men, Mignini and Massei, like Tweedledum and Tweedledee before them, quite forgot their quarrel when it came to assigning guilt to Amanda Knox.

For the prosecution and the court to disagree on so many matters and yet to agree on guilt is not a minor point. The prosecution itself repeatedly changed the supposed motives, evidence, and diverse claims that it made against the accused to advance their case. The only thing that remained constant was guilt. In the *Motivation*, it is clear that to the Court itself the evidence, motive, etc. were mere details, not the important thing at all. The important thing was casting about for a justification for the guilt of Amanda Knox.

It is a critical fact for the understanding of this trial that guilt was preordained; the evidence was an afterthought. Once one sees this cart-before-the-horse mentality for what it is, one can practically sit back and watch as the evidence is twisted to achieve the result rather than being objectively discovered and analyzed. The distortion of the evidence to wrongfully convict Amanda and Raffaele is especially clear in the *Motivation*. I urge everyone with an interest in this case to read it. Even in the translation produced by the anonymous and unaccountable team assembled by the guilters, the *Motivation* is self-damning in its illogical and preposterous assertions.

It is not a coincidence that while those who assert that Amanda and Raffaele are guilty point to this document, they rarely cite its actual contents. Those contents show just how weak the prosecution's case was. As several observers stated shortly after its release, it almost appears to be designed for overthrow on appeal on the basis of its own content. It is as if those who wrote it knew perfectly well that they were convicting innocent people, and sought some form of repentance by including the seeds of self-destruction.

### Shutter Island

Perhaps the most critical conclusion reached in the Motivation is that the break-in of the cottage was staged rather than being an actual burglary. From this reference point the court goes on to claim that Amanda, and only Amanda, had a motive to stage that break-in, and that she must therefore be guilty of murder. Let's walk through this "reasoning" in some detail.

> "It must be held that when Filomena Romanelli left the house in Via della Pergola, she had pulled the shutters towards the interior of her room, (although she did not think that she had actually closed them.)" *P-48*

Filomena "did not think that she had actually closed them" in the Court's words, and yet, the conclusion was "it must be held" that she closed them. Why? Because, the *Motivation* says, the wood was old and swollen, and it was difficult to close them. Anyone who has ever pulled closed an old door or shutter knows about this. You pull it kind of shut but it doesn't really close all the way because it is swollen and doesn't close right. So, it is left partly open. Yet, the Court concluded the opposite, in spite of Filomena testifying that she did not think she had actually closed the shutters. This conclusion, trivial on the face of it, is the first of many sequential and improbable conclusions – improbable conclusions culminating in convictions and years in prison.

Let's call this Improbable Conclusion #1. Filomena did not think she had closed the shutters; therefore, they were closed.

Improbable Conclusion #2 is that because the shutters were closed, they would have had to be opened in some way.

> "Consequently, since the shutters had been pulled together and their rubbing put pressure on the windowsill on which they rested, it would have first been necessary to effect an operation with the specific goal of completely opening these shutters." *P-48*

The Court then reasoned that because no tool for opening them was found at the scene, Rudy would have had to climb up to the window and open them before throwing the rock. A shutter opening tool.... what will they think of next?

So even though Filomena didn't think she had closed the shutters, and was at the minimum not certain that she had, an elaborate line of reasoning was born based entirely on the *conclusion* that the shutters were closed.

It was also claimed that opening the shutters would have been a substantial undertaking. But if they were in fact only partly closed, all it would require is hopping up, using the grating and the wall to gain height, and yanking at the shutter. Remember that the shutters were at about the same height as a basketball net, and Rudy was an accomplished basketball player. It would take only a second or two to accomplish. Yet, the court regards this simple possibility as highly improbable.

> "This scenario appears totally unlikely, given the effort involved..." *P-49*

Remember that opening the shutters is only required if the shutters were closed in the first place. This whole line of reasoning is sequential: each step depends on every one of the previous conclusions being correct, so the probability of the whole line of reasoning being correct is the product of the probabilities of each step; it becomes smaller, and smaller as the improbable conclusions multiply.

Witnesses recounted that they didn't see any signs of climbing up the outside wall. Strangely, however, no close up photos of the wall appear to have been taken. Only a limited investigative effort was made on one of the most important sites in the case.

"She said: 'We observed.... no traces on the wall.'" *P - 50*

A picture would have been nice. Why are the Court's conclusions reached entirely on the basis of reported observations rather than on the basis of recorded images or other documentation?

And, just as damning in the Court's eyes, a nail sticking out from the wall in that vicinity wasn't bent, as the Court believes it would have been, but there are all kinds of simple explanations for this. Rudy didn't happen to step on it, for instance, or he touched it but simply didn't happen to bend it. The nail is situated at roughly the midpoint between the window and the grating below. There is plenty of space between. The nail doesn't occupy some special space where it could not be avoided.

Another point cited as evidence that there was no entry by the window was that the vegetation beneath the window wasn't "trampled."

"...none of the vegetation underneath the window appeared to have been trampled; nothing" P-50

Let's try an experiment. Go outside and walk on the grass some night. Come back the following afternoon and look to see if that grass appears to have been trampled. Or you could skip the experiment, because everyone knows that "vegetation" is alive, and the vegetation planted around homes recovers rapidly from having been briefly stepped on. This is true at your home as well as in Perugia. There is nothing surprising about the plants beneath the window not appearing to be trampled. In this case, not seeing evidence of activity does not mean that there was no activity. And why would anyone assume that the vegetation would be "trampled"? It would be stepped on for a second or two by a burglar hurrying to climb up and through the window. There is no reason to expect signs of a stampede outside the window.

And, in fact, in one photograph that exists of the outside wall there is an apparent scrape mark above the lower window. The window is not very high up, and there is a starting point to the right of it that would make access fairly easy.

And so we have Improbable Conclusion #3: the lack of trampled grass and marks on the wall disproves a break-in.

## Through the Looking Glass

Perhaps the most improbable conclusion of all is the remarkable assertion that the rock went through the window in the wrong direction. This is Improbable Conclusion #4: that the rock was thrown from the inside. In arriving at this conclusion, tremendous weight was attached to the lack of pieces of glass outside the window on the ground below. We will never really know if there were no pieces there, however, because no proper documentation of that area was performed – only the visual observations of the polizia. Did they miss pieces because the glass sifted down under leaves? Who knows? Can we take their word for it? Who knows?

The glass from the broken window was scattered about inside the room and on the sill, exactly as one would expect if the rock were thrown from the outside. Defense expert Sergeant Pasquali discussed the glass distribution and agreed with this analysis, but his testimony was dismissed because he is merely a ballistics expert, not a rock-throwing expert (ballistics being the study of bullets flying about, not rocks). This raises the question of where the defense would have had to look to find a rock-throwing expert – the outback of Australia, perhaps.

> "Pieces of glass from the window pane were distributed in a homogeneous manner on the inside and outside parts of the window sill, without any displacement being noted..." P - 51

In fact, the pieces of glass on the windowsill are not distributed in a homogeneous (uniform) matter at all. There are several large shards of glass that appear to have been removed from the window edges and placed on the sill. This appears to have been done to allow the burglar to reach in and open the latch to enter.

The Court claims to have an ability to read evidence that is little short of mind reading. For instance, the statement that the chaos in Filomena's room is proof of faked burglary rather than the real thing: "The drawers of the little dresser next to the bed were not even opened..." This is a claim that particular drawers should have been opened and others not, if indeed it was a real burglary. How does the court know this? How did the Court know that those particular drawers weren't simply opened and then closed again?

"No valuable item was taken, or even set aside to be taken." Guede had only been in the apartment for a matter of minutes before Meredith came home and interrupted him. Rudy's final act of the burglary before being interrupted was apparently to use the toilet. He simply didn't have time to steal things. Once Meredith returned his prior plans were abbreviated.

The night of the murder was the night before rents were due in Perugia. Students generally pay these rents in cash, so it is well known that they are gathered from the various occupants of apartments on that night. The "banker" for Via della Pergola was Filomena Romanelli, the woman whose room was ransacked by Rudy. It is highly probable that Rudy was searching for 1200 Euros in cash (4 occupants X 300 Euros each) that he believed Filomena would have had somewhere in her room. That cash would be far more valuable to him than stolen items that would be difficult and dangerous to fence. It is highly probable that he started to look for the money, interrupted his search to use the bathroom, and then Meredith Kercher came home unexpectedly.

> "Romanelli's own statements are significant and decisive. In her questioning of Feb. 7, 2009 she recalled having left her computer in its case, 'standing up, not lying down.'" *P - 53*

Snap Quiz: Where, and at what angle, did you leave your laptop computer some night 15 months ago? Someone's life depends upon the accuracy of your memory. Who remembers something like that? The court places "decisive" value on such testimony while ignoring photographic evidence that contradicts it and common sense. This misplaced faith in human memory is inexplicable, unless the court had an agenda to fulfill and was merely using the testimony that they found convenient to pursue their agenda.

After rejecting the simple, straightforward explanation of the broken window, the Court invented an amazing interpretation of its own:

> "This situation, like all the other glaring inconsistencies, is adequately and satisfactorily explained if one supposes that the rock was thrown from the inside of the room, with the two shutters pulled inwards so that they blocked the pieces of glass from falling to the ground below." *P - 51*

Speaking of inconsistencies, if you think about the Court's conclusion on this matter, it comes down to this: Amanda and Raffaele went outside, got a rock, brought it back into the house, and inexplicably threw it *out* through the window to simulate its having been thrown *in* through the window. Why would anyone do something so stupid? Why would they throw a rock through the window in the wrong direction, with the shutters closed, if they were trying to make it look like the exact opposite? Who would imagine that the polizia would be fooled by such an obvious deception? If, in fact they had wanted to fake the rock throw, all they would have had to do was throw it in from the outside.

I'm a materials scientist with a strong emphasis on theoretical mechanics. I have reviewed the evidence of the glass distribution, the pitted inner shutter, the condition of the glass left in and on the windowsill, etc. It is my professional opinion that this evidence is clear: the rock was thrown through the window from the outside, not the inside. In addition to the defense expert Sergeant Pasquali, an unpaid independent forensic engineer, Ron Hendry, has also reviewed the evidence and come to the same conclusion.

But you don't have to believe us, because this is a very simple thing. Ask any kid who has just hit a baseball through a window, which direction the broken glass flew. All that broken glass spread all over Filomena's room got there because the rock was thrown from the outside. It's that simple.

But the Court found the opposite – it claimed that the rock flew through the window in reverse. That finding set up a chain of similar insights that grew ever more absurd, just as the events in *Through The Looking Glass* were unencumbered by common sense. The next flight of the imagination taken in the *Motivation* was that Amanda must have "staged" break-in. The logic in this case is simply silly.

> "Amanda was living with Meredith and had the key to the front door of the house where she lived..." *P-60*

The Court's reasoning on this may be summarized as follows: "Ah hah! Since a break-in was staged, it must have been staged to deflect suspicion. Only someone who had the key to the front door would have such a motive. And only Amanda Knox had the key to the front door and was in town when the murder happened. Therefore, Amanda Knox murdered Meredith Kercher."

If you don't believe me – I know it is difficult to believe that the Court would follow such a weak line of reasoning – read the *Motivation*, page 60. This thinking would be laughable if it weren't utterly tragic. First, we know that the break-in wasn't staged, but let's assume that it was for a moment. Amanda was IT because she had the key to her own home? Ever rented an apartment? Everyone who has ever lived there probably has the key, or could have the key, because landlords generally don't change the locks until someone breaks them. Oh, and, Filomena, who was among the first to draw suspicion to Amanda, was in town too.

Yet from this, the Court leaps to the conclusion that Rudy Guede was let in by Amanda Knox, simply because she had the key to her own front door! Forget the lack of motive, lack of any prior violence, lack of evidence of her presence in the room. The *Motivation* arrives at its conclusion that Amanda Knox murdered Meredith Kercher by outlandishly asserting that the break-in was faked, and then fixating on her as the culprit because she had the *key to her own house*.

## The Elephant in the Room

In justifying a guilty verdict for Amanda and Raffaele, the Court was faced with an elephant in the room; Rudy Guede is clearly guilty of the murder. He had a history of repeated break-ins; he knew that the students would have rent money, in cash, on that day of the month; he was in desperate need of money since he likely faced imminent eviction; he was known to carry large knives (and small ones); his presence at the scene of the crime was indisputable; and he fled the country shortly after. The case against Rudy Guede was overwhelming. How then, to diminish Rudy's role and substitute Amanda, a kid who had no criminal or violent history and no motive, as the architect of this horrific crime?

The Motivation begins this delicate process by attempting to dismiss the import of three of Guede's previous break-ins that were testified to in the trial (there were others). These break-ins took place in just the month before he committed the murder. They were at a nursery in Milan, a law office in Perugia, and at the Tramontano home in Perugia. Incredibly, it downplayed the obvious similarities between these prior crimes and the Kercher murder while highlighting a trivial difference.

It is instructive to review these break-ins, as reported in the *Motivation* itself, not only as a window to understanding Rudy Guede's criminal history but for insights into just far the Court went in its interpretation of events to get the result they sought.

> "...on the morning of October 27, 2007, a Saturday, as she entered the nursery school at via Plinio 16, Milan, of which she was the principal, she noticed coming out of her office a person whom she didn't know, later identified as Rudy Guede.... Rudy Guede had a backpack inside which was a computer. Called at once, the police made him open the backpack, in which they found a 40cm kitchen knife. She recalled that there were other objects in the backpack: a bunch of keys, a small gold woman's watch, and a tiny hammer of the type found in buses to smash windows. The police told her that the computer had been stolen from a law office in Perugia." *P-45*

Rudy had a great excuse for breaking into the nursery school. He claimed that someone at the train station in Milan had told him he could stay there, for which service Rudy said he paid the man 50 Euros. So, the police naturally let him go. I could sell bridges to clients like these.

Just 6 days before the murder of Meredith Kercher, Rudy Guede made this unlawful entry into a nursery school. He was found with a very large kitchen knife and breaking and entering tools, and was subsequently questioned by the polizia. And they let him go on an utterly unbelievable excuse. Why?

And what about the computer that was stolen from the law office?

On the night of October 13, 2007, just over two weeks before the murder, a law office in Perugia had been broken into.

> "The thief or thieves had entered through a window whose panes had been smashed with a rather large stone; the glass was scattered around, and they had found some of their clothing on top of the glass..." *P-46*

Rudy Guede later went to the attorneys to apologize for having been captured with their stolen laptop, claiming to have purchased it legally. Why he did that is a mystery, one of many strange things Rudy did that seem to make no sense whatever. None of this makes sense unless there was something else going on that we don't know about. Rudy's relationship with the polizia is an important anomaly, an unanswered question that we will revisit in a later chapter.

Rudy broke into the office by throwing a rock through a window, the same entry method use in the cottage break-in. There was even a grill beneath the window to climb up, just as with the cottage:

> "...declared that the broken window was "a French window opening onto a small balcony overlooking the inner courtyard of the building; beneath it, corresponding precisely to our window, there is a door equipped with a metal grille..." *P-46*

Finally, Rudy broke into the home of Cristian Tramontano and threatened him with a jackknife when Cristian tried to make Rudy leave his home. This break-in also took place in the month before the murder. During it, Rudy "...tried to exit the house and, finding the door locked, pulled out a jackknife with which he threatened Tramontano...." P-46

Any objective person reviewing this evidence would conclude that Rudy Guede was an active burglar, that his modus operandi was varied, and included throwing rocks through windows and climbing up lattices to gain entry, that he broke into places that were occupied and had threatened the occupants with knives. Any objective person would therefore be not the least bit surprised to hear that Rudy broke into the cottage at Via della Pergola by similar means, with a more tragic outcome.

But the Court concluded the exact opposite. Having passed through the looking glass of logic with the flight of the rock, the Court stuck fast to a path that would have pleased Tweedledee and Tweedledum.

## Friendship and Fun with Rudy Guede

Reaching for the slenderest of threads, the Court observed that while Rudy was not acquainted with the occupants of the nursery school, the law office, or the home, he broke into, he was acquainted with the boys who lived downstairs at Via dela Pergola. This trivial distinction is given uncanny weight and cited as near proof that Rudy would not have broken into the cottage.

> "Even if one accepts that Rudy was the burglar who broke into the law office of the lawyers Brocchi and Palazzoli and into Tramontano's house, it must be observed that Rudy was not known by these, nor by the director of the nursery school in via Plinio, Milan; this situation is entirely different from the one at via della Pergola..."

This situation is entirely different? Rudy had shown no compunction against breaking into a nursery school – *a nursery school*. He had thrown a rock through a window and climbed into a law office. He had threatened a home's resident with a knife. The Court even cited a number of differences between these prior break-ins, showing that Rudy didn't always do the same thing. Rudy committed all of these crimes (and more, actually) in just the month before the murder of Meredith Kercher. And yet, with the twisted logic of Tweedledee and Tweedledum, the Court concluded that he would never have broken into the cottage, because he had played basketball with the boys who lived downstairs.

> "It has already been stated that Rudy Guede was acquainted with the inhabitants of Via dela Pergola and that he had a good relationship of friendship and fun with them (with all of the boys downstairs; with Amanda, in whom he had actually shown some interest; and with Meredith). It thus seems unlikely that Rudy decided to enter this

house in the illicit and violent matter shown by the smashing of the window." *P-48*

It will be news to harassed and uninterested women everywhere that any man that tells another man that he finds a woman attractive has "a good relationship of friendship and fun with them." Amanda barely knew Rudy. There was no "relationship" between them, save in the lurid imagination of the court. Yet the *Motivation* says "...Amanda, in whom he had actually shown some interest..." as if showing interest equates to a mutual connection. Rudy was a well-known harasser of women. He was "the kind of guy who would repeatedly hit on a woman, being completely clueless that she had no interest in him," as one knowledgeable journalist put it to me. There is no evidence that he had done any more than look at Amanda at a gathering with many present and make a comment about her to the boys downstairs. But to Judge Massei this was enough to refer to "a good relationship of friendship and fun with them." This is a term he applies not only to the boys downstairs, with whom Rudy played basketball, but also to Amanda whom he barely knew, and to Meredith, whom he murdered.

Amanda was lucky that she was not the one who happened to be at home that night. Rudy's actions showed that he was not deterred at all by the presence of occupants. He was not deterred at all because he was repeatedly freed after committing crime after crime – allowed to go free by the Perugian justice authorities.

The Court's attempt to dismiss the possibility that Rudy committed burglary at Via dela Pergola would be incredible if the Court were seeking justice, but it is not the least bit surprising if the Court's motive was to condemn Amanda and Raffaele by whatever justification was necessary, while sparing Rudy Guede. In that case their objective would be to cast about for some difference, some distinction, to somehow dispute the obvious similarities between his previous burglaries and this break-in.

The Court goes on. "It is even more unlikely given that at least some of the residents of the house might have been home or might have turned up and surprised Rudy Guede... in the very act of burglary...." Remember that Rudy was interrupted in his burglary of the nursery school, in which he was caught with a knife and stolen property, but he was set free by the polizia for some mysterious reason. Rudy was interrupted in his break-in of a private home, at which point he threatened the resident with a knife, but, again, the polizia set him free. Why would he be concerned about possibly being interrupted in this burglary, when he was in possession of a seemingly limitless "Get out of jail" card? The Court knew this, and yet claimed the opposite.

Once again, one must conclude that the Court's actions are *compatible with* the framing of Amanda Knox.

Then, in what appears to be an attempt at misdirection, the Court devotes several pages to asserting that Rudy, having committed breaking and entering just days earlier, would have no motive to simulate a breaking and entering. "...why ever would Rudy, back just a few days after the kindergarten break-in in via Plinio in Milan, where he had been surprised by the headmistress and... have had to create the appearance of a burglary... when he had done just that recently?"

This is an attempt to claim that the burglary was faked, but Rudy did not fake it so it had to be Amanda. It is a classic misdirection, a straw man argument. Who has ever thought that Rudy faked a break-in?

The error is that the burglary was by no means faked, it was real, and Rudy committed it. This is a clumsy attempt to build support for the preposterous notion that the burglary was staged, on which the Court builds it's case for conviction. No one staged a break-in. There is no evidence whatsoever for it.

### Forensic Fairy Tales

But – enough nonsense – back to Tweedledee and Tweedledum. While Alice hoped to escape from the looking glass world she had entered, the Tweedledee began to recite a splendid poem, *The Walrus and the Carpenter:*

> "The sun was shining on the sea,
> Shining with all his might:
> He did his very best to make
> The billows smooth and bright-
> And this was odd, because it was
> The middle of the night."

149

The *Motivation* reveals a lack of understanding of the forensic science evidence that is every bit as breathtaking as if the sun was shining in the middle of the night. If the *Motivation* was graded as if it were science homework, (and I graded a couple thousand of those back in graduate school), it would flunk. When such crazy absurdities came from the Walrus and the Carpenter, they were amusing. When they appear in a court opinion that ruled that innocent people spend much of their lives in prison, they are anything but.

## Let's Pretend

> "I wish I could tell you half the things Alice used to say, beginning with her favorite phrase 'Let's pretend.'" *Through the Looking Glass*

The *Motivation* doesn't actually use the phrase "let's pretend" when it's about to reach a wrong conclusion, instead, it uses phrases like "could be" or "may have been." Look for them as you read. The timing of a witness "could be" within a certain window even though that was an extreme interpretation. The luminol spots "may have been" blood, even though every one of the tests for blood came out negative. Coincidentally, each time phrases like that were used the conclusions reached were bad for Amanda. The rule seems to have been that if something "could be," no matter how improbable, as long as it supported the guilt of the defendants it had to be positively disproved. If it could not be disproved, it was accepted as ironclad fact and became a building block in the peculiar, sequential logic system used by the Court.

To compile these building blocks the *Motivation* embraced conclusions that not only accepted the tales of the prosecution's forensics witnesses, but which sometimes went far beyond what was testified to. It is clear from reading this document that the standard adhered to by the Court of Assizes was not "guilty beyond a reasonable doubt," the supposed standard in Italian, as well as American law, but the furthest thing from that. This deck was hopelessly stacked against Amanda and Raffaele. *Why?*

## Experts? We Don't Need No Stinking Experts

As in many places, the polizia's forensics people acted as agents of the prosecution, rather than as neutral discoverers of facts. This fundamental conflict of interest was discussed in Chapter Five – *Sherlock Holmes and the Adventure of Forensic Science*. It is a problem in many justice systems, not just in Italy. The conflicts that this advocacy role creates in Italy are more serious, however, because of the presumption of authority that is afforded to the polizia by the courts.

During the trial, the defense requested independent reviews of important aspects of the forensic data by outside experts. The Court rejected those requests. Its reasoning on this was summarized briefly in the *Motivation*, concluding with a remarkable pair of sequential statements, as follows:

> "...an expert report on the computers of the accused was requested, the memories of which were found to have been damaged at the time of the analysis of the supports carried out by the Postal Police, such that the hard drives could not be duplicated/cloned for subsequent examination.
>
> The Court disallowed all the requests, on the grounds that the additional expert reports requested did not appear to be necessary, since the very ample dialectic contribution from the expert witnesses of the private parties offered sufficient material to take a position without additional expertise." P-21

The polizia "experts" that attempted to analyze the computer memories totally destroyed 3 out of 4 of them, a symptom of either profound incompetence or deliberate sabotage of evidence that may have contradicted the prosecution's theories. Yet, the Court attempted to gloss over this fact and glibly dismissed any need for outside review of this, or any other forensic evidence. Experts? We don't need no stinking experts!

## Bathroom Traces

Amanda Knox's DNA was found in Amanda Knox's bathroom. So... what? There is nothing surprising or incriminating about that. My DNA is in my bathroom – grams of it. Your DNA is in your

151

bathroom – perhaps only milligrams, but still *vast* amounts by forensic DNA standards. People naturally shed DNA, especially in places like bathrooms, which probably have the highest concentrations of shed DNA of any room in the house. How could the Court possibly come up with a sinister inference from Amanda's DNA being present in her own bathroom? It goes like this.

The Court recites the testimony that it is impossible to tell when DNA traces were deposited, whether days apart, or simultaneously. It recounts that since it was Amanda and Meredith's shared bathroom "the presence of mixed traces seemed to be a completely normal circumstance, and had no significance." P - 278 The Motivation mentions that the same piece of blotting paper was used to collect multiple samples, so the mixing of DNA is even less surprising. Slop it all together - it's just a murder investigation. All well, good, and mostly correct.

Now prepare for the logical back flip.

> "The Court, however, believes that the presence of the biological trace specimens that were found is of great importance." P - 278

> How is this incredible conclusion reached? Because Amanda said that when she left the house, *the bathroom was clean*. Astoundingly, the Court equates a "clean" bathroom with a DNA-free bathroom.

> "...it should be recalled that Amanda Knox, in the course of her own examination (questioning), declared that when she left the house on Via della Pergola on the afternoon of November 1st, the bathroom was clean." P – 278

Never mind that the PCR amplification method can make a cup of DNA out of a nanogram. Never mind that this is one of the most sensitive tests in existence (*too* sensitive in some respects). The Court actually reasoned that a "clean" bathroom would be without any trace of DNA, so that any that was found there must have been deposited at a later time. This is one of the most preposterously wrong scientific conclusions I've ever seen. Amanda had simply testified that there wasn't blood in the bathroom the afternoon before the murder, but she saw it the morning after. It was only in this sense that the bathroom was "clean." From this error, the

Court leaped to the conclusion that Amanda's DNA must have been deposited when Amanda "washed her hands which were stained with Meredith's blood...." P - 281

The Court transformed the simple, irrelevant, ordinary fact that Amanda's DNA was in her own bathroom into "proof" of her washing the victim's blood off her hands. If you have any lingering doubts as to whether or not this Court was biased towards guilt, you need look no further for the answer. With this kind of reasoning, every single defendant before the Court would be found guilty.

With this conclusion in hand, the Court goes on to read minute details of blood traces as if they were tea leaves, pretending to draw complex logical inferences from details about the shapes of blood drops. These meaningless inferences are just distractions to muddy the waters after the big lies have been told. Remember that not one single fingerprint of Amanda's was found in Meredith's bedroom. No footprints in blood, no handprints, no DNA, absolutely nothing.

This pattern is followed repeatedly in the *Motivation*. First, the common sense interpretation of the evidence is presented and pretentiously considered. Then some additional consideration is tossed in, and common sense is discarded – and replaced with a conclusion that supports guilt. But the additional considerations don't even come close to trumping common sense. They are nothing but shams, lame excuses for deciding the way the Court wanted to decide. The Court's pattern of bias against the defense is beyond obvious, it is blatant.

## Luminol Glow

Blood catalyzes a reaction in a forensic test chemical called luminol, causing it to emit a fluorescent glow. Many other materials trigger the same reaction, yielding a glow that is indistinguishable from that caused by blood (see Chapter Six, *Methods of the Polizia PseudoScientifica*). For that reason, spots that glow with luminol are should be further tested to see if the reaction was triggered by blood, or by some innocuous household item like bleach.

Those additional tests for blood came out negative, indicating that whatever it was that catalyzed the glow of luminol, it wasn't blood. Those tests showed that the spots, which formed no particular pattern or trail, were caused by irrelevant, unidentified crud on the floor, having no probative value as evidence. They were the kind of remnant substance results that might be expected from any old house being subjected to such scrutiny. But here is the Court's reasoning:

> "But it must be noted that the negative result for blood does not necessarily indicate that no blood was present. The result may have been negative because there was not sufficient material to indicate the presence of blood." *P – 282*

"...may have been negative..." This is one of the variations on "could be." In fact, if there was enough blood present to catalyze a luminol glow, that material should have tested positive for blood if it was, in fact, blood. The negative results for blood, *on every, single spot*, means that they were, to an overwhelming probability, not comprised of blood. The court ignored those results to obtain the contorted conclusion that the luminol spots were produced by blood. *Why?*

### Superwitness Protection Program

One of the difficulties Amanda and Raffaele have had in their defense is that their alibis are that they were together at his apartment the night of the murder. The prosecution has dealt with this alibi simply by charging both of them. They can't vouch for each other because they were both charged.

A friend of Raffaele, Jovana Popovic confirmed their alibi by testifying that she saw them both at his apartment twice that evening, at around 6:00 PM and later at around 8:40 PM. This strongly supports their statements that they were there.

To attack Amanda and Raffaele's alibis, the Court first cites the opinion of the prosecution's computer experts that "... at around 21:15 PM, all interaction with Raffaele Sollecito's computer stops." This is the opinion of the same computer experts that totally destroyed three out of the four disk drives that they attempted to analyze (see Chapter Four, *Nineteen Eighty-Four – Perugia Style*).

But the most outrageous assault on the alibis of Amanda and Raffaele came from what the prosecution called "superwitnesses." There was nothing super about them. Their reliability in any honest court would have been highly suspect. Not in this one.

> "Mr. Curatolo said he lives in the street in the area around Piazza Grimana and Corso Garibaldi: a way of life different from the usual one but not for this his testimony may be considered unreliable as this way of living one's life does not affect ones' ability to perceive events and be able to report them." *P - 79*

Incredibly, the testimony of this street person is given added weight because two vendors in the area testified that he did, in fact, inhabit a bench there, and spent the night on it. Not only that, but Curatolo actually states that he saw Amanda and Raffaele, out on the street in front of their home for hours, *during which time the murder took place*. If you believe Curatolo, he actually provides them with an alibi.

Curatolo stated that they were on the street between 9 PM and "before midnight." He stated this nine times during his testimony. Meredith's murder took place at about 9:30 PM. To avoid this inconvenience, the court seizes upon the one time that Curatolo phrases the timing slightly differently, saying, "until 11:30." It further adjusts this expression until it is watered down enough to just allow time for the murder to take place, if you move the time of death to as late as possible.

There is another little problem with Curatolo's testimony. He has the day wrong. He describes seeing Amanda and Raffaele along with people wearing masks, and riding the buses that ferried partiers around to bars. Those buses ran on Halloween, the night before the murder. They did not run on the night Meredith was murdered. The people in masks were in Halloween costumes – the night before the murder.

Curatolo has an accomplished record as a witness for the prosecution, by the way. He has provided critical testimony in at least two other important cases that had received media attention. In effect, this street person has worked as a polizia informant. The

Italian Supreme Court has ruled that such professional witnesses are not allowed as they are all too easily purchased.

It is difficult to convey the sheer craziness of this portion of the Motivation, taking a street person with obvious issues seriously and carefully dissecting his testimony, which was supported by no other witnesses. Read it to get a better idea. Any genuinely skeptical jury would be alternating between eye rolling and laughter, yet the Court takes it as gospel truth, and even then has to twist and turn it to support guilt.

One final twist to the Curatolo saga as this goes to print. There seems to have been a bit of a falling out. Curatolo has been arrested for the sale of heroin. It seems that if, in fact, they were paying him to be a superwitness, they weren't paying him enough.

The second "superwitness," a shop owner named Quintavalle, claimed to have seen Amanda and Raffaele in his shop the morning after the murder at a time before they said they were up and about. His coworker also testified that she was there the entire time and was certain that she did *not* see them.

> "Witness Quintavalle, at the hearing on March 21, 2009, was asked many questions to uncover elements of information that would be useful in verifying his reliability. This was mainly because though his meeting with Amanda occurred early in the morning (at 7:45 am) on November 2, 2007, he only made a statement about it in November 2008 and did not mention it earlier, even when Inspector Volturno questioned him a few days after Meredith's murder...
>
> This Court deems that the testimony of Quintavalle is reliable. It was discovered that Inspector Volturno did not ask Quintavalle if, on the morning of November 2, he saw Amanda Knox in his shop." P-83

Quintavalle didn't say a word about what he claimed to have seen for *nearly a year*, and only then when a reporter persuaded him. When he spoke up, he received instant fame and something to talk about. Yet, his failure to mention something that was obviously important to the investigation was simply brushed aside. True, he was interviewed in detail by the polizia shortly after the crime, and didn't say a word about seeing the accused, however, the generous Court reasoned, he hadn't specifically been asked whether he had seen Amanda, (who had just been arrested with tremendous fanfare). One can almost hear the judges exchanging high fives when they thought this one up. "Hah! They didn't ask that exact, specific question! We have an excuse to believe him!" Again, obviously questionable testimony was accepted as solid fact because it supported guilt.

## The White Queen of DNA

Of all the characters in Through the Looking Glass, the white chess queen is my favorite.

> "I can't believe THAT!" said Alice.
> "Can't you?" the Queen said in a pitying tone. "Try again: draw a long breath, and shut your eyes."
> Alice laughed. "There's no use trying," she said: "one CAN'T believe impossible things."
> "I daresay you haven't had much practice," said the Queen. "When I was your age, I always did it for half-an-hour a day. Why, sometimes I've believed as many as six impossible things before breakfast." Through the Looking Glass

The White Queen of DNA may well be Dr. Patrizia Stefanoni of the Polizia Scientifica, who appears to believe impossible things about her laboratory, her skills, and her results while testifying in court. On the basis of that testimony, (and going beyond it as needed to establish guilt), the court accepted a number of impossible things as fact. The forensic DNA analysis was discussed in Chapters Six and Eight, and won't be repeated here. This section is confined to observations about just a few impossible things Stefanoni has believed, meriting the title of the White Queen of DNA.

Perhaps the most clearly impossible thing that Patrizia Stefanoni has believed is that there has never "heard of" contamination of any DNA evidence in her lab.

> "In response to a specific question on this point, Dr. Stefanoni declared that she had been working as a biologist for seven years, had always used the same methodology, and had never heard that any problem of contamination of exhibits had occurred." P - 220

The forensic DNA literature has many careful discussions about how to combat contamination. Entire laboratory designs are built around efforts to minimize it, particularly for low copy number (hyper-amplified) work. The literature is not full of claims that sample and equipment contamination are no big deal. Perhaps the key here is the expression "heard of" suggesting that unless someone informed her of problems with her own work she did not acknowledge it.

> "The gloves were "changed, in the course of the search, every time an object was touched that was particularly soaked with blood, and when it was obvious that the gloves would be soiled; '...otherwise, it is just an ordinary object... I can move it, but this does not lead to my DNA remaining, let's say, attached.'" P - 203

By her own account, Stefanoni didn't bother to change gloves between handling most evidentiary items, but only if one happened to be *"particularly soaked"* in blood. Little effort was made to prevent the transfer of DNA from item to item other than to avoid getting large smears of blood on them. From this statement it even appears that not even blood stained objects merited a glove change, an item actually had to be "particularly soaked." The video documentation of evidence collection clearly shows item after item being handled without any changes in gloves.

Stefanoni's expressed belief that contamination is only a problem when liquid materials are present had a practical outcome. She apparently did little, or nothing, to avoid contamination as long as there wasn't a visible, liquid, bloodstain.

> "She related how it was possible for her to have touched different findings with the same pair of gloves, and in particular, the bra, first, and then, the underwear. However, she pointed out that, in this specific case, as the video images show (cf. video footage), the part of the bra that was touched was not soiled by any blood." P – 203

Stefanoni felt no need to change gloves as long as video footage reviewed later didn't show blood on that particular part of the specimen.... Think about this statement coming from someone who has never heard of contamination in her laboratory. It is a self-fulfilling prophecy of sort. She does not worry about it, does not take precautions to prevent it, does not test for it, and does not acknowledge it when it happens. It is a happy sort of world, but it is not competent science.

> "...she received that knife, Exhibit 36, in a cardboard box and that it was delivered to the laboratory where it was photographed and analyzed. It did not appear to her that the container of the knife was sterile; she specified however that 'not even samples are sterile...'" P - 214

The Court accepted Stefanoni's reasoning that while the cardboard box that the infamous kitchen knife was shipped in was not "sterile" nothing we have is sterile so, hey, no worries. But "sterility" isn't the issue. The knife was collected and conveyed to the questura, it sat on a desk for a while, was put into an ordinary envelope, put inside the box, and shipped to Stefanoni's lab in Rome. The question isn't whether the box was sterile, but whether the box, the detective's desk, the envelope, or the laboratory might have been contaminated by traces of Meredith's blood.

These same people handled numerous other items of evidence, many of which were contaminated with Meredith's blood. No evidence bag, no clean gloves, nothing remotely resembling the conditions demanded of evidence handling for specimens to be subjected to low template DNA testing (see Chapter Eight, *Canary in the LCN DNA Mine*). The knife was handled like an ordinary household implement (which it was, actually), rather than a critical item in a murder investigation that would be subjected to low template DNA testing. Yet, Stefanoni once again believed the impossible, that there was no chance that it could have been contaminated.

Stefanoni apparently wasn't making a real effort to avoid contamination – she was trying to keep from getting blood on her hands.

### Dust Devils

Stefanoni's idea that DNA contamination only happens by transfer of liquid can be easily tested. Do you have a cat? If not, hunt one down – they are everywhere. Now pet it. Look at your hand. It will be crawling with cat fur, transferred to your hand by the simple mechanism of static electricity. This transfer happens between objects all the time, cat or no cat. It will be pointed out that hair itself does not contain DNA, but hair roots and plenty of other fine particles do, and they are transferred by the same means. You can be assured that you now have cat DNA on your hand. Once transferred these fine particles are held in place by those same static charges, and by additional attractions called van der Waals forces.

These kinds of material transfers were a constant problem when I studied the surface energy of composite fibers. You could take all kinds of precautions to prevent contamination of the fiber, a clean surface being critical for measuring its properties, and then a static charge would develop and a cloud of dust particles, debris, and hairs would leap inches to the surface you were trying to test. There are even businesses based on selling equipment to prevent contamination by solid particles transferred by static. That equipment is especially important in the printing industry, which generates a lot of static.

If Dr. Stefanoni were content to practice DNA forensic work by established standards, her impossible claims of perfection might be merely be troubling, a prideful boast that makes you think-twice before believing anything she says. But her test methods on Raffaele's kitchen knife went so far beyond the pale of established technique that, combined with her boast of never having contamination issues, it is clear that the White Queen of DNA either does not understand what she is doing, or had an agenda.

### Clasping at Straws

Forty-seven days and nights after the investigation began, most of the evidence had been analyzed and not a single shred of it suggested the presence of either Amanda or Raffaele in the room where Meredith Kercher was murdered. Nothing. This was a serious problem for the prosecution. The absence of evidence showed that Amanda and Raffaele were simply not present at the crime. The polizia investigation that was intended to drum up the evidence to support Mignini's theory of satanic sex cults had, instead, found proof that the accused were innocent. So, what to do?

Putting their thinking caps on, someone in the polizia or prosecution remembered that they hadn't bothered to retrieve the bra clasp. It had been photographed and recorded on videos during the documentation of the murder scene, so its existence had long been known. Over a period of 47 days it had moved from place to place in the room where the murder took place, which was visited by an unknown number of unknown investigators; no records exist of how many were there, what their identities were, or what actions they took in the apartment at Via della Pergola during those 47 days. Then Stefanoni went on a mission.

"...both he and I were going in, let's say, in the room, for the sole purpose, at this stage, to look for the clasp." Patrizia Stefanoni, P - 204

They went to Via della Pergola for the specific purpose of retrieving that one piece of evidence.

"The small piece of material with hooks was mentioned as a particularly relevant find from the second inspection, on December 18, 2007." P - 191

Particularly relevant is right. DNA profiling was performed on the clasp and, in contrast to all other materials retrieved from the crime scene, including the bra from which the clasp was cut or torn, it showed a noise-level trace that was compatible with Raffaele. True, there were multiple, other profiles present (see Chapter Six), and the evidentiary value was hopelessly compromised by the 47 days on the floor, but the prosecution at last had something to point at. Stefanoni's targeted mission to recover the clasp had finally found evidence that appeared to tie her quarry to the crime, with luck that was either miraculous – or contrived.

An interesting convergence of events supports the latter. During the same mission that retrieved the clasp, a photo was taken of a particular item. The next day, that photo appeared in the Italian news coverage, it had been immediately leaked by the polizia. The photo showed a *Harry Potter* book, in German, at Amanda's apartment. This news leak cast doubt on Amanda's statement that she and Raffaele had read *Potter* in German at his apartment the night of the murder.

The thing is, there were actually *two* German language Potter books, one of which was clearly shown by evidence photos to be at Raffaele's apartment, confirming Amanda's statement and alibi. The polizia knew this, the press didn't. This inaccurate and illegal press leak, which generated wide press coverage saying that their alibi had been demolished, was committed at the same time that the miraculous bra clasp was retrieved. This is undeniable evidence that elements within the Perugian justice system were willing to break laws in their effort to convict Amanda and Raffaele at the same time that the clasp was recovered.

## The Year of Living Backwards

The White Queen in Through the Looking Glass lived backwards, a confusing state of affairs.

"'There's the King's Messenger. He's in prison now, being punished: and the trial doesn't even begin till next Wednesday: and of course, the crime comes last of all.'

'Suppose he never commits the crime?' said Alice.

'That would be all the better, wouldn't it?' the Queen said, as she bound the plaster round her finger with a bit of ribbon.

> Alice felt there was no denying THAT. 'Of course it would be all the better.' she said: 'but it wouldn't be all the better his being punished.'"

Like the King's Messenger, Amanda and Raffaele spent their first year in prison being punished before being charged with a crime. The polizia hung her picture beside convicted mafia dons long before the trial began. And like the White Queen living backwards, Dr. Stefanoni knew the answers to her tests before she begins to perform them.

Defense experts pointed out that forensic scientists should not know the DNA profiles of the suspects prior to obtaining profiles from the evidence because their knowledge might bias their results. This is a fundamental principle of good scientific practice. If you know the answer to the test, it is *impossible* not to "root for it" in some sense, conscious or unconscious, thereby biasing the outcome. In a partially subjective test like low copy number DNA profiling, where some peaks may be accepted and some rejected by the researcher, it is particularly important.

If the raw data files from those tests were released by the polizia and prosecution, this might be less of an issue, but they have been withheld, so no one outside the Polizia Scientifica and friends knows what really happened, what peaks were selected, and which were dismissed as noise. The Court, however, had no problem with this form of bias because it did not comprehend it.

> "In the first place, it must be stressed that it is not possible to discern any reason for which Dr. Stefanoni would have had any bias in favor of or against those under investigation and, on the basis of such bias, would have offered false interpretations and readings." P-259

Claiming that Stefanoni had no reason for bias shows a lack of understanding of experimental issues by the Court. Confirmation bias can occur whether or not a researcher favors or opposes a certain result. It is a tendency of people to steer results if they know what is expected and it cannot be simply wished away. But beyond that, Stefanoni acted as an active advocate for the prosecution, rather than as an impartial scientist. Her testimony and demeanor in court showed that. It is simply not true that she had no reason to be biased; her career and reputation were on the line.

## Closing Arguments

The *Motivation* postulates a sequence of improbable events to justify the guilty verdicts of Amanda and Raffaele. It substitutes this sequence for the simple, straightforward explanation that Rudy broke in, as he had done repeatedly at other places, was interrupted by Meredith, and wound up murdering her.

A principle in science called Occam's razor states that one should not add unneeded complexity to explain something. Briefly put, "the simplest explanation is usually the correct one." This Court was no friend of Occam. There is also an expression from American cinema for the probability of such a complex sequence being correct. It is from the movie, *Wayne's World*. "It might happen. Yeah, and monkeys might fly out of my butt."

But my favorite model for an utterly improbable sequence of events is a Rube Goldberg mechanism. We have all seen Goldberg's cartoons of elaborate and improbable mechanisms, but for those who don't recall the name, they are "a comically involved, complicated invention, laboriously contrived to perform a simple operation."

Here is the text describing Goldberg's method for keeping shop windows clean.

> "Passing man (A) slips on banana peel (B) causing him to fall on rake (C). As handle of rake rises it throws horseshoe (D) onto rope (E) which sags, thereby tilting sprinkling can (F). Water (G) saturates mop (H). Pickle terrier (I) thinks it is raining, gets up to run into house and upsets sign (J) throwing it against non-tipping cigar ash receiver (K) which causes it to swing back and forth and swish the mop against window pane, wiping it clean. If man breaks his neck by fall move away before cop arrives."

The problem with such a mechanism is that if any, single step should fail, the whole system falls apart; and every single step is highly improbable. The probability of the entire sequence is the *product* of the probabilities of each step. With each step, the probability becomes smaller, and smaller, till by the end, it is vanishingly small. The *Motivation* substitutes a Rube Goldberg murder mechanism for the simple, obvious fact that Rudy Guede murdered Meredith Kercher.

The *Motivation* is *compatible with* the framing of Amanda Knox and Raffaele Sollecito.

*Through the Looking Glass* ends with a poem. An excerpt:

> "In a Wonderland they lie,
> Dreaming as the days go by,
> Dreaming as the summers die"

Amanda Knox and Raffaele Sollecito have now seen three summers die while imprisoned for a crime they did not commit.

## Twelve – Gulliver's Travel Warning

Legendary traveler Lemuel Gulliver had the misfortune to be caught in a violent storm at sea. Driven far off his course, his ship sunk, his shipmates dead and his lifeboat gone, Gulliver swam and waded till he happened upon an unknown island. Safely removed from the terrible weather, Jonathan Swift's famous character awoke to find that he was captive and at the mercy of a perfect storm of political intrigue among a very little people, the 6" tall, Lilliputians.

Amanda Knox had the misfortune of having her roommate murdered while she was living abroad. The tragedy that befell Meredith could just as easily have happened to Amanda – a thought that weighed heavily upon her in the days after the murder. Having escaped that terrible fate, Amanda found herself held captive and at the mercy of a perfect storm of third world justice, corruption, and personal interests, all deeply entrenched in what is theoretically a first-world nation.

The language and culture barriers between Gulliver and the Lilliputians were immense. There had been no known contacts between their worlds, after all. He tried speaking half a dozen languages to them and got nowhere. There was an unfathomable gulf to cross, and yet.... Gulliver found ways to express his respect for his captors, who recognized and appreciated his mild disposition. Soon they were won over. They fed him, freed him, they got along with him, right up until he refused to slaughter their enemies from the neighboring island of Blefescu.

Amanda expressed her respect for her captors and her confidence in the Italian justice system. She has been a model prisoner. She was paraded through the streets when arrested, she had her picture displayed beside convicted mafia dons before she was charged, she was held in prison for a year before those charges were brought, she has been demonized in much of the Italian press, and she was wrongly convicted and sentenced to 26 years in prison. Score one for the Lilliputians.

Italy and the United States share much of our cultural heritage. The U.S. has a large and thriving community of Italian-Americans that are a vital part of our rich ethnic heritage. Amanda spoke some Italian upon arrival, and chose to study in Italy because she loved the country. And yet, every gesture she made seemed to be frowned upon. Every smile at her family, her tone of voice, her accent when she spoke on her own behalf in court, her every outfit – all seemed to be interpreted as sinister and cold, insolent and disrespectful.

## Y'all Let Us Good Old Boys Have Us Some Justice

Some have said that we should sit back and watch respectfully as the wheels of justice grind. But they are wheels of injustice, and they are grinding the lives of innocent people. Should the world have sat back and watched respectfully as blacks were persecuted in the U.S. south? Should other nations have respected the sovereign decisions of South Africa under apartheid? Should the crushing human rights record of North Korea be ignored and happy faced, respectful handshakes and tourism be promoted?

"Injustice anywhere is injustice everywhere," reads the bumper sticker, and with good reason. No nation has a perfect record, but that is no reason not to cry out against a clear violation of human rights. Perugia today has inflicted an injustice every bit as clear and egregious as the racist actions of courts in the United States in the past, and, sadly, sometimes to this day.

One expects serious problems if you run into conflicts with the justice system when you go to a country like North Korea, Iran, or Saudi Arabia. One hopes for support from the State Department should the locals decide to flog you for kissing in public, or if you are imprisoned for taking a picture of a train. But when in a western European nation, one with one of the highest per capita incomes in the world, home to an intelligent, sophisticated people, it comes as a shock to learn that you may be subject to a justice system that is decidedly third world.

Perhaps the worst of it is, if you find yourself in such a circumstance, when you try to tell people that the prosecutor, courts, media, and government have been unfair, corrupt, biased, and there is no hope of getting anything resembling a fair trial – no one believes you. It's a civilized country, no?

When one goes to another country one must certainly respect their laws. But what happens if their laws turn out to be like the marked cards that the dealer in a crooked game of poker pulls out at will? What happens if there is a law for everything, and for everything a law, and your bitter opponents decide which cards to play and which laws apply?

I must admit, that many of my own opinions about the Italian justice system have been formed as I have watched its performance during this trial. For this reason, I am biased: Against. It is difficult to avoid forming a negative view of something when you observe a relentless pattern of corrupt, inbred, and inept behavior. I know I am not the only appalled observer, but sometimes I check my opinions at the door, as it were, and look to other, trusted sources. The Economist, one of the most respected news magazines in the world, and with a European perspective, is helpful for this.

"... Italy is not like other countries. It is notoriously corrupt, so politics and justice overlap." The Economist, June 10, 2010

## Bunga Bunga Berlusconi

All of this would be an easier matter to address if the problems with the Knox/Sollecito trials were merely local to Perugia. Perhaps in that case the broader authorities would have stepped in and taken actions to put a stop to the obvious injustices that have occurred. But the government of Italy is dominated by Prime Minister Silvio Berlusconi, who has other priorities than to put a stop to what has been a lucrative story for the media empire he owns.

There isn't room in this book to begin to analyze the psychological and sexual schisms that seem to characterize modern day Italy, nor am I remotely an expert on that subject. It is relevant to at least briefly consider that Italy has been immersed for more than a decade in Berlusconi's sleaze-oriented media empire, which works alongside the public broadcasting system, also under Silvio's control.

At the same time, Italy has deeply conservative roots and some deeply conservative people. A bit of a cultural clash is going on, as was explored in the *Monster of Florence* by Preston with Spezi.

A recent *Economist* editorial called for Berlusconi to step down. Silvio, it seems has gone too far even for a man who "loves women," his recently divorced wife being but one example. The 74-year old Prime Minister has held numerous... what he calls, "bunga bunga parties" at his mansions, featuring young women who were well paid for their cooperation. Google it, I didn't make this up. Many of these enterprising ladies took photographs, which we can look forward to seeing in tabloids for the next few years. The parties are well documented, and yet it appears that Silvio will remain in power, at least for now.

Investigations are ongoing, however, because while his penchant for paying adult women for sex is well known, and legal, and his fondness for the company of minors (16-17) is also well documented, and legal, actually *paying* minors for sex in Italy *is* illegal. Gotta draw the line somewhere. As of this writing, this is the legal question being addressed.

This political background brings special poignancy to another common refrain one hears in commentary on this case: "When you travel to a foreign country, you are under the control of their laws. It doesn't matter how corrupt, or crazy, or unfair they are. You're in their country and you have to accept the consequences." Perhaps it doesn't matter to the people who write these things from their comfortable homes, but if they were the ones unjustly imprisoned, they might see things differently.

A concerted effort has been made by many in the Perugian and Italian communities to label all efforts to correct this injustice from afar as being "counterproductive," an affront to the Italian people, and unwelcome by both Amanda and her family. These are efforts to silence criticism of on ongoing injustice. I do not presume to speak for either Amanda or her family, so why would anyone hold Amanda accountable for what I, or anyone else says? What sense does that make?

If, in fact, the Perugian justice authorities are people who would take offense at things that Americans and others say, and treat Amanda and Raffaele more harshly, keeping them in prison even longer, then how can one possibly suggest that these people do not deserve to be criticized? That is a characteristic of a hostage situation, not of justice taking its course. This is like saying "Don't criticize the kidnappers or they will take it out on the hostage." If that is how they are, they do not deserve respect, they deserve to be brought to justice.

All of this points to of one of the most difficult problems for the Knox defense. If Amanda were imprisoned in a country with an openly barbaric court system, her situation would be clearly perceived to be wrong by the U. S. government. Diplomatic or trade pressure might be brought to bear to free her. But because she is being held by a subtly barbaric court system in an otherwise advanced, sophisticated ally, the U.S. State Department has barely lifted a finger in her aid.

In fact the recent releases of U.S. State Department cables by Wikileaks has revealed that State does, in fact, regard the government of Italy as being fundamentally corrupt. Italy is also seen by State to be closely tied to the similarly corrupt government of Vladimir Putin of Russia, with whom Silvio exchanges lavish gifts. Some sort of delicate public/private dance is underway here. The life and fate of Amanda Knox is likely of little consequence to the global thinkers who are the dancers.

## DO NOT INSULT US! WE ARE SENSITIVE!

Even the most tepid of commentaries (from others, I don't do tepid) on the methods and decisions of the Perugian court have been met with cries of outrage that they are attacks on all of Italy, attacks on the very nation, the hearts, the honor of the Italian people. "This is an insult!" One shrill response to a mild comment read.

At the same time, these voices point out that there are injustices occurring in the United States. Of course there are. And we should all work to right those injustices, regardless of our nationalities. If someone who happens to be from Italy were to email me and inform me that my local prosecutor and judges were framing an innocent person, who happened to be of Italian descent, my reaction would be to honestly look into it. I would want to know about it. I cannot imagine anyone reacting to such news with an automatic, *circle the wagons* type of defense.

### The Wrong Crowd

Some feel a need to believe that Amanda somehow brought this upon herself. They suggest that she hung out with the "wrong crowd" or that she found her new freedom too much, and so went out of control. These people have read too many tabloid accounts. Amanda was simply in the wrong place at the wrong time, and came to be under the power of the wrong people – the Perugian justice authorities. Once they targeted her, every action she took was fodder for their twisted eyes.

While Amanda lived in Perugia she hung out with fellow students, dated Raffaele, a computer science major she met at a classical music concert, roomed with Meredith, an Erasmus scholar, and with two Italian attorneys in training. Perhaps living with lawyers in training was her biggest mistake, as Filomena aggressively supported Mignini's vision.

She did not live fast and loose, as the tabloids have salaciously lied. She was studying hard, working a part time job, and immersing herself in Italian culture, exactly as she intended. She occasionally smoked pot, and she had a boyfriend.

Rudy Guede was a friend of the young men downstairs, Amanda barely knew him. If her housemates had any idea that Rudy was breaking into homes and businesses, they would have broken off ties with him.

No one means to attack a country. The intention is to right a wrong that has occurred in Perugia, Italy. The intention is to do whatever it takes to shine a light into the dark place that has consumed a corner of Perugia. The hope is that that light will help make life better for those who live there, and not just for those who visit.

### Boycott Perugia?

How would you feel about Perugian justice if this same process and these same standards had been applied to your son or daughter?

Would you prefer to have them study overseas in a country where their legal rights were ensured, or would you think, what the heck, let's go with the one where the law is what they say it is, and often appears to be made up on the fly? Would you like your son or daughter to study where, if the local powers don't like them, they will go to prison for most of their lives? Remember that all this has happened in spite of the fact that Amanda is a likable, gentle person.

One can find articles online dismissing any thought of a boycott of Perugia as outlandish, inappropriate, and ineffective. These articles all seem to appear in Italian tourism sites. A recent article in the Rome Journal, a typical tourism promotion site, began with a discussion of the human rights involved. A large cartoon, helpfully interposed in the article bore the caption, "And while we're on the topic of basic human rights, does everyone know that the coffee machine is broken?" This cartoon trivializes a tragedy.

Scholarships are on offer from the Sister Cities association linking Seattle and Perugia. One wonders if they resemble the scholarship Amanda has been given, to spend much of her life in prison.

> "...right now I feel it all inside me, a hard nut growing bigger and denser from all this – sorrow, frustration, moments of weakened hope. I want you to reach inside me and open it and make the whole thing dissolve, because I don't want to have this hard thing in me forever."
> Amanda's Prison Diary

# PART IV – THE MONSTER OF PERUGIA

# Thirteen – The Little Dictator

In dictatorships and other totalitarian governments, it is a common practice to arrest people, conspicuously without reason, to threaten and intimidate them. This process disavows people of any illusions they may have about possessing civil rights or being entitled to due process of law. The fact that the charges may be frivolous, unfounded, or even nonsensical merely clarifies the bluntness of the exercise. Dictators do this for a reason – to maintain power.

From Mussolini to Idi Amin, dictators have secured their power in part by controlling and preventing criticism. By suppressing the harsh words of those who are not *team players,* dictators bask in a chorus of loving, supportive voices that reinforces their despotic rule. Although Perugia is too small a town to be blessed with a full-scale dictator, it is large enough – and its justice system troubled enough – to have its very own *little dictator*, Giuliano Mignini.

Like these other figures, Mignini has taken extraordinary measures to suppress criticism. Mignini has gone on a prosecutorial rampage, filing an ongoing barrage of defamation charges against many of those who dare to oppose him. This assault has a clear goal: to intimidate and silence that opposition and allow Mignini to remain as Public Minister.

## Mignini's List

Between the Monster of Florence investigation and the Knox/Sollecito trial, Mignini has filed these kinds of charges against more than 30 journalists, lawyers, parents, and others who have criticized, opposed, or simply disagreed with him. A partial list of those charged to date appears near the end of this chapter.

Many of these charges were for "defamation," which is a criminal offense in Italy. This fact brings the power and money of the State into the case: If you are the target of such a charge, groundless or not, remember that *your* lawyers cost you money, while *theirs* are paid for by Italian taxpayers. This inflicts an immediate emotional and financial burden on the target.

*Mignini's List* is a scattershot of human targets with little apparent rhyme or reason to it. Not only do none of the defamation charges have any real merit to them, in some cases, the targets themselves appear to have been almost randomly chosen. But there is method in Mignini's madness. The very fact that Mignini has brought baseless charges against a random multitude is a message in and of itself.

It says: "I have power. I will use it to drain your finances, despoil your name, destroy your freedom, and ruin your life. No one can stop me. Truth is no protection. Justice is irrelevant. Oppose me and you will pay a terrible price."

It is a powerful message. It is the voice of someone speaking as a dictator, not someone seeking justice. This message is conveyed to those who have been charged, and to other potential or actual voices of opposition. Let us see how Mignini has used this voice in Perugia.

## Nobody Knows the Troubles I Have Seen

Dictators have troubles just like anyone else; they just deal with their problems more robustly. A particular problem for dictators is called the "free press." It is a direct threat to their authority because with a genuinely free press, sometimes reporters report the truth rather than the supportive lies that dictatorships feed on. For this reason, dictators large and little attack the free press by going after publishers, reporters, and those who communicate with them.

Perhaps the first charges fired in the current case were against the little-known writer Joseph Cottonwood. In an email to a friend, Cottonwood wrote that there was no physical evidence, no credible motive, and that Mignini was an egotistical bully. The worst of this, from Mignini's perspective, was this line: "I loathe the prosecutor, who has a counterpart in every city in the USA – a preening, intellectually dishonest bully who cares more about making newspaper headlines than in serving justice." Spot on, as the Brits say.

A friend of Cottonwood re-published the email (with permission) in a comment to an Italian newspaper. Seeing this,

Mignini, the consummate prosecutorial bully, filed the first defamation charge of the Knox trial.

In America, the truth is an absolute defense against defamation and libel. If you can prove that what you have said about someone is true, you have won your case. This defamation case will never come to trial, in Italy or anywhere else, but it certainty helps to *make* the case that Mignini is, in fact, a preening, intellectually dishonest bully. Cottonwood made an interesting and early insight at the time: "Perhaps partying American college kids are so hated in Italy that Amanda will be treated as blacks are treated in the USA, and she will be convicted not because of the evidence but because of general resentment of shallow rich Americans."

## Jurisdictional Dispute

Mignini's next shot was fired at the West Seattle Herald (WSH), a local newspaper in Seattle with a circulation of about 12,000. What did WSH do? They quoted someone who said that they thought Mignini was "mentally unstable" and "inadequate." Quoting people is one of the things newspapers do. Mignini charged the WSH with a crime simply for quoting someone. Think about this, they were charged, for reporting, by a locally powerful prosecutor in a different county on a continent with resources paid for by Italian taxpayers.

This makes one wonder what relic of the free press will remain if the world's papers are enjoined from printing any critical article of any locally powerful person – in any place. Fortunately, defamation is not a criminal offense in the United States. Nevertheless, Mignini filed the charges, to fanfare and to Perugian acclaim. He even suggested that the paper should be shut down for the insufferable offense it had dealt him. Was it pointless? Was his action showboating by a "preening bully"?

What was Mignini's motive in bringing this charge? Could it be the same motive that he had in bringing similar charges against Giangavino Sulas, a journalist for the Italian magazine Oggi? And does that match the pattern that Mignini set when he threatened Douglas Preston with charges in such a convincing manner that Preston fled the country? And what about charging Mario Spezi, another well-known Italian journalist, with numerous and unspecified crimes?

Mignini even brought charges against Gabriella Carlizzi, now deceased, the psychic hotline blogger who provided him with the insights that led him to the Narducci case and Amanda Knox in the first place. Perhaps Mignini is less than pleased with the outcomes, prompting him to bite the hand that fed.

By and large, this attack on the free press has been a rousing success. Press reports that are critical of Mignini in Perugia have been few and far between. The same press that trumpeted his outrageous theories and news leaks; the same press that took his morning sound bites, filed them as stories, and took the afternoon off; the same press that turned an honor student into a slut and a murderer, seem to have been co-opted or intimidated by the man who fed them lies. There are at least two notable exceptions to this. The West Seattle Herald has continued its coverage unabated, and Oggi has come out several articles and even a book supporting innocence, as the appeal trial gets underway. But much of the press in Perugia has been silent about an ongoing injustice in their community, and about a prosecutor who has run amuck.

I guess it wasn't surprising that Mignini even charged Amanda with slander for her own testimony in her own trial. Frank Sfarzo interviewed Manuela Comodi about these additional charges against Amanda and published them in his Perugia-Shock blog. Like detective Giobbi, who determined Amanda's guilt psychologically, without actual evidence, Commodi and Mignini determined Amanda's guilt in the matter of slander without any investigation whatsoever.

Q: What was done as investigation?
A: Nothing, what should we have done? She did it in front of everyone.
Q: You didn't think you could maybe investigate if what she said was true?
A: And what should we have done, interview the interpreter?
Q: The interpreter and all other witnesses, the suspect, the victims. Run the investigation, you know how to make them.
A: Please... there's nothing to investigate, she did the slander in public. And everybody was already heard at the trial. Perugia-Shock, January 19th 2010

## The Cult of Mignini

Dictators thrive on creating and cultivating a cult of personality about themselves. These cults are built on remarkable feats and brave deeds on behalf of their beloved subjects. The trappings of greatness often require dramatic dress and impressive titles. For example, Idi Amin, the dictator of Uganda during an even worse than usual era for that sorry nation, and reputed to be a cannibal, adorned himself with the following title: His Excellency President for Life Field Marshal Al Hadji Dr. Idi Amin, VC, DSO, MC, Lord of All the Beasts of the Earth and Fishes of the Sea and Conqueror of the British Empire in Africa in General and Uganda in Particular.

Mussolini, dictator of Italy before and during World War II, was comparatively restrained. In 1936, he assumed the official title "His Excellency Benito Mussolini, Head of Government, Duce of Fascism, and Founder of the Empire." Mussolini also created and held the supreme military rank of First Marshall of the Empire.

It is important to understand that while Mignini and his sex cult-conspiracy theories may be viewed by people outside Perugia as bizarre – perhaps even a product of mental illness – within Perugia he is a popular figure. This popularity remains in spite of, and perhaps because of, his attacks on various and sundry enemies. Mignini has proven to be adept at not only deflecting criticisms that have arrived from outside Perugia, but at turning them to his distinct advantage.

These turns have sometimes come by whipping up a nationalistic or local pride in response to what he perceived as attacks from afar. An example of that resulted when Seattle area Superior Court Judge Michael Heavey writing to the courts in Perugia shortly after Amanda's arrest to suggest that a change of venue was essential for Amanda to get anything like a fair trial. This was necessary, Heavey said, because the sensationalistic local media coverage had poisoned the well of public opinion. Heavey did not spell out where he thought the trial should be moved to, but it was clear from the context that it was to somewhere else in Italy – likely Florence or Rome.

But Mignini saw an opening, and he thrust into it. He proclaimed that Judge Heavey was demanding that the trial be moved entirely out of Italy and conducted in America. This assertion was received with outrage by the Perugian press and people, who saw it as an affront to the quality of their justice system and an attack on their local pride. The imagined enemy was repulsed, and Mignini's popularity rose as the defender of the integrity of Perugia.

The trial then proceeded in the overwhelmingly prejudiced Perugian environment, ultimately proving that Heavey's warning letters were exactly correct. Unheeded, the dire predictions came true, as the trial took place in an atmosphere of bias.

## Mignini's List

There have been many outrageous charges made by Mignini. So many, in fact, that it is difficult to keep up with them. The following is a list of those he charged in the Narducci case, while the Knox/Sollecito list follows. I apologize in advance to anyone who has been charged with defamation or other absurd crimes by Mignini whom I've omitted. Please email me with the charges filed against you and I'll update the lists in future editions.

### Mignini's List, Part I: Victims of the Narducci Investigation

Mario Spezi
Douglas Preston (threatened, only)
Giovanni Battista
Mancini Foligno
Hugh Narducci
Pierluca Narducci
Elisabetta Maria Narducci
Francesco Trio
Alfredo Brizioli
Adolfo Pennetti Pennella
Luigi De Feo
Giuseppe Rinaldi
Professor Fabio
Antonio Brizioli

Giovanna Ceccarelli
Emma Magara
Marcello Zoppitelli
Gianfranco Bernabei
Luigi Ruocco
Ferdinando Zaccaria
Adriana Frezza
Daniela Cortona

Every one of these people was found not only to be innocent, but, to have been illegally investigated and charged by Mignini for crimes that never occurred in the first place. The following is about the decision handed down against Mignini.

> "Ultimately Mignini may find the Florence judge's words hard to shrug off. He and Giuttari, the court said, were guilty of "almost unheard of" criminal activity, carrying out investigations "in no way related ... to their proper competence", launching criminal cases with no evidence, ordering phone taps with "quite different ends" from those cited when the taps were authorized, taps that were made "for reasons of retaliation ... against people towards whom they had reasons for hostility". From The Independent, Peter Popham, June 6, 2010

### All in the Family

In an interview with a British newspaper, Amanda's parents, Edda and Curt, said that Amanda had stated that she was "abused physically and verbally" during her interrogation, and that she had told them she was "hit in the back of the head by a police officer with an open hand..." Amanda later testified the same thing in court.

Eighteen months after the interrogation, and many months after the interview, an unstated number of unnamed polizia could bear the insult no more. They decided to press defamation charges against Curt and Edda *the day before the beginning of the defense's closing arguments*. One can question the speed of Italian justice, but it's timing is impeccable. By throwing this rock into the already muddy waters of the case, they clearly hoped to bury news coverage of the defense's closing with yet another groundless accusation.

These charges had several effects. Among them:

First, the charges mean more lawyers for the family, and yet more legal bills. Guilty or innocent, the crushing burden of legal bills is a punishment not to be underestimated.

Second, if convicted they face 6 months to 3 years in an Italian prison. It is said that those without prior offenses are unlikely to serve time for this crime, but clearly that rule of thumb has no bearing in this case. One need only look at the dragged-out incarceration that has already been inflicted on Amanda to understand this. We don't really know what the courts will decide on this, we don't really know if they will suddenly decide that Edda is a flight risk, and must be imprisoned for the public safety.

Third, having been charged on preposterous grounds simply for speaking the truth and defending their daughter, they are put on notice that further support will bring risks. It is an attempt to silence the defendant's own family.

Fourth, it will make it more difficult and dangerous for Amanda's parents to visit her. If the same justice railroad that convicted Amanda and Raffaele convicts her parents, then any visit to Italy will risk arrest and imprisonment. This could have the effect of isolating Amanda even more.

These legal attacks seem to be part of an effort, not merely to convict Amanda, but to destroy her. There is a pattern of actions that show an attempt to inflict cruel and unusual punishment on someone with no history of violence or aggression, and with no plausible evidence or motive to link her to the alleged crime.

### Mignini's List, Part II: The Knox/Sollecito Trial

During the current trial Mignini has charged the following involved people with miscellaneous, peripheral crimes. Again, this list may be incomplete, as new charges continue to be filed.

Amanda Knox

The West Seattle Herald

Curt Knox and Edda Mellas, Amanda's parents

Luciano Ghirga, attorney for Amanda Knox

Luca Maori, attorney for Raffaele Sollecito

The Sollecito family

Luca Lalli, coroner from the University of Perugia (Not charged, but removed from the case, supposedly for leaking information to the press)

Joe Cottonwood, a fiction writer

*This just added* – Antonio Curatollo, street person and "superwitness" "against" Amanda (though his story would have provided an alibi), charged with sale of heroin for crimes alleged to have occurred years before. Hmmm.

There ought to be a law... an old expression goes. Shouldn't there be a law against the deliberate, wrongful accusation, arrest, prosecution, conviction, and imprisonment of someone who is clearly innocent? And shouldn't it be improper.... bad form, or bad face, even in a country with *sophisticated sensibilities*, to file charges against parents for supporting their own daughter? What manner of crime is it for a prosecutor to pursue, not only the falsely accused, but to lash out with charges against anyone who *supports* the falsely accused?

Mignini's habit of illegal investigation does not appear to have improved between the *Monster of Florence* case and the current matter. He was convicted of prosecutorial misconduct for his work on that case, and sentenced to 16 months in prison. He has been allowed to continue perpetrating the same excesses, inflicting even greater damage – *this satanic conspiracy around*. Mignini's reign of terror should have been brought to a halt by his conviction, or by merely being a prosecutor who was under indictment for his utterly bizarre prosecutions.

Should have been... but, there was a little catch...

## Fourteen – Perugian Catch 22

### *There was only one catch and that was Catch-22*

In Joseph Heller's World War II classic, Catch-22, a pilot named Orr was driven insane by the war. Orr was eligible to be grounded because of that insanity. He didn't have to fly and wouldn't have to die.

Unfortunately, there was a catch. Catch-22. If Orr asked to be grounded because he was crazy, he wasn't crazy after all, because he had the sense to ask to be grounded. So, he wasn't crazy and couldn't be grounded. On the other hand, if he didn't ask to be grounded he was certifiably crazy, but... he hadn't asked. In Catch-22, you were damned if you did, and damned if you didn't. The nuances of this splendid atrocity of circular logic were developed and explored in many forms throughout the book – and in the war, too.

*Catch-22* took place on the Mediterranean island of Pianosa, not very far from Perugia. Perhaps it was that proximity, but the logic of that book, as inescapable as it was profoundly unfair, does not seem to have been lost on the locals. In fact, it appears to be fundamental to many of the rulings there.

### A Change of Scenery

Many people have urged Amanda's lawyers to ask for a change of venue from Perugia because the legal establishment there has been deluged by local media coverage that is clearly biased against her. Unfortunately, they would have had to ask for that change of venue from that same legal establishment, so it would almost certainly be refused. Further, the act of asking for a change of venue might additionally bias the Perugian legal establishment, because they could take offense that they were being charged with bias. That has now happened, and time will tell whether both outcomes have transpired. They didn't ask for a venue change at first instance, and they got a biased court. Then they did ask, and did not receive the change. It remains to be seen whether that court will prove similarly biased.

Catch-22 says they have a right to do anything we can't stop them from doing. - Catch-22

Judge Claudia Matteini was scheduled to hear Amanda's defamation trial. Her attorney's asked the Italian, Court of Cassation, it's supreme court, to change that assignment because that is the same judge that issued the ruling that Amanda be held for trial, writing a document that explained, "I begin my reasoning with the four of them in the bedroom," meaning Meredith, Amanda, Raffaele, and Patrick.

Matteini actually *began her reasoning* by assuming that Amanda, Raffaele, and Patrick Lumumba were present at the scene of the crime. Patrick proved that he was not there a week or so later, providing him with an airtight alibi. No evidence of the presence of Amanda and Raffaele has ever been presented. And yet, this ruling resulted in their being held for a year before charges were brought. She also ruled that they be held in prison while actual criminals with serious prior convictions are commonly allowed to be free while on trial.

The bias of this judge is palpable, but the motion for a change of venue was rejected and nothing can be done. The facts behind her critical ruling are clearly, demonstrably incorrect. They were proved to be incorrect within a single week. Yet that ruling stood. Now that judge is probably even more biased because they accused her of bias. So it goes, in Perugian justice.

"Catch-22 states that agents enforcing Catch-22 need not prove that Catch-22 actually contains whatever provision the accused violator is accused of violating."

## A Brief List of Catches - 22

If Amanda had been guilty, she would have thought to act innocent. But since she was innocent, it never occurred to her to go around acting innocent, she simply was. So, everything she did, every expression, action, crying or not crying, emotional or not emotional, was viewed as more evidence of her guilt.

There was no evidence of Amanda's presence in the room where Meredith was killed. No fingerprints, no DNA, no footprints, no shoeprints. Although the simple explanation for this is that she wasn't there, to Mignini, it was damning evidence. Remember his double-body-swap interpretation of Narducci's body turning out to be none other than Narducci. If there had been evidence of her presence, it would have showed that she was guilty. The lack of such evidence shows that she was guilty, and that she miraculously cleaned up all evidence of her presence. It is the witches' mark, one of the earliest applications of Catch-22.

> "The chaplain had mastered, in a moment of divine intuition, the handy technique of protective rationalization, and he was exhilarated by his discovery. It was miraculous. It was almost no trick at all, he saw, to turn vice into virtue and slander into truth, impotence into abstinence, arrogance into humility, plunder into philanthropy, thievery into honor, blasphemy into wisdom, brutality into patriotism, and sadism into justice. Anybody could do it; it required no brains at all. It merely required no character." *Catch - 22*

The constantly changing motivations ascribed to Amanda fit a similar pattern. First, she had the supposed motive of the powerful lure of satanic sex cults. Who among us hasn't considered participating in a ritual human sacrifice on a boring evening? Then, when the Satan thing had run its course, a new motive was invented. She supposedly harbored a motive of hatred, hatred that had never been expressed or revealed in any way. Then it became clear that both were nonsense, and that Amanda and Raffaele had no motive whatsoever to commit murder. That would ordinarily be a huge boost to the defense, when someone has no motive to commit a crime it's a strong indication that they are innocent. In this case, though, Catch-22 applies. The absence of a motive, we were told, was *especially bad*, as they must have committed a terrible murder for no reason at all.

Rudy Guede claimed remorse for having failed to save Meredith. He boasted of his heroic efforts, lamenting, only, that they fell short. Amanda and Raffaele did not express remorse for a crime they did not commit, they only expressed sadness that it happened. Rudy's ostentatious remorse act contributed to his sentence being reduced to 16 years in the first stage of the appeal.

In Perugia, the innocent are punished more severely than the guilty. It's Catch-22, you see.

> "You know, that might be the answer – to act boastfully about something we ought to be ashamed of. That's a trick that never seems to fail." Catch-22

## Fifteen – The Inevitable Unexpected

## and The Theory of the Crime

It's called the "inevitable unexpected." It dropped your jaw at the end of the movie *Sixth Sense* when you realized that "I see dead people" was why the kid could see Bruce Willis. Bruce's character was dead from the first scene – you saw him die, but it somehow slipped your mind. It was inevitable. It had to be. But even at the very last, it was unexpected.

And it was the inevitable unexpected that turned your stomach in Alfred Hitchcock's classic film *Psycho*, when you found out that Norman Bates' maniacal mother was Norman himself. Of course! It had to be. Why didn't I see that?

It shouldn't be a surprise that the Meredith Kercher murder case harbors surprises that are fully worthy of the term, inevitable unexpected. One such surprise is the evidence that strongly suggests that Rudy Guede was operating as an informant at the time that he murdered Meredith Kercher. Much of the evidence for this is a matter of public record, and yet, the implications of such an involvement, and of such a special relationship, seem to have been slow to sink in.

Perhaps that is because it is not the usual thing that the murderer may have been working for the prosecutor. But, if the reader will take this one, giant leap of cynicism with me, a *theory of the crime* of framing Amanda and Raffaele will take form and many previously inexplicable aspects of the case will fall into place. This is only a theory that I am proposing. It is not proven. I invite others to work to develop their own theories, that we might compare and test them to better understand what has happened in Perugia.

## Anomalies 'R Us

Many aspects of this case do not seem to make sense. I call them *anomalies*.

"An anomaly is any occurrence or object that is strange, unusual, or unique. It can also mean a discrepancy or deviation from an established rule, trend, or pattern." - Wiki dictionary

I've kept a list of anomalies because I believe that they can help to illumine some of the otherwise dark recesses of the Perugian justice system. These anomalies include many things that simply stand out as strange, as inexplicable in terms of what is publicly known. Things like Patrick's change of heart about the kindness of the polizia that arrested him, and Filomena's almost immediate suggestion that the break-in was faked, or her insistence that the glass was on the clothes when the photos showed the opposite.

The anomalies also include major issues, such as the decision by Giobbi and Mignini to fixate on Amanda in the first place, the Court's obviously and deliberately twisted logic in the *Motivation Report*, and the lenient treatment of Rudy Guede. When the murderer's sentence was reduced to sixteen years on appeal, there were no complaints from the prosecution, no problem. Why was that? He committed a heinous crime yet they were content to let him off easy. Amanda got 26 years and it was not enough for them. What lies behind these actions? Cultural differences?

By now it should be clear that Amanda and Raffaele have been railroaded to conviction for a murder they did not commit. That leaves us with a huge question. *Why?* What was the *motive* for the framing of Amanda Knox and Raffaele Sollecito? Discovering that motive might enable a better understanding of the whole, tragic sequence of events that has unfolded.

But first, not to change the subject, let's talk about neutrinos.

## Neutrinos in the Mist

In scientific research, one tries to interpret observations in terms of some model. If everything observed fits the model, it is a very good model. That is nice, but it is not very interesting. When a scientist makes an observation that doesn't match what the standard model predicts, *that* is when it gets interesting. Something is wrong with the model. There is something going on that the scientist does not understand, and that is a call to action.

A case in point was the discovery, decades ago, of a new class of subatomic particles. Neutrinos don't interact much, so they are very difficult to observe. As a result, even though there are vast numbers of them coursing through space, they had gone undetected. The sun spews vast quantities of neutrinos, sending roughly 65 billion of them through every square centimeter of earth every second, *but no one had noticed.*

When something called *beta decay* was studied, however, it was found that something anomalous was going on. The particles that shot out seemed to fly off in a particular direction, but nothing seemed to go in the *opposite* direction to balance the equations. The model of beta decay was incomplete – it omitted something. The fact that something was missing led Wolfgang Fermi to propose a new particle, eventually called the *neutrino* from the Italian for "little neutral one." The neutrino was postulated to carry away the momentum, spin, and energy that went missing in the equations. More than 25 years later, neutrinos were finally observed, in one of the triumphs of particle physics. They had discovered something with their minds that they could not, at first, detect with their instruments.

Here's the thing. Even though detecting neutrinos is famously difficult, they were discovered because of the *anomaly* in beta decay. Beta decay did not make sense because we did not have the whole picture. Once we had the whole picture, it all fell into place and made perfect sense.

Discovering something indirectly, by its momentum, as with neutrinos, or its gravity, as with planets, is a well-known technique in science. Phenomena that might otherwise remain undetected and unknown are often revealed in this manner. Perhaps we can apply something like this powerful approach to gain a better understanding of what has happened in Perugia. The trick will be, not to look for the *thing* itself, but to look for the *effects of the thing* on the "orbits" or "momentum" or behavior of people, their decisions, and their motivations. What unseen forces might have been in play to cause some of these anomalous events?

## The Standard Model

There is a standard model, of sorts, of the Knox/Sollecito trial among the growing numbers of those who are convinced of their innocence. It holds, very briefly stated, that there was a culture clash between Perugia, Italy and the Seattle girl. It caused the crazy prosecutor and polizia to kind of get out ahead of things. In their eagerness to look good and solve the case quickly, they jumped to the wrong conclusion. Then, to avoid embarrassment, "bad face," they refused to admit their error. Refused for years – sending people they knew were innocent to prison for most of their lives.

The standard model, as I will call it (and there are many variations), has many things right with it, but also appears to me to come up short of a full explanation. Although culture clashes, crazy people, and bad face can explain a lot, there are too many things that they just do not explain. It seems that there are too many anomalies that require impossible contortions of motivations, or impossible stupidity on the part of the investigators and judges. It also seems to me that a major component is missing from the standard model, personal motivations. Although people exist in a cultural realm, they also claw tenaciously for their own personal benefit. I see a lot of claw marks from this case.

In science, when a model isn't working out, what usually happens is that someone has an insight. They go "Ah hah!" or "Eureka!" or some such thing and come up with a new model. If the new model does a better job of explaining some of the inexplicable events and phenomena, it is transcendent, and the standard model becomes the old fashioned theory. Parts of the standard model might be absorbed into the new model, it may even form the foundation, but it stands refined and corrected.

My own "eureka" moment came when I first seriously considered the possibility that Rudy Guede was an informant working for someone within the Perugian justice system. Let's explore that thought.

## Information, Please

It is a well-known fact that police often overlook crimes committed by informants, and it is a well-known fact that one of the marks of an informant is that they can get away with crimes.

> "Quite frequently, confidential informants (or criminal informants) will provide information in order to obtain lenient treatment for themselves and provide information, over an extended period of time, in return for money or for police to overlook their own criminal activities. Quite often someone will become an informant following their arrest." -Wikipedia

We have seen from the testimony, discussed in the *Motivation* document, that Rudy Guede committed *at least* three break-ins during the month before the murder. Each time, he was quickly released by the polizia. Why? He did not so much as receive a ticket when he was caught breaking into a home, an office, and a school, and even though he threatened people with knifes. There have been reports that Rudy committed even more break-ins than this, perhaps totaling six break-ins, just counting those *in which he was caught* and released, in just over thirty days before the murder. It was a regular crime spree.

In an article in the British newspaper *The Daily Express*, Bob Graham wrote that Rudy Guede committed an entire series of crimes in the month before the murder of Meredith Kercher.

> "It reveals the third person convicted of killing British student Meredith Kercher had committed six serious crimes over 33 days before the killing. But robberies carried out by small-time drug dealer Rudy Guede were ignored by Italian authorities, raising suspicions that he was a police informer."

I have been told by more than one knowledgeable source that the only person within the Perugian justice system with the authority to order such a release at that time was Mignini himself.

This, at the least, suggests that Guede probably worked for, and was protected by, someone in the Perugian justice system. We don't yet know what Rudy informed about. We don't yet know, with certainty, just whom he informed for. We do know that Mignini occupied a powerful position within the Perugian justice system, and we do know that he exploited informants, Antonio Curatolo, the street person who is now accused of heroin dealing, being a prime example. And we know that Mignini maintained *enemies lists* and had overstepped the bounds of his authority in prior investigations while trying to dig up dirt on them, as his conviction in the Narducci case shows.

It may be difficult to believe that an informant could wind up committing a murder, but it is unfortunately far from unheard of for informant-handler relationships, which are often fiercely charged and delicately balanced, to turn out badly. The fallout from such a break down can be withering for those who handled the informant.

A particularly high profile case of this is now playing out in the terrorism arena. It is the case of David C. Headley, a long time informant for drug and terrorism investigations who was deeply involved in the 2008 attacks in Mumbai that killed 164 people. Between the D.E.A., C.I.A., and F.B.I. there is essentially mutual finger pointing as to whom was to blame for missing the repeated warnings that he was actually on the other side. At least, investigations are underway to determine what went wrong and who might be responsible. In Perugia, no one seems to be investigating the informant-gone-bad, they are too busy giving themselves awards.

### The Perugian Powers that Be

Because we don't yet have complete information on this development in the case, we will need to define some terms to, in part, encompass our uncertainty. Once again, this is a bit like the phrase of the Polizia Scientifica. *It is compatible with...*

I will refer to the "Perugian Powers that Be," or "PPB." By this, I'm talking about an as yet unknown combination of the prosecutors, the polizia, and perhaps even the judges in Perugia. We don't know exactly who was involved, and we don't know exactly what their roles were. That is something that remains to be determined, and which will require extensive investigation, probably taking years to sort out.

I not mean to suggest that the entire Perugian justice system was involved in a criminal conspiracy to frame Amanda Knox. The polizia, prosecutors, and judges in Perugia are not a monolithic group. That group includes many individuals who sometimes work in concert, and are sometimes at odds. But when one looks at the pattern of decisions from this court, the documents produced by various judges, the presentations of the prosecutors and their informal co-prosecutors for the civil clients, it is abundantly clear that many of them worked together to perform the same tragic opera, if you will.

The amazing suspensions of disbelief and the willful distortions of reality and logic in the *Motivation Report* vividly show the extent to which that court would go to arrive at guilty verdicts. The abuses of scientific methodology and simple laboratory practice of the Polizia Scientifica showed a singular dedication to achieving an end result, rather than being objective. And, of course, the astounding leaps of illogic by Mignini, as he choreographed the process of convicting innocent people did not happen on their own. The framing of Amanda Knox was a coordinated team effort.

It does not seem likely that all these people rode roughshod over the spirit and the substance of the laws for entertainment value. They had motives. Every, single, player in Team Perugia had reasons to make the decisions they made. It makes perfect sense that they did so out of some unknown melding of self-interest, team spirit, and nationalistic pride, acted out in, and exploiting, an environment of conflict between indulgence in, and abhorrence of, *sin.*

For all these reasons, the Perugian Powers that Be (PPB) or the Perugian justice authorities will refer to an inexactly known group. We will have to fill in the details at some later time. For now, we are working to paint a picture in broad-brush strokes to gain an understanding, at long last, as to what has happened in Perugia.

## Echoes of the Past

Next, let's recall that in the Monster of Florence case the murders themselves were just the first crimes, while the investigation and prosecution comprised an entire second wave of crimes in which innocents were imprisoned and lives were savaged. This wave of incompetent investigation and criminal misconduct by the polizia and prosecutor continues in appeals form to this day, more than twenty-five years after the couples were murdered.

PM Mignini was convicted for unlawful investigatory activities in that case, as described previously. For Mignini also to have engaged in illegal acts before, during, and after the murder of Meredith Kercher would not only not be surprising. It would be a simple continuation of his ongoing, illegal activity.

In fact, what appears to have happened, what went wrong during the Narducci prosecutions, was that Mignini bit off more satanic sex cult conspirators than he could chew – twenty of them, including polizia, journalists, and other influential people. He went after a substantial number of people in the legal establishment of an adjacent town, Florence. Because there were so many defendants, they were able to mount a defense – in Florence – that defeated him. In the Knox/Sollecito prosecution, he selected just two people for his prime targets, neither had any local support, and he did it in his power base, Perugia. Later add-ons, such as the parents and various journalists, had little political power within the Perugian court system. By pursuing less powerful targets and doing it on his home field, he was able to achieve convictions this second time around.

## I've Been Working on the Railroad

Let's get back to Rudy now, because I've been working on the railroad. The idea that Rudy was an informant is a kind of missing link. It can enable us to better understand things that have puzzled us all along. Now we can begin to connect the dots. When you connect the dots, you tie together the pieces so that you can see the big picture from the little parts.

We need to develop a theory of the crime of railroading Amanda Knox and Raffaele Sollecito that can be tested against the data, to be refined if it works and corrected if it doesn't.

There are many things that we know, but that are denied by a few observers who have their own agendas. Let's accept them as facts and see where it takes us. We know that Amanda and Raffaele are innocent because there is no valid evidence against them. We won't bother to debate that here. It is a fact, and one of the critical starting points for really understanding what has happened. Now we are moving beyond those debates.

## The Dots

Now it's time to list some "Dots," things that we are pretty sure we know, or can surmise by connecting other Dots. This is an attempt to gain a 30,000-foot view of what has happened in Perugia. Think of the next two sections, *The Dots* and *A Few Questions* as further priming of the mind for trying to understand what has happened, and why.

Dot # 1 – Amanda and Raffaele are innocent. Everyone knows it. Virtually everyone knowledgeable about the case and not blinded by bias, self interest, or hatred has known it all along.

Dot # 2 – Rudy Guede is guilty of the murder of Meredith Kercher, and everyone knows that, too. The evidence against him is overwhelming. Rudy killed Meredith. Amanda and Raffaele were not even there.

Dot # 3 – In the small town of Perugia, nothing significant in the Perugian justice system escaped Mignini's awareness.

Dot # 4 – We will assume that Rudy was, in fact, an informant, probably for the Perugian authorities. While he was protected as an informant, he committed burglaries and was caught with stolen property and a 10" kitchen knife. Every time he was caught, someone from PPB set him free. When he was merely spotted, someone gave the word and he was not investigated.

Dot # 5 – At some time after the murder the Perugian authorities realized that Rudy had committed the murder.

Now let's connect some Dots, starting with #3 and #4, Mignini knew what was going on in the Perugian justice system, and Rudy was an informant for someone in that system. This tells us that Mignini would have to have known that Rudy was an informant.

When it became known that Rudy Guede had committed the murder of Meredith Kercher, it would simultaneously be realized that he did so while under protection as an informant. At the least, Mignini knew about it, more likely, he was deeply involved in it. Mignini wasn't just the prosecutor, he was in charge of the investigation from the outset.

This is not something that would be under the radar – it is something that would be huge. The murder that had electrified the community and brought the world's press in was committed by an informant who was engaged in a one-man crime wave while under the protection of some highly placed person in the Perugian justice system.

Dot #6 – Rudy could have revealed his status as an informant at his trial or otherwise, but he chose not to. He could have used that fact to argue "good behavior" as part of his plea for leniency, but he chose not to. He had an ace in his pocket, but he chose not to play it, even in a desperate game for his freedom. Why?

Dot # 7 – Rudy has been treated with a degree of lenience that is amazing. He had his sentence reduced to 16 years in the first level of appeal. The prosecutor did not appeal that reduction, so the

Supreme Court could not increase his sentence. Even after the confirmation of his conviction and sentence, he could walk in less than nine years, while he is still a young man. There is talk of work release in *half of that*. He has even had his reputation somewhat restored for showing "remorse" and apologizing to the Kerchers for not having "fought hard enough to save Meredith." Rudy has been shown great lenience by PPB. They have worked with his attorney as if he is a member of the old boys club.

Dot # 8 – Giuliano Mignini was under tremendous pressure during this entire period from the ongoing investigation into his misconduct in the Monster of Florence case. He was ultimately convicted and if he doesn't get the conviction overturned on appeal, he will be banned for life from serving as either a prosecutor or a judge. His career will be finished. Mignini was desperately seeking to keep his career and life on track during this entire trial. Further, Mignini has a history of "upping the ante" by forging ahead on the same path, even when it is obviously wrong.

Dot # 10 – Amanda and Raffaele have been clearly railroaded by the PPB. Their wrongful convictions are a direct result of a broadly based, aggressive effort to misrepresent or manufacture evidence, poison public opinion, and accept utterly tortured, illogical assertions as documented in the *Motivation Report*. While efforts to gain convictions are commonly organized and hard fought, this railroading is particularly conspicuous and egregious.

Dot # 11 – The polizia grabbed a single, seemingly random item from Raffaele's kitchen drawer, a big kitchen knife. They labeled it "the knife" and claimed that it was the murder weapon with no real evidence.

Dot # 12 – Rudy Guede was brought to the attention of the polizia and prosecutor investigating Meredith's death in at least three different ways, as soon as *the day after the murder,* yet there is no indication that he was investigated in any way. On the contrary, the prosecution pursued Patrick Lumumba instead. Amanda listed Rudy by his nickname (she didn't know his real name), Stefano Bonnasi, who lived downstairs, informed officers about him, and said that he had a habit of leaving his excrement in the toilet, as did the burglar. We now know that Rudy had just committed at least three, and probably several more break-ins in the preceding month alone, some of them with methods similar to the cottage break-in. At least some of the multitude of investigators present must have been aware of that similarity *on the day that the murder was discovered.* None of these leads appears to have been pursued.

There are many other facts at our disposal, of course, but I want to keep these particular points in mind as we proceed here.

## A Few Questions

Next, a few of the questions that have gone unanswered in this case. Some of these questions arise from the anomalies.

1) Why did Mignini railroad Amanda and Raffaele? We have speculated that he is obsessed, that he believed in the ridiculous satanic ritual story of the spirit-channeling blogger Carlizzi. Perhaps he does, but it was never really convincing as his sole motive. It was never really satisfying in the way that the truth is. There was no driver, no motive beyond crazy, pointless obsession. I spoke with one journalist who has knowledge of the case and has met with Mignini. They said, "He is crazy, but crazy like a fox."

2) What was the PPB's motive for being so lenient with Rudy? It must take a lot to make a criminal justice institution sympathize with the person who committed a horrific crime.

3) When Rudy was arrested and found to match extensive DNA, handprint, and shoeprint evidence, why weren't Amanda and Raffaele released? When they captured the guilty party, why didn't they release the innocent?

4) Why did the polizia pluck a single, large kitchen knife from Raffaele's drawer? Of course, they needed a murder weapon to point to, but why this irrelevant piece of cutlery?

5) Why did the PPB pressure Amanda to accuse Patrick Lumumba? What was special about Patrick?

6) Why was Filomena so quick to point a finger at Amanda? She was interning to become a lawyer in the Perugian legal system. She was one of the first to claim that the break-in was staged and also claimed to have seen glass atop her clothing, something no one else saw and something that is contradicted by the evidence photos. Why?

Filomena and Laura turned against Amanda with a vengeance. They were in a position where favor with Mignini was valuable to them. Their testimony did not correspond to the testimony of their friends. This changed over a few days, shortly after the crime. They did what they could to characterize Amanda as evil, in spite of seeing no particular conflict between her and Meredith. Why?

7) Patrick Lumumba went from complaining about being struck himself during his interrogation, to having one of the worst, pit bull lawyers who went after Amanda the hardest. Patrick had a reputation for being a nice guy, but his behavior, and remorseless condemnation of Amanda contradicts that. Why didn't he see that her mistreatment could have led to her implicating him? Why didn't he empathize with her imprisonment, since he claimed to have been so damaged by his own, undeserved week behind bars? Why did he radically change his story of his own treatment? Who got to Patrick?

8) Why did Giobbi decide that Amanda was guilty based on psychological insight alone? Is he really that confident in his abilities? Is it possible that Giobbi was just looking for an excuse to bring Amanda in? Has he ever leaped to such a conclusion before? We have always accepted that he did this out of arrogance, but that interpretation is somewhat astonishing. Could there be a simpler, more calculated reason? Remember that Giobbi is a high-ranking polizia official and is probably not an idiot. Also, notice that you don't hear him bragging about his keen insight any more.

## A Theory of the Crime

We have always really lacked a theory of the crime – the act of knowingly and deliberately prosecuting two innocent people for murder. Let's see if we can now produce a scenario for what most likely happened, one that makes sense and that is compatible with the evidence.

We must remember that this is only a theory. Proof for this does not yet, exist, it is only a model of what may have happened. One takes such a model and compares it with the facts. If the facts don't match, the model must be corrected. But if it explains a lot of things, and if it has what is called "predictive power," that is, if it leads to predictions that can be tested and verified, then it gains weight as an accurate theory. Only time will tell how this theory fares.

Some may object that this is sheer speculation. But if it is speculation, it is based upon a great deal of information. Most of the forgoing is in the public record. Some may also object that it is unfair to try to unravel the mysteries around the framing of Amanda and Raffaele until solid evidence has been compiled. But no official investigation of prosecutorial or investigative misconduct whatsoever appears to be underway. Time, and perhaps direct efforts are moving such evidence further out of reach with every day. The trail of the PPB is growing cold.

Finally, we should remind ourselves of the profoundly original concept of fair play displayed by PM Mignini and his co-conspirators during the trial. He manufactured horrible stories about things that never happened, backed them up with a computer animation of his own lurid fantasies, presented them to a gullible and biased jury, and used all these tools to obtain convictions of two innocent people. He even sought solitary confinement in an effort to crush the hearts of those innocent people.

## A Theory of the Crime of Framing Amanda Knox and Raffaele Sollecito

As accurately as I can now discern, the framing of Amanda and Raffaele proceeded in something like the following manner.

Rudy was caught committing some crime, and so came to the attention of the Perugian justice authorities. He cut a deal with them, becoming an informant in exchange for being released. They needed his help for something. Perugia was a small crossroads for the drug trade and the mob. Rudy was reportedly a small time drug dealer and burglar, but he was also raised in a wealthy, adoptive family, and so might have had connections, and might know things. Mignini, meanwhile, had an ongoing pattern of engaging in illegal investigations in the Narducci matter, which involved an imagined network of wealthy families. Mignini also had a record of using informants of dubious quality, such as Antonio Curatolo.

While working as an informant, Rudy continued his other career, burglarizing homes and offices. He wasn't a very good burglar, since he was spotted in action and even captured a number of times. When this happened he would play his "Get out of Jail Free" card by calling the PPB. They would call whoever was holding him and he would be released. Then he would commit more burglaries. In the course of getting away with one crime after another, Rudy grew in confidence to the point of arrogance. He had a virtual license to commit break-ins.

On November 1, 2007, one of Rudy's badly flawed burglaries turned out even worse than the rest. Meredith Kercher came home and interrupted his break-in. Being a fighter, she fought – and lost. Rudy murdered her, abused her, quickly grabbed some valuable items, her cell phones and money, and fled. Either because he had come to think of himself as nearly invulnerable, or perhaps because he was drugged out, he didn't cringe in fear at what he had done, but went out dancing, both that night and the following. Then, perhaps coming to his senses and realizing that he had overstepped his authority, he fled to Germany.

At some point after the discovery of the murder, someone in the PPB realized that the killer was their own man, their own informant. This knowledge may have come very soon, if someone recognized the M.O. of Rudy, or if they bothered to follow up on the tips from Amanda and Stefano, or it may have taken some time, perhaps until the first fingerprint and DNA evidence came back.

At some point, someone had an "Oh my God!" moment, and the enormity of what had taken place came to the attention of the PPB. Calls were made, conferences were held. What to do? A criminal who was working for them and under their protection had committed murder. The murder never would have occurred if Rudy had not been protected. His ongoing pattern of serious crimes, including ones using weapons, was a clear indication that he should have been reigned in, but he was not.

Whether Rudy worked as an informant or not, the failure of the Perugian justice authorities to stop his crime spree when they had multiple chances to do so is unquestionable. The PPB bears some of the responsibility for the murder of Meredith Kercher.

## Scapegoats and Bargaining Chips

In fact, it is even possible that the break-in at the cottage may have been an assignment given to Rudy by someone in the PPB. Filomena, whose room Guede broke into, and whose room he was sacking, worked as an intern at a local law office. Another of Rudy's break-ins was at a law office. Mignini had previously launched illegal investigations that included various efforts to intercept information relating to other lawyers, judges, detectives, and reporters, using wiretaps and other means later deemed illegal.

As a specialist, if an incompetent one, at breaking and entering, Rudy Guede may have been working "black bag jobs" as part of his work as an informant, not to obtain goods, but to secure information in the form of laptops, cell phones, etc. He did so in at least two cases that we know of. The famous Watergate break-in by agents working for Richard Nixon was the most famous bungled black bag job.

The PPB discussed the situation and realized that it had hit the fan in a way they never intended. A murder certainly wasn't part of their plan. To them, it was an unfortunate consequence of decisions they made to achieve justice. At some point, the cover-up began.

Rudy knew things that could destroy careers, bring down important work, and damage valuable investigations. There were a thousand excuses to cover up what had actually happened. How could Rudy's silence be ensured?

They had to have something to offer him, but if the responsibility for the murder of Meredith Kercher landed squarely on Rudy, they had no bargaining chip. Rudy's best hope would have been to say he was working as an informant, just doing his job. That would have brought down the house of cards.

They needed a scapegoat. They needed someone to blame to get Rudy off the hook. The PPB weren't looking for the murderer, they knew perfectly well who that was. They were looking for someone to blame for the murder. Of course, the men in the field didn't know that. They were doing their jobs, and you never tell the little guys anything. But the higher-ups knew who did it - and they were looking for someone to blame.

At first, they tried to pin the blame on Patrick Lumumba. They tried to substitute Lumumba, a black man, for Rudy, another black man. Perhaps the thinking was that that might have helped explain at least some of the forensic evidence, such as black hairs found at various sites, and any distant camera views or witness sightings. This is why they put such bizarre emphasis on the casual text message, "See ya later." They browbeat Amanda into her sleep-deprived vision of Patrick committing the murder, and brought him in. Unfortunately, it soon developed that Patrick had an airtight alibi. Soon after, the news came that Rudy had been captured in Germany.

Once the masses of evidence against Rudy came in, DNA results (the ones that were properly done), handprints, footprints, shoeprints... they knew that they couldn't escape the fact that Rudy was there and that he was clearly involved. It was a disaster. Not only had they lost Lumumba, now Rudy was definitively placed at the scene of the crime. At this point, many observers, especially Amanda, believed that she would be released. But now more than ever, the PPB needed someone to take the rap. If they were to have anything to offer Rudy, they needed someone to play the central role, the mastermind, so that Rudy could be... demoted, so to speak, to a secondary role. Perhaps even a sympathetic one.

It has always been a mystery why the PPB didn't release Amanda and Raffaele when they captured Rudy. He was clearly there, clearly the murderer. He had all kinds of prior crimes. Why not stick it to Rudy, declare victory, and release Amanda and Raffaele? Why would they go through all this sheer *bother*, when there was a seemingly straightforward path? Why, unless they had a reason they could not do so, a reason that goes well beyond saving face.

Rather than releasing Amanda and Raffaele, the PPB "substituted one black guy for another" and kept them in custody. It doesn't make sense, unless they needed a scapegoat for the crime and were trying to save their skins by cutting a deal with Rudy. Ironically, it was actually a double substitution, first Patrick for Rudy, then Rudy for Patrick. It's an echo of the preposterous Narducci double corpse swap claim. (Monster of Florence, p. 210, 213)

Without Patrick to use as scapegoat, all they had were these kids... close to the crime. They discovered it. These lovebirds. Arrogant, different, they didn't act right. She was American, pretty – too pretty, and he was from a family about which rumors swirled. There were other roommates, but they had fled back home, or they were Italian, and not as interesting. This Amanda Knox, she has the blue eyes of a devil, and she swiveled her hips. She was a perfect target for the repressed PPB.

This is why Amanda Knox and Raffaele Sollecito were found guilty before the evidence was even gathered. They *had to be guilty* for the cover-up to work. The evidence was merely details to fill in later. What better scapegoat than a "she devil" a controller of men, who could manipulate poor Rudy? Amanda was nearly perfect for the role they cast her in.

With scapegoats in place, Rudy was demoted to a secondary role in the murder. The astounding judicial redemption of Rudy Guede by the PPB is a matter of record. They couldn't let him go free, but they could offer him lenient treatment, and they have come through with that offer. Without it, he would have done thirty years, with it, he may be out on work release in as little as five years. They had the necessary bargaining chip to ensure his silence.

## The Inevitable Unexpected

Perhaps we now have an understanding of some of the unknowns in this case. These answers were as inevitable as they were unexpected, and yet they ring true and are compatible with the evidence. The above theory of the crime suggests that the following is *probably* true:

Rudy worked for the Perugian justice authorities. He murdered Meredith Kercher while under their employ and protection. The Perugian justice authorities bear responsibility for the murder of Meredith Kercher.

Amanda Knox and Raffaele Sollecito were railroaded into a wrongful conviction because they were needed as scapegoats. Without them, the PPB would have nothing with which to buy the silence of Rudy Guede.

The polizia grabbed a knife, one single knife out of many from Raffaele's kitchen drawer, not because they imagined that Raff kept the murder weapon there and they had magically guessed which one, but because they knew that Rudy had a habit of carrying big kitchen knives when he committed burglaries, and they thought he might do so when he committed murder. The autopsy report showing smaller knife wounds was not yet available, remember, and they could not wait. They believed that a large knife would match the wounds. This later proved to be a mistake requiring an awkward, two-knife theory. They also knew that, by remarkable coincidence, that one knife would just happen to have Meredith's DNA on it. Stefanoni's arcane laboratory techniques ensured that finding. The irrelevance of the knife also gave her free reign to manipulate the profiling system, as described in Chapter Twelve.

They drove Amanda to accuse Patrick because they were looking for a black man to substitute for Rudy in the murder. Best to have the closest substitute murderer available.

Amanda and Raffaele weren't set free when Rudy was captured because they knew all along that Rudy was guilty, and they were trying desperately to get him off. They needed Amanda and Raffaele as scapegoats more than ever.

And finally, we can perhaps understand some of the vilification of Amanda Knox. When you do something terrible to someone,

one process that kicks in is to find justifications for why you did that wrong. Psychologists call it transference.

The PPB didn't do terrible things to Amanda because they despised her. They despised her because they did terrible things to her. They had to rationalize what they had done. They needed Amanda as a scapegoat to save themselves. They needed to view Amanda as an evil person to avoid realizing that they themselves were evil.

While this is just a theory of the crime that I've developed, to me it rings stunningly true. Viewed through this lens many unexplained actions fall into place. It implies that there has been serious misconduct within the Perugian justice system, not merely quirky behavior, or incompetence. For that reason this is a call to arms, a call for an investigation of what has taken place by journalists, by an independent prosecutor, and by other observers.

## Sixteen – The Monster of Perugia

Now we must speak of Monsters, for that is ultimately what this story is about. It began with young people pursuing dreams, coming to a beautiful town out of a fairy tale. But monsters too, are the stuff of fairy tales. And while there are monsters that dwell in the sea and monsters from outer space, so, too, there are monsters that thrive in the hardened and misshapen hearts of men.

Two tragedies have occurred in Perugia, Italy. Meredith Kercher was murdered, her life taken from her just as it began. That tragedy can never be undone.

The second tragedy continues, unrelenting. Amanda Knox and Raffaele Sollecito, young people who have never harmed another person have been convicted without evidence, without reason, without conscience. Every day that passes with Amanda and Raffaele imprisoned marks another day of that tragedy. Their lives have already been shattered by the experience. Even if they are released soon the years taken from them can never be returned. The dashing of their trust and innocence can never be undone.

These tragedies didn't just occur, they are *crimes* that were committed by a monster that remains on the loose. It damages and destroys people's lives and will continue until it is stopped. We must somehow find a way to not only free Amanda and Raffaele, but to bring an end to the rampage itself. Pitchforks and torches, the implements of warfare against monsters past – will be of little use here.

### Of Monsters and of Men

Giuliano Mignini wrote that he hoped to help establish the kingdom of heaven upon earth. He wound up attempting to make monsters out of ordinary people. First, it was the unfortunate victims of his prosecution in the Narducci case. Twenty people pursued for years by a prosecutor who fantasized a satanic conspiracy with no basis in reality. Yet, Mignini was left in power, so his rampage continued. He was convicted of crimes in that case but they brushed it aside, suspended his sentence, and the rampage went on. He lodged the same kinds of absurd or insane charges in this case, and everyone knew it. And his rampage rolled on.

It is tempting to label Giuliano Mignini the Monster of Perugia. His role has been central, his words and maneuvers have steered the course of this framing and incarceration more than any other. He has woven a web of lies and sensational speculation that have ensnared the minds of many in the court and the media. Without his twisted perspective, none of this would have happened.

But that is far from the whole story. Mignini did not act alone. He may have been the prime mover of this outbreak of malevolence, but if it all came down to him and him alone, he would long ago have been brought to a halt. He has acted in an official capacity without which he could have done nothing. He has been left in that capacity, despite convictions for misconduct and clear evidence that his misconduct continues. While Mignini was charged, tried, and convicted by officials from nearby Florence for crimes committed there, the system of justice in Perugia did nothing to restrain him during his pursuit of Amanda and Raffaele for over three years.

Rudy Guede committed a horrific murder, tearing Meredith's life from her even as it began. His sociopathic descent from clueless, would-be womanizer, to incompetent burglar, to murderer served as trigger point for the devastation of lives and families on two continents. He too, would be a tempting candidate for the Monster of Perugia.

But Rudy, too, did not really act alone. He was allowed to continue a break-in spree that culminated in Meredith's murder even though those in power could have easily brought it to a halt. There are likely many people with knowledge that could yet pry loose the truth from him and end the scourge on the lives of Amanda and Raffaele. Many others have made decisions, given testimony, and performed despicable acts, as part and parcel of the Monster's rampage.

It would also be easy to settle with the idea that it all just sort of happened, a culture clash, honest people trying to do honest jobs with unfortunate consequences, but that explanation just doesn't make sense. Certainly, Italian culture was in play, and certainly, the culture clash between the attitudes in a small, conservative Italian city and a lover of life from laid-back Seattle didn't help.

But those attitudes are only the exposed, public tip of a vast and deadly iceberg of rage, greed, arrogance, and denial. The real Monster of Perugia was kindled by that rage, nourished by that greed, given confidence by the arrogance, and sustained for years by a longstanding denial of the truth.

The murder of Meredith Kercher unleashed a perfect storm of lurid delusions, endemic corruption, nationalistic insecurity, and unprincipled ambition. It is that perfect storm that is truly the Monster of Perugia.

That Monster laid Amanda and Raffaele's lives to waste in full view of the world. It committed kidnappings and held hostages while people on two continents watched and commented.

That Monster enjoys the flourishes of the nimble pens of journalists who fed at the prosecution's trough of lies in the morning courtroom sessions then took the hot afternoons off while the defense spoke to a half empty courtroom. So many of them filed sensational stories, cashed paychecks, and did not care that their stories simply were not true. This Monster has no compassion and shows no remorse.

The Monster found supportive politicians from Rome to Perugia, who enjoyed mugging for the cameras in finely tailored suits as the Roman holiday played out. Their smug self-congratulations confirmed the fine jobs done by archaic institutions at the inexorable destruction of youthful hopes and dreams.

The Monster finds exhilaration in the facile minds of Patrizia Stefanoni, the White Queen of DNA, and the Polizia PseudoScientifica's team of Procrustean investigators. It delights in their arrogant belief in their own abilities, and in their desire for advancement at any cost in integrity.

The Monster loves Maresca, the lawyer both of the Kercher family, and of the polizia in their defamation suit. He ranks among the fiercest of those pushing for guilt at any cost. Rather than pursuing the truth, he worked hand-in-hand with Mignini in a way that would never be allowed in other courts. What was it he whispered his client's ears? The Monster is gorging on his greedy quest.

Does the Monster even find comfort among those whose sorrow seems to have crystallized into misplaced malice and revenge?

The Monster haunts the consciences of the jurors, who often slept through court proceedings, apparently giving little thought to their duties as discoverers of truth. Not one of them stood up to the court and the judges and cried "No! This is wrong!" They went along with it all, draping themselves in the colors of Italy on the day that they unanimously rubber-stamped a verdict shaped by corruption and delusion.

The Monster was especially welcomed by anonymous, Internet hate mongers who have formed a tiny army of tiny people posting lies, distortions, and half-truths on every article that can be so soiled.

The Monster glistens on the silent lips of the polizia, who know the truth but do not speak it. The twelve who raged against her in an all night interrogation ordeal who now continue their lie, even seeking money for what the have done. The officers of the law who conducted the terrible parade of Amanda and Raffaele, winding through the streets of Perugia – their helpless prey in tow, exhausted minds reeling in confusion and disbelief. And the Monster is proud of the many able polizia who accepted awards for performances in a passion play of injustice.

The Monster resides in every mind that twisted itself about the truth while seeking reward amid a shower of lies. Those minds will not find peace until they have found the heart within their hearts. They will not find rest until they have summoned their inner pitchforks and torches and driven the Monster back into the darkness from which it came.

211

## Seventeen – The Best of all Possible

## Italian Justice Systems

"It is demonstrable," said Professor Pangloss, "that things cannot be otherwise than as they are; for all being created for an end, all is necessarily for the best end. Observe, that the nose has been formed to bear spectacles–thus we have spectacles. Legs are visibly designed for stockings –and we have stockings." *Candide*

So did Pangloss begin to explain to Candide, Voltaire's famously hapless protagonist, that he lived in the best of all possible castles in the best of all possible worlds. Candide was soon thrown out of that castle and Pangloss with him, but right up until he was hung to death for speaking his mind, Professor Pangloss continued to believe in the perfection of the world and therefore, in the lack of any reason to seek improvement.

Some may find it unfair that Amanda and Raffaele have had their lives ravaged by a preening, criminal, possibly mentally ill prosecutor. Some may object that they weren't allowed to meet with an attorney before the hearing that determined they would be held in prison for a year before even being charged. And some sensitive souls and civil liberties types may regard it as unjust that they have been convicted of a murder they obviously did not commit.

Nevertheless, there remains reason for good cheer. Like Candide, 250 years before them, Amanda and Raffaele set forth into the world with great hopes and met with many woes. But like Candide, they live in the best of all possible worlds, for in Perugia, we are told Amanda and Raffaele receive the fairest of treatment by the best of all possible justice systems.

"Things cannot be otherwise, than as they are…"
"If this is the best of possible worlds, what then are the others?"

Studying *Candide* and too perplexed to understand the almost whimsical injustice of the Perugian court of first instance, I envisioned a meeting with an Italian friend who could explain their perspective on it all. Such a friend would be well versed in politics, jurisprudence, and the case.

This friend is not a real person, but he is an amalgam of real reactions to the case from Italians. The following conversation did not really take place. It is merely, as part of my closing arguments, an *animation* of a conversation that could have happened with an avatar of Italy – I'll call him – *Panglossini*.

## We Invented Justice

We were to meet at a Starbucks in Seattle, but it was crowded, so we went next door to a different Starbucks. "I have trouble understanding your justice system," I told Panglossini, sipping my expensive coffee something, "it doesn't make any sense to me. May I ask you some questions?"

"You may ask if you like, but it isn't my justice system, and anyway, it explains itself. You have only to think to see the beauty," Panglossini replied.

"That may be, but I am easily confused," I said. "For instance, I can't understand why your jurors are not sequestered or even asked to not discuss the case. They were exposed to all the lies, distortions, sensationalism... they were exposed to it all. Why is this?"

"We have no jurors, that is an American thing, we have only judges," Panglossini replied.

"But they are ordinary people...."

"Who are judges when they sit in the courtroom. And this sequestration would be silly. Reading the news is a wonderful thing, they get to watch the 'Amanda show' which they are a part of, after all," Panglossini explained, delighted to be able to help me. "You would want them to miss that? By reading about the case they have a more interesting picture than they receive during the boring trial, when, after all, they are on the verge of sleep...."

"What about 'innocent until proven guilty' and 'beyond a reasonable doubt'? Those are supposed to be the standards of justice, even in Italy, but they were utterly ignored."

"In Italy we make sure to convict," Panglossini said. "Remember that we *invented* justice, two thousand years ago. Once you are captured, you can count on being guilty, at least in court of first instance. We don't let any O.J. Simpsons get away unlike America."

"Two thousand years ago the Romans fed Christians to lions and gladiators to each other," I said as Panglossini smiled and nodded. "You routinely convict innocent people. Over 50% of the time, over half of all criminal convictions in Italy are overturned on appeal!"

"Yes, but it is okay. In fact, it's the best thing possible. We don't consider someone *really* convicted until all their appeals are through so it doesn't matter if you find guilty a few innocent persons, because in our best of all justice systems, the appeal is automatic!"

"But people get held in prison for years while their trials crawl along, even though they're innocent."

"No, no of course not. In Italy, defendants are free while the trial is underway, during the appeals, everything. It is the best thing possible. Even convicted murderers are free until all their appeals are exhausted. Look at this murderer guy who was filmed at a Swiss ski resort. He will be guilty someday but now he can ski. It does not matter how many years the trials take to get right."

"But Amanda and Raffaele were not free, even before conviction, even before being charged they were held in prison...." I began to swirl my chocolate-coffee-something around in my degradable cup.

"It is best this way. Amanda might have fled. And if she made it to America, or anywhere at all, how could she be extradited with only Mignini's stories to tell? And she has had the best of all possible prisons you know – it is a very nice place, Capanne prison. No? Very scenic, very famous. Amanda loves the view from her prison window. I read it in the newspaper, it must be true. She thinks everything is fair and wonderful. I read that too."

Panglossini was very well read. He had learned all about the case from the international media.

"I hear that the prosecution can actually appeal an acquittal. So even if most of the jurors, not just one or two but an actual majority find a defendant innocent..."

"Well, of course it takes many jurors to be innocent. There are six citizen judges, and two professional judges. If four citizens think innocent, but two professionals know guilty, the defendant is guilty. Two plus two equals five. It is the best arrangement because what if citizens are wrong? So a majority is not enough... they would still be guilty anyway."

"Okay, but even if *all* of the jurors believe the defendant to be innocent, after years of investigation and trial, even then, the prosecution can appeal the acquittal and make them go through it all over again?"

"Yes, of course, this is one of the best of the best things about Italian justice," Panglossini said. "This way, it doesn't matter if the judges make a mistake and let a guilty person go. The prosecutor can keep right on prosecuting, right on pursuing, hunting, until they get them."

"That would be double jeopardy in the States."

"Double, triple, who counts jeopardies?" Panglossini asked. "You miss the point. The idea is judges can feel okay about not having to convict if they are not so sure. They can go ahead and acquit if they happen to feel like. Because they know, it will all be fixed up later if wrong. That is why it is the best of all justice systems, because everything that can go wrong, does go wrong. But, hey, who cares? It all gets fixed in the end. "

"In the end.... After how many years in prison?" I asked, "and what about Mignini?"

"A fine man," Panglossini reflected, "what about him?"

"He was under indictment throughout the trial. They kept delaying his case, delaying it, delaying it. The prosecutor was under indictment! Then he was convicted! He did absolutely crazy things in the Narducci case and now he has done them again to Amanda and Raffaele. It is unbelievable that a person should be allowed to perform in a professional function when they have been convicted of misconduct at the same profession."

"Yes, unbelievable, and yet, it somehow happened. He was the best of all prosecutors."

"Wonderful? Amanda's prosecutor was indicted, and convicted, for prosecutorial misconduct! It's not like it was a noise ticket…"

"Yes," said Panglossini, "what could be more perfect than that? You see, he himself was under indictment during the trial, and so he was especially sensitive to the rights of the accused…"

"Sensitive? He abused…."

"How better to be sensitive to someone under indictment, than to be under indictment yourself? And he was not only indicted, he was even convicted. If he does such a thing again, and is caught…"

"He will have to go to prison!" I said, with just a touch of delight.

"Oh, no. That will never happen. He is a prosecutor, a judge – they would never make him go to prison like a common criminal! But he may be disbarred. Therefore, he is now above reproach."

I swirled the tiny remnants of my coffee drink around at a dizzying pace as I tried to bridge the gap, tried to understand how people, good people, could do such a thing. They are not evil, I reminded myself, again, and again. They are different, Italian – they have different ideas. And I tried, as I have tried many, many times to smooth things over, but I slipped, a bit, in my diplomacy, perhaps.

"Don't you understand the shame, the absolute *shame* that this has brought to Italy?" I said it, and I did not say it nicely.

"Shame? What shame? We are proud of our ways!"

"Don't you understand what an embarrassment this trial is? The world is watching you. What we are seeing is appalling. Don't you get it? Don't you get what a humiliation it is to have so many see how deeply flawed your system is…"

"There are no flaws! Dozens of judges agree Amanda is guilty!"

"They agree with a verdict that is obviously wrong! That is part of the shame! This trial makes your justice system look like a bunch of criminals. It makes your scientists look like idiots."

"Stefanoni is a great scientist! She shows the world how to do DNA…"

"She makes a mockery of the scientific method. She shows how ignorant she really is by imagining that she is perfect and can do no wrong..."

"She is the best of all possible DNA profilers, that is why there is no need for review...."

"We are watching you. People who represent your nation to the world, whether you like it or not, have done something terribly wrong, obviously wrong. No matter how many fancy robes you trot out who all agree completely, it is wrong, and everyone with a brain can see it. Don't you understand that?"

He did not. Even though it was all in my mind, all in my own *animation*, I could not get my Panglossini avatar to understand, just as I will never understand Italian justice, Perugian style.

I thought about Amanda, and Raffaele, still in prison – more than three years now, and every day another agony of waiting. I thought about the many people who had put them there, walking free, proud of what they have done, presenting themselves with awards for it.

I sat back down, dropped my head in my hands, and wept.

## Epilogue

Candide ends with Professor Pangloss, who it seems, had been ineptly hung, clinging to the belief that all was as it should be in a perfect world. Candide, however, had found meaning in his gut wrenching life. "Let us cultivate our garden," he decided.

Many have found this a puzzling ending, but it makes perfect sense to me. The world does not just happen, but is of our own making. Let us cultivate our world, let us make it a better place, in Perugia, in Seattle, everywhere.

We can do better than this.

# Appendices

## People
The Roommates
Upstairs
Amanda Marie Knox
Meredith Susanna Cara Kercher
Filomena Romanelli
Laura Mezzeti

Downstairs
Giacomo Silenzi
Stefano Bonassi
Marco Marzan
Riccardo Luciano

## The Families

Amanda's parents:
Edda and Chris Mellas - Mother and Stepfather
Curt and Cassandra Knox - Father and Stepmother

Meredith's parents:
John and Arline Kercher

Raffaele Sollecito: Francesco and Marta Sollecito
Rudy Guede: Pacome Roger Guede (father)

## Others

Patrick Lumumba

## The Polizia
Edguardo Giobbi
Armando Finzi
Rita Ficarra
Monica Napoleoni

## The Lawyers

For Amanda:
Luciano Ghirga
Carlo Dalla Vedova

For Raffaele: Giulia Bongiorno, Marco Brusco, Luca Maori
Delfo Berrretti
Daniela Rocchi
Donatella Donati

For the Kerchers: Francesco Maresca, Serena Pena
For Guede: Nicodemo Gentile, Valter Biscotti
Prosecutors: Giuliano Mignini, Manuela Commodi

For Patrick: Carlo Pacelli and Giuseppe Sereni

Judges:    Claudia Matteini, Paolo Michelli, Giancarlo Massei,
Beatrice Cristiani

Prosecution forensics experts and coroners:
Dr. Patrizia Stefanoni
Dr. Renato Biondi

Defense experts: Carlo Torre, Dr. Sarah Gino, Luca Lalli

Anna Donino - The interpreter

## Places

#7 Via dela Pergola - The cottage where Amanda and Meredith
lived upstairs with two others and four young men lived
downstairs.
The questura - The polizia headquarters where the
interrogations took place.
Piazza dela Grimana - a Plaza with a basketball court very near
to the cottage.

## Things

"The Knife" a large kitchen knife retrieved from Raffaele's kitchen drawer because "it looked clean." It was touted as the murder weapon despite not matching 2 out of 3 wounds or a knife imprint left in blood at the scene.

The clasp - The bra clasp cut from Meredith Kercher's bra during the murder, photographed by the polizia during the initial investigation, then left at the scene until retrieved 47 days later.

Luminol - A forensic chemical that produces a fluorescent glow when catalyzed by blood, or any of a number of other substances. More information on luminol appears in that appendix.

TMB - Tetramethyl benzidine is a sensitive, presumptive test for blood. TMB is a chemical that is catalyzed by blood to undergo a chemical reaction that results in a color change. It is regarded as less sensitive than luminol. More information on TMB appears in that appendix.

## Sherlock Holmes Forensics (long)

Sir Arthur Conan Doyle's famous character, Sherlock Holmes, the world's first investigative detective, could discern your occupation from the way you wore your hat. He could sniff at your tobacco and determine that you had fallen on hard times, or glance at your shoes and know which borough of London you resided in. His skills and insights were nothing less than remarkable. Of course, they were also pure fiction.

"Pipes are occasionally of extraordinary interest," said he. "Nothing has more individuality, save perhaps watches and bootlaces. The indications here, however, are neither very marked nor very important. The owner is obviously a muscular man, left-handed, with an excellent set of teeth, careless in his habits, and with no need to practice economy." *Sherlock Holmes*

Some of today's forensic scientists say they have similar skills. They claim they can tell how many people were involved in an attack from the number of wounds, can deduce a day's activities from a few cell phone calls, and improve the fundamental performance of analytical equipment with the twist of a knob. Unfortunately, this is also pure fiction. On a worldwide basis, the quality and reliability of forensic evidence has all too frequently been distorted, blown out of proportion, and not properly vetted by scientific methods.

The entire field of forensic science is currently under review – some even say it is under attack. This review isn't just led by defense attorneys, but by governments, scientists, and others who believe that the proper role of forensic science is to assist in identifying and convicting the guilty– that they might be stopped– and freeing the innocent. Not the other way around.

That is placing it in stark, simple terms of course, but forensic science has been at the heart of a fundamental and ongoing failure of the criminal justice systems of even the world's most advanced nations. For those nations that are on the borderline, the situation is far worse. Far from the public's common CSI show-inspired misconception that the field comprises brilliant and attractive forensic scientists operating state-of-the-art equipment to solve intractable cases by the end of the hour, the reality is a

221

hodgepodge, patchwork quilt of over-worked researchers with wildly varying capabilities, training, and facilities.

In the wake of discoveries of wrongful convictions that were at least partly caused by mistaken forensic science work, the U.S. Congress requested a review of the entire field by the National Academy of Sciences. That report, which will be discussed later in this chapter, concluded that there are serious issues with the field and made recommendations for reform. Even within the United States, forensic science facilities vary enormously in their capabilities and staffing, ranging from sophisticated purpose-built laboratories to the back room at the county courthouse. Expand the view to an international perspective and the variation is even wider. The result is a far-too-common failure to identify and convict the guilty and to free the innocent.

I do not mean to criticize the great majority of the world's forensics experts, who try their best to honestly do their jobs. They need help, and often, they are not receiving it. Many of the most critical problems in this field could be addressed with adequate funding and proper support.

But there are also problems that result from shortcomings in the techniques of forensic science, and from a failure to separate the responsibility for performing forensic science investigations from the responsibility for convicting criminals. This results in a fundamental and systemic conflict of interest between the funding and career prospects of forensic researchers and the judgment calls they must make.

Before we explore these issues, a basic question: What is "forensic science"? What does that term really mean and how does it differ from "regular" science? In general, forensic science is defined as a set of scientific, or *scholarly,* methods used to investigate matters of interest to a court. The word "scholarly" is of interest here, because that means learned, but it does not necessarily mean scientific, and there can be a world of difference. More specifically, forensic science is a set of different investigative disciplines such as fingerprint analysis, ballistics, bite mark analysis, and DNA profiling.

The ultimate objective of forensic science is to apply the powerful techniques of modern science in the service of justice. It is not just science, in and of itself, but developing scientific evidence to determine what transpired at a crime scene. To better understand forensic science let's take a fairly large step back for a brief review of science itself. I do this because it appears to me that there is not a lot of understanding of the relationship between science and forensic science, and because that lack of understanding seems to be particularly prevalent among the Polizia Scientifica. So let's go back to school for a bit and talk about *science*.

## The Scientific Method

Scientific research is performed by a fairly well defined set of methods, collectively called the "scientific method," which have been developed mostly over the last century. Although they vary somewhat from discipline to discipline, briefly these methods go as follows. After observing some phenomenon, a hypothesis is formed that tries to explain what has been observed. This hypothesis, a learned guess as to what is happening, is a kind of model, an idealized version of reality. The model is then tested in a set of carefully designed experiments and control experiments. If the experimental results agree with predictions of the hypothesis, it is supported by the observations and researchers gain confidence that it is a good description of what is happening. If the experiments contradict the predictions, the hypothesis must be revised, or rejected.

This research is further subjected to a rigorous process of peer review in which other researchers ask probing and difficult questions about the work. Peer review takes place both by presenting the experiments and explanations in a public forum before other investigators with credentials in the field, and by publication in the peer-reviewed technical literature. In this process, an article must pass peer review – must make sense to the peers and be clearly and completely stated without any obvious faults, and all of that is before it can even be published. All of this, and it is only after publishing that the real tests begin.

If an experiment produces results that are interesting enough to pursue, other researchers will reproduce it in an independent facility to validate, refute, or refine the research and its conclusions. This comprises the vital step of determining reproducibility. If an experiment cannot be reproduced, it cannot be said to be valid, it is irreproducible. The famous *Journal of Irreproducible Results*, a satirical science magazine, is full of outrageous experiments that could never be reproduced (nor would anyone want to). The JIR recently held a contest for funniest graph, for instance. The winner: *All Theories Proven With one Graph*. It's a very impressive graph.

The process of the scientific method is far from perfect. It is not a flawless logical construct that is entirely divorced from human influence, human prejudices, and human limitations. I once heard a talk by the man who won the Nobel Prize in physics for predicting quantum tunneling, a breakthrough in understanding that has led to many useful devices. A peer reviewer rejected his paper on the subject on two grounds. It was "highly speculative" and contained "no really new ideas." These directly contradictory criticisms came from the same reviewer.

People perform science, and it is blessed and burdened, as is any other human endeavor, by our strengths and weaknesses. But the design of the scientific method is intended to achieve a real understanding of existence that is independent of the researcher. The method was conceived to transcend human failings and foibles to discover things about the real nature of existence.

This process of review, of pounding on new ideas to see if they hold water, is at once, a rigorous, demanding, and exhilarating process. Standing in front of fifty or so Ph.D.s to present your research is a daunting experience. It is entirely possible that you've made a mistake, and they will not hesitate to point it out (politely) during the question and answer session at the end of your talk. These sessions can be positively withering. I've withered a few presenters, and I've had my own mistakes pointed out in the full glare of public forums. It is intense and exhilarating.

Often, the witherers and the witherees go out to dinner later that evening. Rancor is rare, collegiality, combined with intense competition is the norm. Some of the keys to surviving the process and retaining self-respect are a measure of humility, recognition that humans can make mistakes, and a healthy understanding that this is all part of the process. Criticism of your work makes it better, validates it, or corrects it if it is wrong. You hope for that, actually. Who wants to pursue a research path that has a fundamental flaw?

This has been a brief explanation of how real science is conducted. I provide it as a background for comparison with the claims of science that will follow. Real science benefits from exposure, criticism, and review. The light of day is welcomed, demanded, it is a fundamental part of the process. Pseudoscience, in contrast, hides its dirty work in the shadows while putting on a pretentious show.

To say that the scientific method has been successful is an understatement of biblical proportions. Perhaps no other exploit of humankind has achieved anything like the success of science. With it, we have learned to make computers, space ships, half-mile high skyscrapers, and to unravel the genetic code. And yet, depending on how you define it, the scientific method is only a century or two old.

## Guilds and Craftsmen

The power of scientific methods to unlock information cannot be disputed. Unfortunately, not all of the techniques that comprise forensic science were developed that way. In fact, some of those techniques are skills that were accumulated over time in a manner more closely resembling a medieval craft than a science.

Long before the development of scientific methods there were other ways of attaining knowledge of the physical world that achieved varying degrees of success. The system of guilds and apprenticeships that existed for hundreds of years, and still exists in some forms today is a prime example. Guilds were comprised of skilled craftsmen in a particular field, such as stone masonry or glass making. These craftsmen inherited various trade secrets from previous members, worked to apply and develop those arts, and passed them along to young people through apprenticeships.

The crafts so developed reached high levels of proficiency, and produced many artistic and architectural masterpieces. But the limits of this method of developing knowledge were also apparent. Many talented people were excluded from the guilds and could not contribute. The secrecy of the knowledge and of the methods to develop it limited exposure to review and refinement. Methods that *kind of* worked, but were really not well understood, persisted for centuries in this environment. And methods that worked, but which were never documented because of secrecy, were lost forever when the chain of apprenticeship was sometimes broken.

A famous example of this is the mystery of Damascus steel, from which high quality swords were forged. This steel, which was produced from about 1100 to 1700 CE, has remarkable properties, superior in some ways to the best current steels, but no record exists as to how it was made. To this day it cannot be fully replicated. It was, perhaps, the highest achievement of the materials developers of the pre-scientific era, and it has been lost.

Using the body of knowledge accumulated under the guild and craft system, people built cities, bridges, and machines. The method worked, but it could only take us so far. When these approaches were largely supplanted by the scientific method the current explosion of progress in technology began. A guild could figure out how to make a pretty good stone bridge, but they stood no chance of inventing a computer, or putting a satellite into orbit, or of discovering how DNA works. Craftsmen discovered, through trial, error, and ingenuity, how to make Damascus steel, but they would never have succeeded at synthesizing diamonds, or making silicon semiconductors, or nano-machines. Once a certain level of sophistication is reached, that method hits a wall that it cannot overcome. To move beyond it, one has to embrace the more sophisticated procedures that we call the scientific method.

All well and good, science can reveal deeply hidden mysteries of nature; guilds and apprenticeships – not so much. The scientific method isn't just a stuffy bunch of formalities performed by people in white outfits, it is a profoundly important and powerful system with rules and requirements that must be met or it simply does not work. The problem here arises with the term "forensic science" which, in some cases is a misnomer, and with public perceptions of the field.

When people confuse the abilities of full tilt scientific research with a technique cooked up by some guy that took a correspondence school course, you have a problem. When someone makes up a brand new test method that hasn't been subjected to *any review whatever*, let alone fully vetted by a peer review process, and then he pretends that it is "scientific," you have the potential for grossly misleading judges and jurors, leading to terrible miscarriages of justice.

## They Blinded Me With Science

From the adventures of Sherlock Holmes at the turn of the last century to the popular and numerous crime scene investigation series *CSI* many of the common conceptions of detective work in general and forensic science in particular have been shaped by fictional accounts rather than the far-more-mundane reality. Real investigators are human beings; they are not all brilliant analysts with superhuman insight. Real "forensic scientists" often aren't even scientists at all, but "practitioners" who may have little or even no formal scientific education.

This isn't too important for the plot of a TV adventure. The crime will be solved before the final station break no matter what. But if you happen to be a suspect in a murder case, or if a loved one was the victim of a crime, the gulf between the reality and fiction of forensic science takes on critical importance. It is important because the actual abilities of forensic science to lay bare mysteries and solve crimes simply do not begin to approach either the expectations of lay persons or the claims of some forensic scientists. It is also important because the final determination of innocence or guilt is made by some of the same lay persons who are fundamentally ill informed on the matter: the jurors.

This misinformation is a double-edged sword. It can cut the prosecution, or it can damn the defense. Having seen neat, clear, convincing scientific evidence on CSI type shows, many jurors now expect a scientist to walk into the courtroom and present rock solid DNA evidence. They expect a beautiful full color chart or a computer animation that tells who did what and how and that points a virtual arrow of guilt at the defendant. There is even a name for the phenomenon: the "CSI effect." This helps the defense, because real world evidence is rarely so cut and dried, nor so impressively presented.

On the other hand, jurors can also regard forensic practitioners with unwarranted reverence, accepting their word as the word of "science" rather than seeing it as what it sometimes is, an opinion voiced by someone who is in league with the prosecutor, and whose livelihood depends on coming up with material to support the claims of that prosecutor. Such a practitioner may be anything but objective – anything but fair. This conflict of interest has led to calls for the separation of forensic laboratories from police, prosecutors, and other parts of the criminal justice system.

## The Advent of DNA Profiling

In the 1980s, a technique called *DNA profiling* was developed. We'll talk more about this method in upcoming chapters because it plays a critical role in this investigation. What is important here is that when DNA profiling was developed, for the first time it provided a genuinely scientifically developed technique to *individualize* evidence from a crime scene. Individualizing evidence means that it was possible to specifically connect physical evidence from a crime scene with a particular individual as the source of that material. That's different from methods that merely suggest a class of people, such as a male in his thirties or a left-handed suspect. When biological traces are left behind that are clearly associated with a crime, DNA profiling could often label a specific person as the source of that material.

This new ability brought with it an unintended benefit. Not only could this technique give powerful evidence to aid current investigations, it could be used to reanalyze evidence from crimes that had been committed years – even decades – before.

This was a great boon to prosecutors, who could look at cold cases from the past and finally bring criminals to justice, but it had yet another consequence. The new technique of DNA profiling was also applied to cases in which people loudly proclaimed their innocence. Many of these people had been convicted, at least partly, on the basis of forensic science techniques. Yet when DNA profiling was used to review the evidence, hundreds of convicted people in the United States alone *were proven to be innocent*. The stunning implication was that the results from these other forensic techniques were wrong. Moreover, while those hundreds of overturned convictions were important, they were just the visible tip of the iceberg. Many times that number of false convictions must exist, but simply weren't amenable to review by DNA profile techniques.

Groups under the name *Innocence Projects* performed much of this work. Defense lawyers who had run up against dead ends teamed up with the new DNA forensics experts and tested the biological evidence left behind in many of these serious crimes. In hundreds of cases the DNA proved them right. And they were set free.

All of this raised a fundamental question. If the results from some of these other forensic science techniques implied that innocent persons were guilty, what did that say about those techniques? It said that they did not work as advertised. Their reliability was called into question by the unequivocal discovery that in many cases their application led to the wrongful convictions of innocent people.

All of which makes us wonder; where did these forensic science techniques come from? Why were they applied for decades when they didn't really work?

Although forensic practitioners frequently use the term "science," it is sometimes a bit of an exaggeration. In fact, there are wide discrepancies between the various forensic science disciplines as to how carefully they were developed in the first place, and how well they have been reviewed, tested, and analyzed over the years. The result is that a few of them are quite sound, such as the analysis of fingerprints, but several others are on far shakier ground. Yet they are routinely applied in cases that affect people's lives and freedom.

When techniques are applied even though they are not really understood, their results, interpretation, and evidentiary value are simply not reliable. When verdicts are rendered on the basis of these unreliable results, innocent people to jail, and guilty, dangerous people are free to commit further crimes. The loss to society is tremendous. The loss to victims, past and future, and to the wrongfully convicted, may devastate their lives.

## The Drive for Reform

As a result of this discovery of flaws at the heart of forensic science, the United States Congress requested a review of the field from the National Academy of Sciences, one of the most prestigious scientific bodies in the world. The NAS performed that study and released *Strengthening Forensic Science in the United States: A Path Forward*.

*Strengthening Forensic Science* called for a comprehensive set of reforms that will rebuild the forensic science disciplines. It was nothing less than earthshaking. It calls for a program to build forensic science techniques upon the solid platforms of peer reviewed science. It calls for the separation of forensic science institutions from the prosecutorial side of justice systems. It calls for programs to certify programs and ensure compliance with standards. It calls for reforms that will do nothing less than put the *science*, into forensic science. These calls were long overdue, and similar recommendations should be enacted on a worldwide basis.

Although this report has produced heel dragging and pushback from some in the forensic science community, leadership has also come forth. Thomas L. Bohan, Ph.D., J.D., President of the American Association of Forensic Science, addressed the NAS Review and related issues in an editorial in the Journal of Forensic Sciences that cut to the heart of the issues. Rather than digging in his heels, he joins the NAS in issuing a clarion call for reform.

"It was quickly found, again largely through efforts of the Innocence Project, that the (hundreds of) wrongful convictions arose from incompetent defense attorneys, unethical prosecutors, misguided reliance on "eyewitnesses," and flawed forensic testimony, occurring either singly or in combination. Scores, and then hundreds, of persons were discovered to have been convicted of heinous crimes of which they were innocent."

"For the most part, that flawed testimony was delivered by an incompetent or overreaching practitioner. However, the National Academy of Sciences report that arose in part from concern about wrongful convictions quite rightly went further than simply calling for better supervision and certification of forensic practitioners. Stating that many common crime-lab forensic practices had never been scientifically validated, the report called for research to determine which practices were valid and over how broad a range of application the validity existed."

The latter comment highlights the fact that part of the problem with the discipline called forensic science is that it is a collection of fundamentally – and sometimes radically different – techniques and capabilities. When the same practitioner presents DNA results that were produced by methods that have been vetted by real scientists, and bite mark analyses that are mere semblances of real science, there is a problem. The doubtful techniques are carried along on the bandwagon of real technical expertise. The dubious conclusions that can be reached by these methods may be presented as if they shared the same peer-reviewed, carefully developed, scientifically sound heritage as the few techniques that actually were vetted in that manner.

Kenneth E. Melson, a former President of the American Academy of Forensic Science from 2003-2004 expressed concern about the validity of these un-vetted techniques.

"In any legitimate justice system, ... truth must play a paramount and integral role... The very survival of the rule of law depends not only on a justice system that administers the law fairly, but a system that is just by being well-grounded in ... truth ....[M]ore research is needed in the techniques and science already in use. With the importance of forensic science to truth and justice, the science employed and relied upon by judges and juries must be valid. It does not matter how well forensic scientists abide by testing protocols, or how reliable the techniques are, if the underlying science does not actually reveal what the expert says it does. "

What this ultimately means is that the best-informed people agree that the tests themselves must be tested. One cannot assume that some method that is in use, even if it has been used for some time, is reliable unless it has been subjected to rigorous scientific evaluation to see if it really means what is claimed.

Brandon L. Garrett, Associate Professor at the University of Virginia School of Law and Peter J. Neufeld, co-founder of the Innocence Project recently published a review of the sources of wrongful convictions that were identified by DNA profiling. The report, entitled *Invalid Forensic Science Testimony And Wrongful Convictions* was recently published in the Virginia Law Review. Garret and Neufeld analyzed the testimony of forensics experts and found that regardless of the validity of the tests performed, often that testimony was exaggerated, inaccurate, or incomplete in ways that caused significant deception. In fact, this study claims that 60% of these cases involved invalid forensics testimony, while still others involved withheld exculpatory material.

Since the cases analyzed in this paper all comprised wrongful convictions, it is not a valid basis for saying that forensic testimony in general is often invalid. It may well be that this particular subset of court cases, most of which involved rapes because those cases are most likely to allow corrections through DNA analyses, were especially prone to exaggerated or misleading testimony. The zeal of the forensic experts to obtain convictions in emotionally charged situations might have played a role.

An additional form of bias appears to have been uncovered by this study. In the cases in which the forensic testimony was deemed valid, most of that evidence was either non-probative, or exculpatory. In contrast, most of the cases in which the forensic testimony was not deemed valid, it was inculpatory. In other words, most of the invalid forensic testimony was done to be favorable to the prosecution.

This invalid testimony was rarely challenged by defense lawyers, who, in general, did not have the resources to do so. Except for occasional high profile, well-funded defenses, there is a consistent imbalance between resources available to the defense compared with the prosecution in forensic science.

In the United States, the court ruling that determines the admissibility of forensic evidence is called the *Daubert Test,* it was established in 1993. It reads as follows:

(1) whether the theory or technique can be and has been tested, (2) whether the theory or technique has been subjected to peer review and publication, (3) the known or potential rate of error, (4) the existence and maintenance of standards controlling the technique's operation, and (5) whether the theory or technique enjoys general acceptance within a relevant scientific community.

Remember these requirements, or at least the gist of them. 1) To be worthy of inclusion as evidence a test must have been tested. That makes sense. If I whip up a brand, spanking new test, I ought to put it through its paces a few times to be sure that the results mean something before I condemn or release someone on its basis. 2) The theory or test ought to have been peer reviewed, as described in the previous sections, so that knowledgeable people can have a good look at it and validate or dispute it. 3) The number of errors the test makes should be known, so it if is always right, you know it, and if it works.... usually, judge and jurors should know that too and can take it into account while weighing it as evidence. 4) There should be standards as to how the test is performed, so it isn't every forensic practitioner for him or herself.

And 5) the technique should be widely accepted within the scientific community, not just embraced by a wild-eyed flat Earth society offshoot.

These are standards and ideas that apply to U.S. law, not to Italian courts, but the common sense, logic, and scientific validity has application anywhere. Science and logic sometimes cross borders with ease. Other times, not so much.

## Inculpation and Exculpation

A few more background concepts are important to understand when looking at evidence and how it is collected and interpreted. Like forensic science itself, these concepts are sometimes either taken for granted or not thought of in a consistent, rigorously logical manner. The idea here is to lay a foundation of common language and concepts before looking at how this crime was investigated, and how the evidence from it has been interpreted.

Exculpation and inculpation are critically important aspects of evidence with some nuances that should be well understood to wisely interpret that evidence. Exculpation is the process of ruling a suspect out by suggesting or proving their innocence. Evidence is said to be *exculpatory* if it suggests or proves innocence. Inculpation is the inverse, implying that a suspect may be guilty of the alleged crime. Inculpatory evidence suggests guilt, but it does not prove it.

Notice that I use some important qualifying words here, "implying" and "suggesting." Physical evidence, in and of itself, doesn't prove guilt or innocence. It is only raw information that must be combined with other information for a judge, jury, or investigator to decide whether they believe that a suspect committed a crime. The standards for using this physical evidence are what we are considering now, because they are different for the cases of exculpatory and inculpatory evidence.

There is a critical difference in the quality of information that is required in the two distinct cases of inculpatory and exculpatory evidence, i.e. they are not just reverse cases, they are fundamentally different. To inculpate a suspect, there must be a correspondence between the mark left at the scene and the mark that the suspect would generate. It may not be perfect, because there could have been some sort of smearing or distortion, but it must correspond and not have ANY significant differences. Say most of the loops and whorls in a print at a scene and from a suspect are the same, but a few, even just one or two, decidedly are not. The fingerprints do not match. Those few loops that are different prove that they are not from the same source.

To be inculpatory, the evidence needs to exactly correspond to within the margin of the quality of the best measurements. This is pretty close to the same idea as "close only counts in horseshoes." Fingerprints that are close, but that show differences, do not show that a suspect was at a crime scene; they show the opposite. When you leave fingerprints, they are always coming from the same fingers. You don't have three loops and a whorl one time, and two loops and a whorl the next. Similar prints are not identical prints. The fact that they are merely similar shows that the bearers are different people. So there is a high standard of correspondence required for evidence to be inculpatory.

To be exculpatory, on the other hand, the evidence only needs to show that the traces are different from the suspect in some sense. They may be similar in many other respects. It's an all-or-nothing situation. For this reason, it is tougher, in a sense, for evidence to be inculpatory than it is for it to be validly exculpatory.

It is the difference between simply ruling a possibility out, and determining it to be the fact. An alibi is a common form of exculpatory evidence. If someone can show that they were somewhere else when the crime was committed, then they're almost certainly innocent (unless they hired someone). That's a lot easier than showing that they were present, that they took a gun and fired it, etc.

**Probative Value**

*Probative value* is an important aspect of evidence because information doesn't help a bit in an investigation unless it has that. Although this may seem obvious, I believe that failure to understand it lies at the heart of some of the most important misunderstandings in this case.

Consider three fingerprints left at three different crime scenes. The first print – call it "Print A"– was found at an apartment where a murder occurred and is an exact match to someone from a community 50 miles away. That person had no business ever being in that apartment. He had no relationship with the apartment: he wasn't the landlord or a former tenant. There is no innocent explanation for his print being there. This fingerprint is clearly inculpatory. It suggests that he may have been present at the crime, and therefore involved in it.

In and of its self though, it doesn't prove that he committed the act. Perhaps it will be found that he picked up a piece of furniture at a garage sale and the victim later purchased the item. If, however, further evidence shows that he was in the area when the crime was committed – that he had a motive, that he had a violent past – then the importance of the fingerprint increases, and it becomes a vital part of the evidence showing the suspect's guilt.

Now consider a second fingerprint, "Print B," found on a random item at an apartment that was shared by several people and where a crime was committed. It is found to be a match for one of the roommates at the apartment. So what? It probably doesn't mean anything relevant to the case. The roommate lived there, and there is nothing surprising that he left traces of his presence at the scene. The evidence matches, but it is not inculpatory because it doesn't really provide any information that he was involved in the crime. There is, in other words, a perfectly innocent explanation for the fingerprint to be present at the place where the suspect lived. Your fingerprints are present at your home, for example, and yet you probably haven't committed any heinous crimes lately.

The difference between these two fingerprints is captured by the idea of whether the evidence is *probative*, whether it tends to prove a *relevant* point. Print A appears to have been left behind by someone who had no legitimate business being in a place that was a crime scene. That discovery has significant value in determining guilt or innocence. Print B was left by someone on a mundane object at his own home, where he had every right to be. It provides no information that is relevant to the case. The probative value of evidence is whether it is useful to prove, or contribute to proving, something important in a trial.

Probative value is one consideration that factors into the rules of evidence, in American law, which govern whether a court will determine that the evidence is admissible, allowed to be presented in the first place, or should be excluded. If the evidence has no probative value, there is no reason to present it to the jury. It doesn't have any bearing on the crime and accusations.

There is another critical factor that weighs into American court's determinations of admissibility of evidence, its *prejudicial* value. The prior sex life of a suspect or a victim might have some relevance – it might provide some meaningful information about a crime– but it might be so lurid, so largely beside the point, that its principle effect would be to create prejudice in the jury that could interfere with their ability to arrive at a correct, unbiased verdict. For this reason, such evidence is usually excluded even though it might have some relevance to the case.

## Mistakes do Happen

Let's return to the fingerprints because I promised to give you a third one. This fingerprint was found on materials used in a terrorist bombing in Spain. Running it through an enormous database of fingerprints, it was found to be a match to someone in Oregon, almost on the opposite side of the world. That person became a suspect in the bombing, even though that was a bit of a long shot. Little or no other evidence connected him to the crime. Even though the evidence was inculpatory, it only suggested that he might have involvement. Corroboration of that evidence by additional links was needed.

This last print was found in a high profile case involving an Islamic extremist terrorist bombing and a *partial* fingerprint found at the scene. Fingerprint experts from the FBI believed it to be a match for Brandon Mayfield, an attorney in Oregon who also happened to be a convert to Islam. On that basis, Mayfield was arrested with considerable fanfare. A couple weeks later, the Spanish police, who did not stop investigating and declare victory just because they had a suspect, matched the fingerprints more precisely to an Algerian man. The FBI determined that the match was an error and the lawyer was released after 17 days in jail.

The implications of this case are having a substantial impact on the interpretation of partial fingerprint evidence. The match to the lawyer was ultimately found to be a result of a substandard image of the partial, original print and it was determined to be sheer coincidence that many aspects of the prints happened to be similar. The fingerprints obtained from crime scenes are often of poor quality. They may have been smeared, distorted, or poorly imaged.

This apparent match was also a result of comparing the found print to many, many different stored fingerprints in extremely large databases. If matches are between prints at a scene and suspects who were in the area and are valid suspects for other reasons, then matching characteristics are critically important. But efforts are being made that tend to undermine the significance of some matches. This is the accumulation of vast databases of fingerprints, DNA profiles, mug shots, and other personal data on millions – even billions – of people worldwide.

There is a second important take away from this last fingerprint. A mistake was made because one of the most reliable forensic science techniques produced a wrong result. That mistake prompted a re-evaluation of the technique to revise and correct it so the same mistake won't be made in the future. It also prompted an admission that a mistake was made, and the release of the suspect, (who then filed a lawsuit). That admission and release is what institutions with integrity do when a mistake is made. They don't double down on a bad bet, they correct their error and move on.

## A Man's Gotta Know His Limitations

Sherlock Holmes may not have needed Dirty Harry's edict, "A man's gotta know his limitations," but mortal forensic scientists might benefit by keeping the Clint Eastwood character's insight in mind. Crime scenes almost invariably bear evidence of what took place during the crime. One of the fundamental ideas of crime scene investigations, and one that has proven extremely useful, is that it is nearly impossible to be involved in a violent act without leaving some kinds of traces behind. They might be fingerprints, or DNA traces, footprints, tire marks. If they look carefully, investigators can find clues as to what happened and who was there when it did. But that record is imperfect. It does not provide some kind of video recording of what took place.

In mathematics, this is similar to something called an *underdetermined matrix*. When there isn't enough information present to solve the matrix equations, it is underdetermined, so one can only solve for a *solution space*, a range of solutions that all fit the information available. The actual solution could be any one of them. They are all possible given the information at hand.

In a crime scene the pattern of blood, glass, footprints, etc. might have resulted from any of a number of possible events. You can't figure out exactly which one happened no matter how long you look at the evidence. You can get the general picture, but if you know your limitations like Harry, you recognize that a general idea of what happened is the best you can do. This fundamental limitation appears to be sometimes lost on forensic scientists, who must work on the edge of this information boundary and are often pressed to give answers that they just don't have.

## Control Experiments

Scientists are serious control freaks, when it comes to experiments anyway. Without proper controls, you have no idea what you are measuring. Control tests are such a fundamental matter that they are almost lost in the grass, yet an experiment without a control is like a old style thermometer without a scale. You see the mercury inside, but you have nothing to compare it with. There are two choices at this point. You can understand that the mercury level is meaningless, because there is nothing to compare it with, or you can point at it and make up any temperature you want. This is a very important concept to understand in assessing the evaluation of evidence in this case, so I want to use an example to explain control tests in some detail.

James Lind performed one of the first controlled experiments in 1747 to study scurvy, a serious medical problem that we now know results from vitamin C deficiency. Scurvy sometimes caused more deaths among sailors than attacks by the enemy. People had known since antiquity that scurvy could be cured by eating fresh food, but no one knew why or what kinds of fresh food. Lind had a idea that he wanted to test to solve this problem. His idea was that acids were cures for scurvy. That idea turned out to be wrong, but his experimental methods were logical, and because of this logical approach, he was able to refine his idea – even though it was wrong at the outset – and make real progress towards a solution.

To test his idea Lind set up an experiment in which 12 sailors suffering from scurvy were split into 6 groups. All were treated in the same way and fed the same things, with one exception. He made a single diet change in each of the six groups. The fact that it was a *single change* meant that he could have some confidence that that particular change caused the different results. In such an experiment, one hopes that the *controlled variable* is responsible for any changes in outcome. If that variable is combined with a dozen other changes, no one can be sure that it made any difference in the experiment's outcome.

Lind fed his six groups of sailors the same diet, but with each group receiving one additional ingredient each: cider, seawater, sulfuric acid, vinegar, oranges, and barley water. The sailors fed the oranges rapidly recovered from their scurvy symptoms, the others – not so much. The vitamin C in the citrus fruit prevented the scurvy. In fifty short years, it became common practice to provide sailors with foods containing vitamin C, and scurvy was largely eliminated.

Lind's simple method of testing his idea may seem obvious looking back, but it was not common practice at the time. The key was to perform an experiment in which everything was kept the same except for one controlled variable. In this case, it was the added food, whether oranges or sulfuric acid. By comparing the results for sailors with these different added foods, Lind could determine which added food helped – and which did nothing.

Lind also used what is called a negative control, in this case plain seawater. There was no reason to believe that drinking seawater would do a sailor any good against scurvy, so that was a test in which the expected result was nothing at all. If something did in fact happen, that would show that there was a problem with the experiment. This was a real possibility. Perhaps the mere fact that the sailors were being studied would change some aspect of their health, maybe simply by giving them hope for a cure would help. To show that an experimental result is a real result rather than an artifact a negative control test must be run that shows that unless the controlled variable is present, nothing will happen.

If Lind had known in advance about vitamin C, or about citrus fruits being a cure, he could have also set up what is called a positive control experiment. To do this he would have fed one group of sailors something that he knew from prior experience would cure their scurvy. The expected result of that test would be for the scurvy to heal. If it did not, the results of the positive control would be negative, and one could, again, see that the test was flawed in some way.

Positive and negative control tests are vital checks that help to ensure that a test is testing what you think it is testing. If you include the factor that you are testing for, you had better get a positive test result. If you don't include that factor, you had better not get a positive result. If can't get the results you expect when you are controlling what goes into the test, how could you expect to know what the results mean when you have an unknown variable?

## Blind Experiments – The Blind Leading the Blind

Careful scientists also take steps to keep their own researcher bias from influencing results. They perform what are called blind and double blind experiments to avoid introducing experimenter bias, whether deliberate or not, into their results. In a double blind experiment even the researcher doesn't know which specimen is which. Careful researchers do this to prevent themselves from knowing what the results "should be." That way, when they get a result, they can trust it, because they know they didn't unconsciously choose it. In any experimental situation where there is any kind interpretation or data massaging possible, it is critically important that the experimenter not know results are hoped for.

"Scientific controls are a vital part of the scientific method, since they can eliminate or minimize unintended influences such as researcher bias." Wikipedia

## Forensics at the Crossroads

This has been a brief primer on the state of forensic science in the early 21st century. It is a discipline at a crossroads. There have been great successes and important advances, but there have been terrible abuses as well. Opportunities to better exploit scientific advances to identify and convict guilty people have been missed because of inadequate funding, and inadequate attention to the needs of the field. Innocent people have spent their lives in prison because of inadequate techniques, shameful incompetence, and deliberate wrongdoing on the part of investigators. Other people have become victims when an innocent person was convicted and the guilty person went on to commit more crimes.

Consider that situation. If a guilty person is simply not yet identified and captured, they are at least on the run, fearful, and concerned about bringing attention to themselves. But when an innocent person is convicted of a crime that someone else committed, the person who is actually guilty is, in a powerful sense, liberated, nearly free from legal pursuit. The authorities are no longer after them. They have a conviction for that crime in hand, and, with limited resources will usually move on to other matters.

Freeing innocent people who have been wrongfully convicted is often seen as something in the province of "liberals." But for every innocent person wrongfully serving time for a crime they did not commit, there may be a guilty person still at large: A person who is likely to commit additional crimes. For every wrongful conviction, there may be multiple future victims of crimes. It is a terrible price for those victims and a terrible price for society – not just a price for the wrongfully convicted.

Forensic science is at a crossroads at which the demands that are made on the discipline and the people practicing it exceed the resources and the body of knowledge that are required to do a proper job. And we have a situation where fundamental conflicts of interest were built into the forensic science system from day one, contaminating many of the findings that can determine the safety of our citizens, and threatening the liberty of innocent suspects.

This has been a look at where things stand in forensic science "on a good day," with good faith efforts being made all around. Now let's take a look at what happens under less favorable conditions. Let's take a look at forensic science, Perugian style.

## DNA Profiling (long form)

The intent is to provide an introduction to DNA profiling with an emphasis is on aspects of that technology that are relevant to this case and on some basic background. It does not begin to cover details, and it is far from a comprehensive treatment but you can see the bibliography for some of those. One more caveat, I am a materials scientist, and also a chemist, and I've developed several experimental techniques so I have good familiarity with this type of field, but I am not a molecular biologist or forensic DNA practitioner. I consulted with a couple of those to fact check this material.

For those whose eyes glaze over when the talk gets technical, the object here isn't to bury readers in technical mumbo jumbo. The object is to explain in clear terms what DNA is, how it can be used to identify people, and enough about the process of profiling to convey the fact that it is a *process*, it doesn't just happen. It may take a little work to get through it. I advise a little patience, and maybe a little re-reading if a section isn't clear at first. To really understand the issues with DNA profiling that have come up in this trial, it's important to understand what profiling is, and how it is performed. That understanding is our goal.

Here's the plan. First, we'll have a primer of basic background information on DNA, so that we're talking the same language. Then, some material about the tools used to perform forensic DNA profiling, so we know what we're going to talk about. Then, the actual procedures used to perform the process called PCR-STR DNA profiling. By then it should start to make sense and we can talk about what can go right, what can go wrong, and why. In the next chapter, Canary in the DNA Mineshaft, you'll get an idea of how unprecedented and unreliable some of the procedures used in the Knox/Sollecito prosecution were.

### The Secret of Life

DNA stands for deoxyribonucleic acid. It is the molecule in the center of our bodies' cells, in their *nuclei*, and it is the carrier of the information that makes almost all life on earth possible (many viruses depend on DNA's close cousin, RNA, ribonucleic acid.) In both plants and animals DNA and RNA work together with proteins and other organic molecules to create the molecules we are made from, organize them into cells, organize those cells into organisms, and reproduce the entire system. Not only are they the blueprints of life, they are the architects, the engineers, and the construction crews.

With just a few exceptions, every cell in the human body contains two copies of that person's DNA, organized into units called chromosomes. Each chromosome is a single chain of DNA and protein, coiled up and then coiled up again to wind an extremely long, incredibly slender chain into a fairly tight unit. This double coiling of DNA makes it practical to fit it into a cell and to move it around, otherwise, handling it would make handling a single strand of a spider's web seem easy. This is important in the present matter because DNA is a relatively compact, stable material that is encapsulated within a cell nucleus, and that nucleus is encapsulated into a cell. These layers provide some protection, and also make it a fairly "portable" material, it can be moved around in dust, etc.

There are 23 different chromosomes in people. Regular cells are "diploid" containing two of each for a total of 46 chromosomes. Sperm and egg cells are different, containing only one copy of each, so they are called "haploid." Aside from this difference, all somatic cells in the human body contain the same kind and form of DNA. Red blood cells, a major constituent of blood, do not contain any DNA at all and are incapable of reproducing or performing many other normal cell tasks. Their job is carrying oxygen and carbon dioxide as efficiently as possible, so they don't need, and don't have room for, the rest of the equipment. The DNA in blood comes entirely from the white blood cells, which comprise only about 1% of the total blood.

The elegance of this system for producing and reproducing organisms is without parallel. It is, at once, perhaps the most beautiful, simple, complex, robust, sensitive, and spare system that exists.

DNA consists of extremely long chains made of four kinds of nucleic acids, called "bases." Those bases are bonded end-to-end to form long chains. They are also loosely bonded to pair with each other, following particular rules. Between the bonding and the pairing, extremely long, spiraling chain molecules are formed. The longest grouping of human DNA, Chromosome 1, contains about 220 million of these bases, 110 million in each side of a double chain, the famous double helix. The exact nature of these nucleic acids isn't important to us. What is important is that they are shaped in such a way that adenine pair only with thymine, and guanine pairs only with cytosine – A to T, (or T to A) and C to G, (or G to C). These combined bases are called "base pairs" because they always go together in the complete DNA molecule. The whole molecule, the entire double helix, resembles a ladder that has been twisted about its center.

Because of the selective bonding of base pairs, DNA has a remarkable property from which most of its other remarkable properties stem. It can make copies of itself.

The two sides of the DNA double helix are held together by a special kind of bond between each of the pairs of bases along its length. These are like the rungs of the ladder. These bonds are called hydrogen bonds. These have an intermediate level of strength, which makes them perfect for joining the two sides of the DNA ladder. Although the *hydrogen bonds* are pretty strong, they are nowhere near as strong as those primary bonds. If you heat them up to 50 °C or so, they will come apart. But the much stronger primary bonds that hold the rest of the molecules together will remain intact.

This is why heating up a solution of DNA in the right conditions will "unzip" the two halves of the molecule, with the hydrogen bonds between the two halves separating, while the chains themselves remain intact. So, you have special, double chain molecules, which are like tape recordings of information. They are very strong, and yet the two halves of the double chains can be readily split apart without damaging the chains themselves. Imagine heating up a ladder a million feet long and having it unzip along the rungs, leaving the two sides of the ladder intact. That's about what happens when you heat up DNA the right way.

When you unzip this ladder and cool it again in a "soup" of free nucleotides along with a special enzyme, DNA polymerase, those nucleotides add onto the open sides of the ladder, rebuilding each side of the original double helix. You now have two double helix chains where before you had one. The DNA molecule has duplicated itself. It has split into two halves, taken up separate bases from a nucleotide soup, and formed two complete molecules.

This is a simple version of what happens when something called the polymerase chain reaction (PCR) takes place. This reaction is used to replicate DNA in a laboratory. PCR proceeds in a cyclic process, with each cycle doubling the DNA. Here's the thing. If you can make 1 DNA molecule into 2, you can make those 2 into 4, those 4 into 8... and after 28 cycles of this, the typical number performed in a PCR reaction for profiling, you have roughly $2^{28}$ power molecules of DNA for every single one that you started with. That's roughly 268 million copies made of every starting molecule.

To perform the PCR process, you first need extracted DNA from a forensic sample. That sample needs to be carefully collected from a certain, specified source. The association between the DNA and the source is critically important, as we will see in the next chapter.

## Short Tandem Repeats (STRs)

There are two classes of people in the world, those who classify everything into two classes, and those who do not. There are also two classes of DNA, coding, and non-coding. Coding DNA carries the information for the genes, the parts that specify how to make people, plants, hair etc. These parts of the DNA molecule have to work just right, or the organism they code for won't work and will not survive. For that reason, coding DNA is tightly *conserved*, it does not change much over time and does not vary much from person to person or from dog to dog.

Non-coding DNA on the other hand, and there is far more of it than coding DNA, doesn't yet have an identified function. It may have some mysterious, undiscovered function, but it appears to be remnants of old, unused genes, or to serve as some sort of spacer, or maybe, just maybe, it is *a primal memory of dinosaurs past*. Probably not, but because non-coding DNA doesn't seem to have much to do, it can vary substantially without killing the organism.

Because it varies greatly between people, non-coding DNA is the part that is used for identification.

The portions of non-coding DNA that are now used for identification are called "short tandem repeats" or "STRs." These are short sequences of DNA, 4 or 5 bases long, that are repeated some variable number of times in a particular location on a person's DNA. For example, in one person the sequence CTAG, with 4 bases, might be repeated 5 times, giving the STR sequence CTAGCTAGCTAGCTAGCTAG. In another, it might be repeated seven times, giving CTAGCTAGCTAGCTAGCTAGCTAGCTAGCTAG.

Because of the different number of repeats, these STRs have different lengths. Because they are different lengths, they can be separated by a technique called electrophoresis. By compiling a list of the different lengths of several different STRs in a DNA sample and comparing that with the lengths of the same STRs from different people, the source of the sample can be identified. In a nutshell, that is how DNA profiling works. There are some more tricks involved, but this is a simple starting point to understanding it.

By comparing a number of different STRs, and there are many STR regions, one can be fairly certain what DNA came from who, – provided that some other things are done right.

The people who have developed the PCR-STR profiling technique have chosen a number of STRs that have useful characteristics for identification. First, they work with STRs that have 4 base pairs in each repeat unit. This is enough to be a clear unit, but not so many that they tend to be degraded and made useless by environmental exposure. Three or fewer repeat STRs are not used because they tend to cause "stutters," errors in the analysis resulting from shifts in the replication process.

## The Polymerase Chain Reaction (PCR)

The process of splitting the two halves of the DNA double helix apart, then adding complementary base pairs onto each, doesn't just happen on its own, it is initiated by a molecule called "DNA polymerase." The word "polymerase" is a combination of the words "polymer," referring to a large molecule that is built up from small molecules and "ase" referring to an enzyme that makes a reaction happen. So, DNA polymerase is a molecule that promotes the combination of nucleotide bases into larger DNA chain molecules. The discovery of this molecule filled a gap in the understanding of how DNA worked, and also opened the door to the polymerase chain reaction. In 1965 an enzyme was discovered that initiated the replication of DNA, and that could survive at fairly high temperatures.

By working with polymerase molecules it is possible to set up a chain reaction in which a DNA molecule is split apart and replicated, starting at a specific site. When PCR is applied to PCR-STR profiling, the entire chain isn't replicated, but only those portions of interest, the STRs that are used to distinguish one person from another. This is done by yet another clever trick that was developed by the molecular biologists that invented the technique, the use of DNA primers, which are used to spot an exact location on a strand a hundred million bases long.

### Primer School

Primers are tools for recognizing a particular, exact point along the millions of bases that make up a DNA strand. They are about 20 base pairs long, and they will only bind to the complementary set of pairs on the strand being worked on.

By making the recognition sequence long enough, the replication of the DNA can be restricted to a single point in the entire base sequence of DNA in the human genome. This is because the number of possible combinations of $4^{20}$ base pairs equals about one billion. Only one such combination out of a billion random base pairs will fit the bill and be replicated.

The bonding points of the primers are very carefully chosen for forensic purposes. Two points are chosen for each STR locus of interest, one "upstream" and one "downstream" from the variable length STR region. In this way, the STR region is selected out of the much larger DNA molecule, and will then be replicated and analyzed.

Yet another trick to speed up the analysis involves deciding how far away from the STR region will be the point at which the primers will select. Once one has settled on 10, or 13, or more STR regions to use for identification, it would be nice to be able to process all of those regions simultaneously, in a single operation. A single process has several advantages. The different STR lengths can all be readily compared with each other in a single test, rather than being compared between different tests. They can all also be compared to one or two "internal standards," segments of known length. It is also less expensive to run one test rather than two or more.

For these reasons, the primers are chosen so that the lengths of non-STR DNA on either side of the STR segment are of different lengths for each STR region. The final molecule winds up with a length that is the sum of the variable STR section, plus the two non-STR regions on either side of it. By deliberately selecting different lengths for the adjacent regions, one can create non-overlapping DNA segment lengths that can all be measured at the same time.

Think of it this way. Start out with the first selected STR region. It will vary in length by some amount. Select short side regions by cutting right next to the STR. When the priming and replication are through, the products are variable length DNA pieces, but all them are all fairly short. Select the next STR region, and begin the replication further away from it, leaving longer side sections. This will give variable length pieces, but all of them will be longer than the longest, of the first group of STRs, no matter what length that samples particular STRs were.

The variability in length of each type of section comes from the variability in length of the STR section. Two, constant length section adjacent to each STR region are added to make the overall length of that piece of DNA be different enough from the lengths of all other sections so that they will separate and be distinguished by the electrophoresis process.

One last trick before we measure the results (I know, you're tired of tricks). By using three or four different colored fluorescent markers with the different primers, you produce different length DNA fragments, tagged with different colored fluorescent markers. You now have two different ways of distinguishing things, color, and length. Point an ultraviolet light at the fluorescent markers and they light up in different colors. A detector can sense these different colors, distinguish them, and measure their intensity in units called relative fluorescence units, Rufus. These units are *relative*, that is, they are all proportionate, but not pegged to an absolute standard, such as the number of STRs present. In general, higher RFUs indicate a greater amount of DNA in the detection system.

## Electrophoresis for Fun and Profit

Once the PCR process is complete, you have hundreds of millions of fragments of DNA with different lengths, depending on the number of repeats in the original STR segments, and on the length of the side chains. Those STR lengths are characteristic of the particular person the template DNA came from. There are also four groups of different fragments, with each of those groups labeled at the end with a different color fluorescent dye that is part of the primer that began the replication of the DNA in the first place. Four groups of different length DNA pieces, each group tagged in a certain color. Now how can you measure the lengths of all those molecules? That's where electrophoresis comes in.

An electrically charged molecule can be pushed around by an electric field. If you take a charged molecule, an *ion*, and put it in an electric field, the field will propel it. Positively charged ions will move towards the negative side of the field, while negatively charged ions will move towards the positive side.

When a field is imposed by applying electrical charges to opposite ends of a very fine tube filled with a conductive liquid, a capillary tube, you wind up with two opposing flows of ions moving in opposite directions. Any positive ion that is in that field will want to drift toward the negative end. Any negative ion in the field will move toward the positive end. They will slowly flow through the tube in opposite directions.

How slowly? That's the trick. The smaller the ion, the faster it is able to move. The long chains of DNA are huge, bulky things compared to a most ions, yet they only have the same amount of propulsion force, because they carry only the same amount of charge. If you put an outboard motor on a tiny speedboat, it will go pretty fast. If you put the same motor on a tanker, it is going to move very slowly. The larger the tanker, the slower it will move.

For this reason, the longer the DNA chain, the slower it will move through the electrophoretic capillary tube. The shorter chains will move faster, and will get to the positive end faster. If you start out with all the different pieces in the same place, in a line of material, then as they migrate through the tube, they will fan out, shorter pieces moving to the head of the race, and all the others spread out like runners in a marathon.

The capillary tube is filled with electrolyte solution, and a small amount of the sample DNA is introduced at one end. The ends of the capillary are connected to opposite poles of the electrical supply so that an electric field is created along the inside of the capillary. The negatively charged DNA fragments move through the capillary at different speeds, depending on how long they are. You start out with a mixture of different lengths of DNA all bunched up together at the beginning of the tube, and wind up with different lengths of chains flowing past the end of the tube at different times.

That's where you detect them. As each length of DNA fragment flows past the detector, it is exposed to a very bright ultraviolet light that excites the fluorescent dyes attached to the ends. The dye glows, and each color of glow is detected by a photodetector and recorded, making a little peak on a graph. Even if the lengths of two distinct groups of STRs are very similar, they can be clearly distinguished because the colors of the fluorescent dyes attached to their primers will be different.

What you wind up with is a series of peaks as each group of selected, amplified DNA fragments with different colored dyes flows past the detector. Remember that there is a large number of every type of DNA segment because of the PCR amplification. It's still a tiny amount of DNA, but it is enough to sense. The height of each peak is an indication of how many fragments are in that group. The time that each peak passes the detector is an indication of how long the fragments are.

A DNA profile, then, is a series of peaks on a graph. Each peak represents a bunch of fragments of DNA that have some number of short tandem repeats in it. The position of that peak tells you how many repeats. The size, or area of the peak gives an idea of how much of that fragment was present. And the color tells you which one of the fluorescent tracers it was tagged with.

## Jigsaw Puzzle

Each person's DNA profile has either one, or two, alleles, genetic variants, at each STR locus, (plural, loci). The mother and the father provide one allele each. If these happen to be the same, the individual has only one allele present at that STR locus. Among a population, there are many different alleles for each locus. By producing a DNA profile for a suspect, and comparing the alleles that are present to the alleles that are present in a profile drawn from an item of evidence, it is possible to establish, or reject, a match.

To be a match, the correspondence must be perfect. Every allele in the suspect must correspond to an allele in the evidence item. This is a bit like matching pieces in a jigsaw puzzle. For a piece to be the correct, matching piece for a location, it must correspond in every, single respect. It must agree with the shapes of all the pieces around it. It must agree with the color at the edges, again, for all pieces around it. If it is only close, it is not the correct piece and does not belong there. If it agrees on three sides but does not match in one, single sense, it is not the correct piece. Stuffing it into that position would leave another piece, one that does belong there, with nowhere to go. Making an incorrect matching of a DNA profile can put an innocent person in the position of a felon, and let the felon walk free.

## And The Point Of All This Is....

If all this sounds a bit complicated, that's because it is. That is the point I am making. DNA profiling doesn't just happen, it is a process that has to be performed to produce results. The process has to be performed in what amounts to a specialized wet chemistry laboratory, with laboratory apparatus, beginning with evidence collection bags (ideally, anyway), and continuing with swabs, centrifuge tubes, PCR reaction tubes, sample tubes, and electrophoresis capillaries. These vessels are stored, handled, and cleaned in the real world, not in outer space somewhere. That same laboratory, and some of that same equipment, may have processed many samples of the victim's blood. Things can, and do, go wrong in this process.

The possibility of contamination of DNA samples in forensic laboratories is a fact of life that must be dealt with.

# TMB – Tetramethylbenzidine and Luminol

Tetramethylbenzidine, usually known by its abbreviation, TMB, is a sensitive presumptive test for blood. TMB can indicate other substances than blood, so it does not provide a definite identification.

TMB is commonly used at a crime scene to screen stains that appear to be blood. If a possibly blood stained item does not give a positive indication with a TMB test, it can usually be set aside, since the stain does not consist of blood and the item is likely irrelevant to the crime. This results in a major savings in time. If a TMB test gives a negative result, there is a very low probability that the stain in question is comprised of blood.

A positive result with TMB is less decisive, because it is only presumptive of blood. Further testing with some confirmatory test is required to be certain. These confirmatory tests examine detailed aspects of the blood, rather than looking for a chemical reaction. An example of a confirmatory blood test is a microscopic examination that looks for red blood cells. DNA testing is not a confirmatory test for blood since there are many sources of DNA other than blood.

Testing at crime scenes is often performed with TMB in the form of Hemastix® test sticks. The Hemastix® is moistened with distilled water, swiped against the stain to swab up some of it, and observed for a color change. A blue green color means that the specimen is blood or another substance that causes the reaction.

## Chemistry of TMB

When TMB is oxidized, it turns a brilliant blue green color, providing a means of indicating a test result. Because the color is so intense, it can be seen or detected even in very small amounts, and can be observed by spectrophotometry. By controlling the oxidation of TMB, the creation of that indicating color can be controlled.

In use, TMB is usually combined with hydrogen peroxide, a powerful oxidizing agent. With both the TMB and the oxidizer present, you have a chemical mix that is ready to react, it only needs to be catalyzed to do so. Their reaction cannot proceed without the presence of that catalyst, which is called a peroxidase.

A peroxidase is a material that triggers the breakdown of the hydrogen peroxide into active oxygen, which is then available to oxidize the TMB. The peroxidase catalyses the reaction, but it is not consumed in the process. For that reason, a very small amount of catalyst can continue to promote the reaction of the TMB. The TMB itself is strongly colored in the oxidized state, but not in the reduced state. This allows for the tremendous sensitivity of the test, a very strong color produced by a very small amount of test material. The substance being tested, blood, further lends itself to an extremely sensitive test.

## To Heme or not to Heme

Dried blood contains iron in the form of heme, the critical component of the larger hemoglobin molecule that transports the bodies' oxygen. Red blood cells are practically made of hemoglobin, which comprises more than 95% of their dry weight. With four heme groups in each hemoglobin molecule, drying blood leaves behind a large amount of heme, which just happens to be a powerfully active molecule.

One can think of heme as an organic chemical cage, a tight fitting net of carbon and other atoms, wrapped around an iron atom. The iron atom inside provides chemical services, accepting and releasing electrons, for instance. The cage is the first layer in a two-layer system that uses the powers of the iron atom to move oxygen around. The outer layer of the system is the hemoglobin molecule. That molecule's four heme groups work in concert, breathing in and out $O_2$ and $CO_2$ as the blood circulates.

Because heme is a biologically evolved, chemically *adept* molecule for manipulating oxygen, it also acts as a peroxidase, something that catalyzes the decomposition of peroxide, releasing its oxygen. That available, active oxygen is perfect for the subsequent oxidation of TMB. Because the heme is only acting as a catalyst, it is not consumed in the reaction, but can promote it again and again. The result is that a tiny amount of dried blood can catalyze a clearly visible reaction in the powerfully colored TMB.

Many peroxidases will catalyze the reaction, and the test does not distinguish which one it is. One especially famous peroxidase is called *horseradish peroxidase*, presumably because it was first isolated from horseradish. Many sophisticated analytical tests are based on controlling the catalytic action and distribution of horseradish peroxidase.

In addition to being catalyzed by peroxidases, TMB can also be oxidized directly by ordinary bleach and other oxidizing materials without the presence of a peroxidase. These reaction products will have the same blue green color and will cause false positive results.

The hemoglobin mechanism is amazingly effective at transporting oxygen and carbon dioxide, and we would not be alive without it. But the chemistry of heme/hemoglobin is even more adept at binding with another molecule that is less friendly, carbon monoxide. When hemoglobin is exposed to carbon monoxide, the monoxide bonds with so much energy that it doesn't release again. It remains stuck on the hemoglobin molecule, so it is no longer available to transport oxygen and CO2. Not good. That's why carbon monoxide is tremendously toxic, probably killing more people than any other poison.

The fact that by an accident of nature, carbon monoxide sticks to hemoglobin far better than it does to oxygen, reminds us that the chemical activity of heme and these other chemical test components, are not specific to what we want to learn. They are tools that perform particular chemical reactions, they are not magical indicators that read out "Blood," "Saliva," "Whatever." An indication means that a chemical change has happened, but that change does not necessarily result from what we expect. Care must always be taken in understanding the context of these tests.

## Sensitivity of TMB

The relative sensitivity of TMB and luminol has become an issue in this trial because of a remarkable finding that appears in the Motivation Report. The report concluded that luminol-glowing prints that were randomly scattered through the hallways were comprised of blood, even though they all tested negative for that with the TMB test. These are random prints in the hallways of the cottage, not the prints left by Rudy Guede as he exited the scene. For this to be the case, every one of the half dozen prints would have to have just enough heme to set off the luminol, but not enough, even when collected with a swab, to trigger the TMB.

When luminol is distributed over a surface bearing heme, or any other peroxidase, or any other viable oxidant, a reaction occurs and the luminol glows for a brief period. Capturing the light from that glow in a completely darkened room allows for observation with a very low level of background noise. That means an extremely high signal-to-noise ratio, an important figure of merit.

The indication from TMB is a color change, not an emitted light. It can only be observed against a background of light from other sources. The change in color can be noted, or measured, but the signal-to-noise ratio will never be as high for an indicator that does not emit its own light. This difference provides a theoretical edge to the sensitivity of luminol compared with TMB.

But sample collection and contamination factors weigh heavily in this equation. How much sample was swabbed up, exactly? The *area* of the material collected from the glowing spots and concentrated onto the swab will have a major impact on the amount of heme available to trigger the TMB, and the resulting sensitivity.

Dr. Stefanoni did not even reveal that she had performed the TMB tests on the luminol glowing spots in her testimony on the subject. It was only months later in the trial that the testing was discovered, and the results learned to be negative in every case. The details of how the tests were performed remain unknown, to the best of my knowledge. Those details are essential to estimating the relative sensitivities of the luminol and TMB testing.

But there are some things that we do know about this. TMB is an exquisitely sensitive test, in many cases its sensitivity is very close to that of luminol. It is also known that heme will swab up easily from a non-porous tile surface with standard sample collection or Hemastix® swabs. That is what the swabs are made to collect. We also know that if the luminol glowing spots were formed in dried blood, they would have some uneven distribution of blood and heme on the surface of the tile.

If the luminol glow spots were comprised of dried blood, and they were swabbed and tested with TMB, the amount of heme picked up by the swab from the tile surface should be substantial, because the swab would be very efficient at lifting the material. It should also be somewhat randomly variable, because of the uneven distribution of the blood. With a substantial, and variable amount of heme on each of several TMB swabs, it is extremely improbable than not one of them would give a positive indication for blood.

This contradiction leads us to reject the theory that the amount of blood material was, in every case, just enough to trigger the luminol, but not enough to indicate with TMB. The probability of that is extremely low. It is far more probable that the spots were not blood.

Why did the luminol glow spots fail to test positive with TMB? After all, both tests respond to the same general classes of materials. One possibility is that some agents that could trigger luminol might be resistant to swabbing with an aqueous solvent. They might also have come to be bonded to the tile floor, so that they provide a surface catalyst, but don't come off with a swab. This kind of bonding can be observed any time one leaves a spill in place, and it congeals and sticks much tighter than if quickly cleaned. Not that I've ever done that.

Neglecting contamination, the absolute sensitivity of the TMB test itself depends on several factors. First, it is necessary to be clear about what is meant by sensitivity, and that requires that the type of TMB test be clearly specified. If the test is with a Hemastix®, properly performed and in a well lit room, a fairly well defined sensitivity can be specified, with the main uncontrolled variables being contamination and lack of discrimination.

If the test is performed in a laboratory with spectrophotometric recording of the TMB reaction, then the sensitivity will be a parameter to be determined by running control samples of known concentration. If contamination issues can be excluded, such a laboratory version of a TMB blood test could be designed to be sensitive to a very small number of heme molecules.

The lack of discrimination between blood and other agents are the main limits to the sensitivity of either of these test agents. The level and kind of contamination of samples with other peroxidases or oxidants is generally unknown without further tests.

## Luminol

Much of the chemistry of luminol is similar to that of TMB. The heme groups left behind by blood form an active triggering device. Energy that is stored in the luminol reagent system is released when the heme, or other substances that act as peroxidases are present.

When luminol is oxidized, some of the energy released by that reaction goes to produce an excited electronic state. This excited state can then decay to a stable ground state by emitting light. The energy from the reaction has been channeled to produce light. Observe or photograph the light and you have an indicator method. Controlling the oxidation of the luminol is therefore the critical step. An oxidant, such as hydrogen peroxide is made available, and all that remains is the presence of a catalyst to trigger the reaction.

## About the Author

I need to explain some of my background because my credentials in regard to the current matter are a little complicated, and there has been some confusion about them. I've been referred to as a "DNA expert" for instance, and I am not, although I do bring some relevant expertise to those questions in this case.

My education was as a materials scientist, with B.S., M.S., and Ph.D. degrees in materials science, and another B.S. degree in chemistry, all from Michigan State University. That's not as inbred as it perhaps sounds because MSU is a big place. My dissertation was in the area of fiber/matrix interactions in organic polymer composite materials, with emphasis on surface phenomena, surface chemistry, wetting, free energy, and so on. The case issues relating to DNA and blood transfer, adhesion, and contamination fall under that field.

I now have 20+ years of post-Ph.D. experience in a wide range of science and technology fields. My specialty is to be unspecialized and multi-disciplinary, rather than to be tightly focused on any one area of science or technology. In the course of that time, I've worked for, with, or under the thumb of, numerous world-class organizations, including the Air Force, NASA, Army, Navy, special forces, some of the largest consumer products companies in the world, intelligence agencies, many advanced technology science and engineering firms, investigators and attorneys.

I've worked as both a scientist and an engineer, hold seven U.S. patents, and have developed some new measurement techniques, so I have some appreciation of the stringent requirements for doing that properly. I've also developed some consumer products, including vertical gardening systems, high brightness phosphorescent panels, and a water dissolvable labeling tape for labeling food storage containers.

Over the course of a number of years developing and supporting forensic identification tools for investigators and other security personnel and nearly a decade reviewing technology offerings in the security field for large corporate clients, I've learned to spot exaggerated or distorted technical claims and distinguish them from reality.

# Bibliography and Links

## Websites of interest

www.monsterofperugia.com (News about this book)

www.sciencespheres.com  My blog, mostly about this case.

www.injusticeinperugia.org  Blog created by Bruce Fisher with many contributors.

blog.seattlepi.com/dempsey/  Candace Dempsey's blog, most often on the case

perugia-shock.blogspot.com/  Frank Sfarzo's blog from Perugia

www.friendsofamanda.org  Friends of Amanda website, the original defense site.

www.amandadefensefund.org  The defense fund and site for donations.

knoxarchives.blogspot.com/  Ray Turner's blog on the case.

www.amandaknox.it/  Articles by myself and Steve Moore translated to Italian.

viewfromwilmington.blogspot.com/  Professor Chris Halkides blog on this case and others.

www.injusticeinperugia.org/SteveShay.html  A compilation of Steve Shay's articles about the case.

www.causes.com/causes/506038?m=eb7a7bc2  Facebook Cause in support of Amanda and Raffaele.

Note: The Wikipedia entry for the Meredith Kercher case has been corrupted by partisan activity and, as of this writing, it is deliberately biased and inaccurate. That bias shows a fundamental weakness in the otherwise amazingly effective Wikipedia structure. If an article is on a controversial topic, one side or the other can hijack it, creating a serious conflict by placing an inaccurate reference in the midst of an otherwise authoritative source.

Other books on the case of note:
*Injustice in Perugia*, Bruce Fisher
*A Murder in Italy*, Candace Dempsey
*The Fatal Gift of Beauty*, Nina Burleigh

Some accessible books on DNA:
*DNA on Trial*, Tina Kafka
*DNA and Body Evidence*, Brian Innes
*Forensic Science, Modern Methods of Solving Crime*, Max M. Houck
*Forensic DNA Analysis*, Lawrence Kobilinsky, Ph.D., Louis Levine, Ph.D., Henrietta Margolis-Nunno, Ph.D., J.D.

Some technical references on Luminol and TMB:

K. Weber, The Use of Chemiluminescence of Luminol in Forensic Medicine and Toxicology. I. Identification of blood stains, Deut. Z. Gesamte Gerichtl. Med. 57 (1966) 410-423.

F. Barni, S.W. Lewis, A. Berti, G.M. Miskelly, G. Lago, Forensic application of the Luminol Reaction as a Presumptive Test for Latent Blood Detection, Talanta 72 (2007) 896-913.

J.L. Webb, J.I. Creamer, T.I. Quickenden, A Comparison of the Presumptive Luminol Test for Blood With Four Non-Chemiluminescent Forensic Techniques, Luminescence 21 (2006) 214-220.

I. Quinones, D. Sheppard, S. Harbison, D. Elliot, Comparative Analysis of Luminol

Formulations, Can. Soc. Forensic Sci. J. 40 (2006) 53-63.

S. Luczak, M. Wozniak, M. Papuga, K. Stopiniska, K. Sliwka, A Comparison of the Bluestar and Luminol Effectiveness in Bloodstain Detection, Arch. Med. Sadowej Kryminol. LVI (2006) 239-245.

A. Castello, M. Alvarez, F. Verdu, Accuracy, Reliability, and Safety of Luminol in Bloodstain Investigation, Can. Soc. Forensic Sci. J. 35 (2002) 113-121.

L.J. Blum, P. Esperanca, S. Rocquefelte, A New High-Performance Reagent and Procedure for Latent Bloodstain Detection Based on Luminol Chemiluminescence, Can. Soc. Forensic Sci. J. 39 (2006) 81-100.

http://en.wikipedia.org/wiki/3,3',5,5'-Tetramethylbenzidine
http://en.wikipedia.org/wiki/Peroxidase
http://en.wikipedia.org/wiki/Horseradish_peroxidase
http://en.wikipedia.org/wiki/Luminol

For updates and additional information

**www.monsterofperugia.com.**

For other science blogging by Dr. Mark Waterbury

**www.sciencespheres.com**

Made in the USA
Lexington, KY
24 August 2012